# Pacific Crossing Notes

## *A Sailor's Guide to the Coconut Milk Run*

Nadine Slavinski
and
Markus Schweitzer

*Illustrations by*
*Nicholas P. Schweitzer*

Rolling Hitch Press
New York

*Copyright © 2015 Rolling Hitch Press*

*Until one is committed, there is hesitancy, the chance to draw back, always ineffectiveness. Concerning all acts of initiative and creation there is one elementary truth, the ignorance of which kills countless ideas and splendid plans. That the moment one definitely commits oneself, then providence moves too. All sorts of things occur to help one that would never otherwise have occurred. A whole stream of events will issue from this decision raising in ones favor all manner of unforeseen incidents and meetings and material assistance which no man could have dreamt would have come his way.*

– William H. Murray,
Mountaineer and writer

# Contents

## Part III.  Underway                                                   67

## Part IV.  US East Coast to the Caribbean                               111

## Part V.  Panama                                                        135

## Part VI.  The Eastern Pacific                                          159

# Introduction

Having recently returned from sailing across the Pacific Ocean in our thirty-five foot sloop, we hear the same question all the time: *So, what is it like?*

We still struggle to answer in brief layman's terms, because words like "nice" and "great" hardly do justice to the world's largest body of water or the biggest adventure of our lives. To help guide the aspiring cruiser, however, we'll take a different tack and provide a more thorough answer in 100,000 words (give or take). The South Pacific beckons with its trade wind sailing and fantasy islands – but what can a sailor expect along the way?

As we sailed west, we wrote a number of magazine articles and blog posts relating what we found: the challenges, the rewards, the everyday realities. Having amassed a huge body of useful information, we decided to tie it all together, augment it with important new material, and make our work available to sailors getting ready to cast off for their own adventures. In *Pacific Crossing Notes*, we aim to provide coverage that's broad enough to be useful while detailed enough to remain practical. And while no single volume can claim to be fully comprehensive, this book does compile a vast body of information in a single volume, all for less than the price of a six-pack of cold beers in the tropics.

Subjects include preparation for a Pacific crossing, weather, safety, and the island groups of the Coconut Milk Run: that is, the trade-wind route from the Americas to Australia. You'll find detailed information on Panama, the Galapagos Islands, Marquesas, Tuamotus, Society Islands, Cook Islands, Tonga, Fiji, Vanuatu, and New Caledonia. Separate sections cover a trip down the US East Coast, the Panama Canal, New Zealand, and Australia (including tips on selling a boat there for a one-way trip).

Since it's easier to digest advice if you have a sense of the source, we'd like to introduce ourselves here. We're a family of three who have undertaken two extensive "seabatticals" aboard our 1981 Dufour 35, *Namani*. The first was a one-year, 10,000 mile journey in which we sailed the Mediterranean, crossed the Atlantic, cruised the

Eastern Caribbean, and eventually headed north to Maine. Later, we set off on what would become a three-year trip from Maine to Australia, where we eventually sold our boat. In tastes and budget, we tend toward simplicity and consider ourselves cautious sailors. On the whole, we're glass-half-full types who find positives in every country we visit.

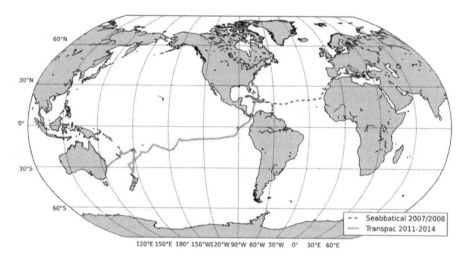

Our two extended voyages aboard *Namani*

For us, sailing the Pacific was a special time of living in tune with the elements as we explored some of the world's most beautiful and remote locations. If we could do it all over again, there isn't much we'd change – except perhaps to have somehow prolonged those magical years cruising as a family.

Here's wishing you the voyage of a lifetime – and always a hand's breadth of water under the keel!

# Overview

We'll open this book with an overview: a chart of the journey ahead, so to speak. *Pacific Crossing Notes* is organized into sections with overarching themes such as *Preparation*, *Safety*, and *Underway*, as well as location-specific sections. Be warned: headers such as *East, Central*, or *West Pacific* are more relative than absolute. They divide the journey into the same chunks most cruisers use to divide their sailing seasons. That's why you'll find the Galapagos Islands together with French Polynesia in the East Pacific, while the Cook Islands, Niue, and Tonga are lassoed together in the Central Pacific.

Each section is subdivided into chapters that break that subject into manageable bits. For example, in the *Preparation* section, you'll find sub-chapters on building up experience for an ocean voyage, outfitting a cruising boat, and calculating solar power. Similarly, the *West Pacific* section includes full-length chapters on Fiji, Vanuatu, and New Caledonia, along with shorter sections that vary in tone and subject. Some are entertaining anecdotes we call "The Spice of Life" while others are "Fact Files" that list practical information (currency, fees, shopping, cruising guides).

Throughout, we strive to balance facts with flavors, making this a book to keep you company during the countdown to your trip as well as a pragmatic guide to pull out as you face each successive landfall in the voyage of a lifetime. Admittedly, we can't cover everything without having crossed the Pacific a few more times – but give us time for additional "research" and we'll be happy to get back to you in a future edition of this book.

In the meantime, you'll find plenty of bang for your buck in the information and tales within these pages. There's something for the planner, the voyager, and the armchair adventurer. Enjoy reading, and above all, enjoy sailing!

# Part I

# Preparation

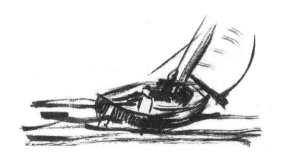

# Preparation

Getting ready to cross an ocean can often seem like harder work than the crossing itself. Buying and fitting out a cruising boat present exhausting choices, and the effort it takes to put land life on hold can be overwhelming. That may be why so many dreamers stay on the wrong side of the starting line. But across those mental barriers lies the voyage of a lifetime and the type of cruising that will make you wonder why you didn't go sooner.

While we drew heavily from our Atlantic crossing experience when we set off across the Pacific, we knew that the challenges would be very different. For one thing, the overall distance is far greater and supplies are correspondingly fewer and farther between. And while sailing across the Atlantic boils down to a single three-week hop with good services on either side, the Pacific is an entirely different kettle of fish. Most cruisers take at least one season (while many others take several years) to island-hop across the world's biggest body of water. As rewarding as the voyage is for a sailor, it can be punishing for a boat. You can never have too many tools, spare parts, or radio conversations about how to overcome the challenge of the week, whether that's something as mundane as gooseneck barnacles sprouting in mid-passage or as worrisome as a fraying shroud.

This section covers various preparatory topics, from working your way up to blue water passages to buying and equipping a boat. Daunting as it all may seem, the anticipation can provide its own high. You're on the cusp of achieving the dream of a lifetime – a period in your life you'll eventually look back on as fondly as you do the trip itself.

# Chapter 1

# From Weekend Warrior to Ocean Voyager: Stepping Up to Blue Water Sailing

Day sailors with big dreams might leaf through the pages of sailing magazines and wonder how to work their way up to an ocean crossing. It's a question we often asked ourselves and one we field now that we've achieved a dream many years in the making. There's no single right way, but we can tell you about our route to the open sea – one that eventually led us across the Atlantic and Pacific Oceans aboard a 1981 Dufour 35 together with our young son. Those four years of cruising gave us magical travel experiences and family time we wouldn't trade for anything – a prize we earned by taking it one step at a time.

We started in our twenties, when we re-launched a long-neglected seventeen footer and explored southern Maine's Casco Bay. As our dreams and paychecks grew, we stepped up to charter vacations and gradually got serious about the idea of sailing away from it all. The next logical step was to enroll in a correspondence course to fill in our spotty knowledge of navigation and seamanship. But after that... well, there's nothing logical about selling up and sailing away, not the way our culture sees things. That may be why so many dreamers stall out before upping the ante to blue water sailing. Because just how does one progress from local sailing and textbook exercises to the wild blue yonder?

Looking back, we find three experiences that stand out in terms of making blue water sailors out of the weekend warriors we once were. The first is obvious enough: gaining open water experience, either by sailing with experienced friends or through a sailing course. The second point is one that's often overlooked by people determined to fast-track their way to the wild blue yonder – that is, getting thoroughly familiar with the boat you intend to cruise. Overlapping with that is the third major point: developing a mindset of resourcefulness. In many areas of the world, you'll be totally on your own in terms of repairs, and every boat will quickly develop issues out on the open sea.

## On Your Mark. . .

So, first things first: every prospective cruiser should gain open-water experience. Like many casual sailors, we tested the waters with a couple of charter vacations before setting the bar higher. When we did, the two experiences that were most valuable to us were a coastal skipper course and a week-long delivery we joined as crew.

Because we live in Europe, we chose a British RYA Coastal Skipper course (the rough equivalent of ASA 106/108) in Gibraltar. Having completed the theoretical part of the course at home, we could apply the knowledge in a real-life setting. It was a fantastic experience that packed a lot into one intense week, including overnight sailing in a heavily trafficked area with significant tides. Those were lessons we drew directly upon years later when we sailed our own boat through the Straits of Gibraltar and the Panama Canal, as well as along the busy east coasts of North America and Australia. The course also whetted our appetite for cruising because of the cultural variety of the area. We sailed from British Gibraltar to Morocco and back over to Spain, taking the time to sample local culture along the way.

We recommend looking for a course that takes place in tidal waters and includes night sailing in long, open water stretches where there is significant shipping. The best way to get your feet wet with such intimidating factors is having an experienced sailor hold your hand – or act as a drill sergeant who demands that all maneuvers (especially those you'd rather avoid) are repeated until you've got them down pat. Our instructor devoted a couple of long mornings to docking maneuvers in quiet marinas, for example, and the white-knuckle experience paid big dividends when we eventually cruised the Mediterranean on our own. And as far as cost went, we found that liveaboard sailing courses aren't more expensive than chartering since you share the boat with other students.

The second valuable experience we had was serving as crew on a delivery trip in the Mediterranean. For us, it was a test: could we actually handle and enjoy multi-night open-water sailing over longer distances? Our ten-day trip from Malta to Mallorca via Sicily fit the bill exactly. We found a charter company that offered crew berths on its delivery trips at very low rates, with the added benefit of serving under a professional captain. Sailors based in North America might find a similar experience by signing on to help with a return delivery after one of the East Coast-to-Bermuda races. As things turned out for us, the weather was awful and the delivery was rushed – the perfect test! Though we came away on shaky legs, we learned that we really could handle round-the-clock watches in poor conditions and that night watches needn't be terrifying – not when you have a watch buddy and an experienced captain to call on if needed. As it turned out, several other crew members in the three-boat delivery were just like us: casual sailors wondering if they truly wanted to commit to the next step. One became a close friend and crewed for us when we crossed the Atlantic three years later.

With those two experiences under our belts, we felt confident that our dream was worth pursuing. Still, we knew we hadn't mastered all the skills we needed to run our own boat – something many fast-trackers seem to overlook before plunging straight into open ocean. This next point is key: sailing is the easy part. What's much more difficult is dealing with traffic in tight quarters, anchoring in challenging conditions, making decisions on things with as high a degree of uncertainty as weather forecasts, and coping with the constant repairs that are part and parcel of long-range cruising. That's why gaining blue water experience is only one facet of your learning journey. The other is becoming familiar with and handling a range of challenges on your own boat.

## Get Set. . .

Too many people expect to simply buy a boat and sail off into the sunset, but there's nothing simple about it – a lesson that becomes all too clear in mid-ocean. We've seen the sad remnants of other people's dreams rotting away in marinas around the world, often at the first port of call after a major crossing. That's why we strongly recommend buying and sailing the boat you will cruise on for at least a year before setting off on your grand adventure. Every boat has its own history, its own quirks, and its own aching joints. For your own safety and peace of mind, you should get to know a boat before you sail away from the safety net of home.

We owned our boat for eighteen months before we set sail and look back on that cycle of seasons as one of our most valuable learning experiences – a time in which we learned to walk before we ran. Over those months, we completed several short passages and made countless repairs that helped us get to know our boat – not just superficially, but deep down at the bottom of lockers, up the mast, and under the keel. The mistakes we made and lessons learned helped get our first cruise off to a good start. We discovered what our tool box lacked and bought what we needed while still in a familiar place stocked with parts. We also discovered that the aging engine that had checked out beautifully in our pre-purchase survey was developing problems – and that replacement parts were no longer manufactured. In a year of weekends and short vacations, we bashed knuckles and toes, dragged anchor once or twice, and soaked in many a contemplative sunset. Generally, we learned to call her home. Eventually, our "patience" (though at the time, I felt anything but patient) paid off in two enjoyable long-range cruises.

Putting in overtime on boat work

It's not just about preparing the boat, but the crew, too. A person who buys their first cruising boat within a few months of departure of their big adventure risks being rushed and distracted by the process of cutting their ties to land. Conversely, the sailor who buys a boat a year or more ahead of time will get to know the vessel and can customize details to accommodate their priorities, whether that includes up-to-date electronics and safety gear, details like bunks for the kids, or just a place to stow a guitar. This well-prepared owner can take the boat out (or work on it) on fifty critical weekends.

The advantage of learning aboard your own boat is that you're the boss, and you can carefully design trips to fill gaps in your knowledge. Once again, I'll stress that sailing is the easy part. Before setting off into the sunset, make sure you can fix your boat, anchor confidently, deal with shipping and night sailing, and learn to err on the side of caution when interpreting weather reports. Use your pre-departure year to work your way up gradually. From weekend day trips, you can move on to anchoring overnight. Eventually, you can try night sailing by picking a fair weather window and a familiar stretch of water; then simply head out and back. The prospect of night sailing frightens a lot of novices, but it can actually be very pleasant – and it's amazing how much you can learn in a single night. Early on in our second extended cruise, we gained a valuable refresher in night sailing within the space of a few hours by leaving Portland, Maine at sunset. Buoys were flashing everywhere, ships were coming in and out of port, and making sense of the big picture – even in a familiar port – got us right back into the swing of things. A short overnighter like that one to the Isle of Shoals gave us a manageable challenge before we knuckled down in earnest for a three-year trip to Australia.

You'll learn more by doing overnighters or short passages on your own than you will by taking any additional sailing courses on other boats. You'll get the feel of the boat and discover her ugly secrets. During this time, take the family out for a week or two-week cruise and anchor every night so you'll learn how to manage power resources, how the dinghy handles, and what types of meals are practical on board. This is especially important for sailors dreaming of a Pacific crossing, since there are so few marinas along the way. If you feel you still need guidance, think about hiring an instructor to join you on your own boat instead of taking additional courses. The cost will likely be the same (or cheaper, if you have to fly several people to the course location and pay multiple tuitions).

One caveat: as valuable as a preparation year can be, I wouldn't recommend extending it too long. You can spend a lifetime inching up to the big league, but sooner or later, you just have to take the leap and go. That's the other lesson we learned by looking at the boats we left behind: for every sailor who succeeds in cutting their ties to land, there are a dozen others still immersed in "getting ready" for a someday that never comes. Marinas around the world are full of boats that are bigger and nicer than ours, yet we're the ones who made our dream a reality. We didn't wait until every detail was perfect because we knew that repairs are a constant. No sooner do you cross one thing off the list than the next item comes along, begging for attention. Being cautious is smart, but being over-cautious will get you nowhere.

## Go?

So, you've taken a couple of courses and gotten to know your own boat. Are you ready to go? Don't forget point number three: learning to become your own rigger, mechanic, plumber, and general tinkerer. I'm not suggesting you wait to become an expert in all these areas before setting off, because then you might never leave. However, you should try your hand at a number of different projects on board and develop a mindset of self-sufficiency. Get to know your tool box, have a look at what's hiding behind the panels, and attempt a number of repairs on your own.

Consider this: an ocean cruiser will put more hours on the hull in the course of a seventy-two hour passage than some weekend warriors will do in an entire season. A boat has all the systems of a house, packed closely in a corrosive salt-water environment where there's no repairman on call. You'll need tools, spare parts, and above all, resourcefulness if you're going to sail off into the sunset. We often had to cobble together solutions for things that didn't have a direct one-to-one replacement – from a busted diesel injection pipe to a fitting in the galley sink and a patch of deck rot we discovered in the middle of the Pacific. There's no course in resourcefulness except that which you teach yourself, and every boat, no matter how new, will develop problems. Case in point: our 1981 sloop needed just as much work as some very fancy modern yachts. In either case, it's a frustrated owner indeed who waits for parts and expert help rather than attempting repairs on their own.

Therefore, you should take any opportunity you get to observe fellow sailors work on their own engine / rig / hull / deck / electronics / plumbing. You cannot plunge into ocean sailing (especially the South Pacific) with the mentality that you can find and pay someone to help with repairs. Even if you can find help, the people offering services often make shoddy repairs. The best resource is a good manual, your brain, and your fellow sailors, because the cruising fleet quickly develops into a community in which everyone helps each other. A diesel repair course may be a worthwhile investment, but looking over someone else's shoulder or tinkering with your own engine can be just as valuable. Think of your build-up phase this way: every time you pay someone else to do a job for you, a learning opportunity is lost. If you must pay an expert to do the job, act as their helper so you can learn.

So there they are: our three key steps toward blue water sailing. There are a few smaller points I'd add to the list, such as first aid certification and a mariner's long-distance radio certificate. The latter will allow you to legally operate an SSB radio, which we list among the top couple of pieces of equipment on our boat. With it, we could receive weather information, have two-way conversations with people thousands of miles away, and send/receive short email messages.

If it all sounds like too much, don't worry: all of this preparatory work can be great fun, not to mention rewarding. Think of every step along the way as its own adventure, not just an adventure in the making. Many of us use sailing to escape the endless grind of the rat race, and these activities will give meaning to every weekend and vacation before you set off. In the rest of your free time, you can research destinations, charts, and other equipment. That's another lesson we learned: anticipation can be – well, if not the best part, then pretty darn close.

# Chapter 2

# Getting the Most Out of a Survey

If only we knew then what we know now! Over eight years of owning our boat, we had four professional surveys of vastly differing qualities. Comparing our experiences taught us how to get the most from a survey, as did discussions with a seasoned professional, Tony Theriault of Theriault Marine Consulting in Cape Elizabeth, Maine.

Our conclusions? First, we learned the importance of setting clear expectations, as well as understanding the owner's role before and during a survey. We also discovered that surveys are not just for sailors interested in buying a boat or renewing insurance. Surveys can also be excellent evaluative tools to identify any weaknesses to address before heading out for another season – or around the world.

## Finding a Surveyor

Whether you're interested in a pre-purchase survey, an insurance renewal, owner's consultation, damage assessment, or a value appraisal, you must first locate a credentialed surveyor. In the United States, the accrediting agency is the National Association of Marine Surveyors, which requires that members show adequate experience and pass an extensive test. Look for a surveyor who is past the associate status and has full certification. Next, check where your surveyor's experience lies. Some specialize in wood, aluminum, or steel hulls, or even in tall rigs. The right surveyor will carry the tools needed for the job at hand and have experience in the appropriate area.

Equally important is talking with the surveyor to see if you're compatible. As Tony Theriault points out, it's a job that calls for strong communication and people skills. A good surveyor is a person you can trust to help make important decisions, and who can bridge the potential divide between a buyer and a seller (in a pre-purchase survey, the buyer hires the surveyor).

Once you have found a surveyor, make sure you clearly specify and agree on the scope of the survey – the more detail, the better. In a pre-purchase survey, will the surveyor go aloft to look at standing rigging? To what extent will the electrical system be examined? Be sure to describe your level of experience so that the surveyor knows whether to assume you have a high familiarity with boat systems or not.

Explain what exactly you want to achieve in the survey so that the outcome will match your expectations. A consultation, for example, may be requested by an owner who suspects trouble in a particular area, or it might extend to a full survey that will guide an upcoming re-fit. Then the surveyor can provide a realistic time and price quote and you can both plan accordingly.

## Preparing for the Survey

In our very first, pre-purchase survey, we failed to properly prepare the boat. As a result, the surveyor only took a perfunctory look beneath settees and into cluttered lockers. He failed to get to the bottom of things – literally – and didn't examine some of the vessel's fundamental support structures. At the time, we didn't know enough to insist on more, or to recognize that we had failed to provide the structure for a thorough survey.

In contrast, Tony Theriault spent hours on our second, consultative survey in which we sought to identify areas to address in re-fitting the same boat. Watching him move masses of gear and maneuver into the most uncomfortable reaches of the boat made us appreciate the work of a true professional dedicated to our cause. In the end, we had a truly thorough and candid look at the health of our boat. However, this was only accomplished at the expense of valuable time (in fact, it required a second visit to complete the job).

Lesson learned: prepare the vessel in order to permit a thorough examination. Don't waste the surveyor's valuable time – and your money! Empty every locker, shelf, and cubbyhole. Buy extra-large, inexpensive containers to store surplus equipment and get as much as possible out of the way. This will allow the surveyor to immediately focus on critical systems. Key areas to provide access to are the chain plates, hull-deck joint, and high stress areas around bulkheads and the compression post. It's equally important to expose the steering system, engine transmission shaft, batteries, and central electrical areas.

Ideally, try to find a time slot not followed by any pressing engagements. That will allow the survey to attend to all areas without rushing. A full, pre-purchase survey on a used thirty-five foot sailboat should take the greater part of a day (or two half days), so if the potential surveyor quotes you an hour, look elsewhere. On the other hand, a consultative survey limited to a specific area of concern may take only a few hours.

It is absolutely critical that you, the (potential) owner, are present for the survey. Ask questions, listen, and take notes. Learn from the surveyor and draw his attention to your areas of concern. Let him know what type of sailing you plan to do and in what conditions. If you race, tell him. If you heard a creaking sound last season, make sure he knows. As a boat owner, you must act as the voice of your vessel in the same way that a parent reports on the health of a young child to a pediatrician.

## During a Survey

A full survey will have three parts. First, the vessel should be examined out of the water to inspect the hull, keel, rudder, and propeller. The second section is a dockside component, inspecting the deck, internal structure, and all systems while the boat is afloat. The final part is a sea trial to check the rigging, sails, and engine at work.

Normally, a surveyor will avoid destructive testing, taking readings with a moisture meter and tapping the hull with a rubber-tipped hammer. An experienced inspector will notice a spongy feeling on deck and pick up subtle differences between the hammer's pings. If the surveyor suspects damage or weakness, he might recommend exposing a section of fiberglass or taking a core. A few key areas on some hulls might be impossible to access without destructive measures (on our sloop, for example, the keel bolts are glassed over). This means an owner must decide whether to leave well enough alone or go all the way by opening up these areas. This decision can be based on the boat's age, history, and any evidence of possible damage.

There are two specialty areas that many surveyors do not cover in detail: most will not go aloft to inspect standing rigging, nor are they qualified mechanics who can make more than a general engine inspection. Buyers interested in older vessels should consider bringing in a specialist rigger and mechanic. The fees do add up, but it can be a worthwhile investment considering the costs of rigging or engine failure (not to mention the potential for endangering the crew).

A true professional is like a teacher and safety coach in one, making sure you have the best boat for your purpose and budget. A boat that is not suitable for one sailor may be perfect for another, and the surveyor will act as a matchmaker between boat and sailor in a pre-purchase survey. For owners who already know their boats well, a surveyor can

*Namani* being hauled out for a survey in Maine

bring the tools and fresh perspective needed to find any weaknesses lurking beneath the surface.

## The Survey Report

The surveyor will summarize his or her findings in a multi-page report in both paper and digital format, complete with photos. Be cognizant that the report takes time to write up – an important consideration if you're trying to squeeze the survey, launch date, and new insurance coverage into a short period of time. It can be useful to compare old surveys to a more recent version, so hold on to all the material you have. Some insurance companies will grant coverage on the basis of an older survey together with a letter of compliance (in which the owner states that all recommendations of the old survey have been met).

Foregoing a pre-purchase survey is just plain foolish unless you're extremely experienced – not as a sailor, but in repairing all systems of a boat. One sailor we know bought a thirty-year-old boat without a survey and ended up paying top dollar for a vessel that needed new sails, a new engine, and other big ticket items that should have been knocked off the asking price. A surveyor will be candid and help prevent ugly surprises.

A good survey can be an illuminating learning experience for novices and experienced boat owners alike. Remember, a survey is not just a chore to complete once and avoid forevermore. A consultative survey can also be an extremely valuable diagnostic tool that guides a re-fit, as we can attest. Having addressed the findings of the survey, you can enjoy anything from a summer cruise to an ocean crossing with well-grounded confidence in your vessel.

## Summary of Points

Before the survey:

- Check your surveyor's credentials and referrals.
- Specify the scope of the survey.
- Prepare the boat and empty all lockers.
- Schedule a time slot that allows for overtime if necessary.

During the survey:

- Be present throughout the entire survey.

- Ask questions and take notes to supplement the report.

- Describe how you use the boat and any concerns you have.

- Provide a snack and drink to help you both maintain your concentration.

Tip: If your surveyor is willing to work on a weekend, you might be able to save money by arranging to have the last haul-out on a Friday. The boat can remain in slings over the weekend and be the first back in on Monday morning, keeping your haul-out bill to a minimum. However, this only works if the forecast calls for dry, hot weather that will allow the hull to dry quickly for reliable moisture readings.

# Chapter 3

# Fitting Out a Small Boat For a Pacific Crossing

Outfitting a boat for an ocean crossing is no easy task. Like so many aspects of cruising, every decision represents a trade-off: cost versus utility, safety versus comfort, savings versus preparedness. Given a finite amount of space, what should your priorities be?

Having completed an Atlantic crossing on an earlier trip, we were able to make informed decisions about exactly what gear we wanted for the Pacific. Crossing the Pacific on a relatively small boat brings its own set of challenges and rewards. We knew we'd have to remain self-sufficient for long periods of time and manage our resources carefully. Economy of space and price were top priorities: our wish list was long, but our pockets and lockers only so deep, so we knew we couldn't have it all.

Bit by bit, we settled on a final list and set off. Of course, every sailor has a different definition of what constitutes a "necessity." What follows is our version, tailored toward outfitting a small boat for a big ocean on a moderate budget.

## Safety Gear

In preparing our sloop for departure, our biggest expenditures were safety gear and sails. We upgraded to a Viking Resc-You life raft for two reasons: first, it's service interval is three years, and second, there are service stations around the world. At the same time, we repacked our grab bag with fresh flares and supplies and made sure to update the emergency contact information on our EPIRB.

Just as important as that gear, however, is preventative safety equipment that costs a fraction of the price, such as quality life jackets, tethers, and jacklines. Many boats run jacklines along the length of the deck, but surprisingly few install a jackline in the cockpit. We find the cockpit jackline equally important since it allows us to clip in before leaving the cabin. It's easy to make your own: just use a length of heavy line attached to U-bolts that are securely mounted to the cockpit.

In terms of safety equipment, we also consider an SSB transceiver an absolute must. With our SSB and a Pactor Modem, we could download email messages and weather reports, as well as report our position to radio nets during blue water passages. SSB radio nets are a great resource where problems can be solved using the collective knowledge of the cruising fleet in multi-party conversations. Radio nets also build camaraderie and provide entertainment during long days at sea – something difficult to achieve with a satellite phone.

## Electronics

Our budget allowed for a radar that we rarely used – but when we did, we were glad we had it. We also carried an AIS receiver which was useful off the coast of North America and Australia, though rarely in between. The Pacific is full of small fishing boats of dubious accountability, and only a fraction transmit an AIS signal.

Our GPS, radar and AIS units were standalone devices with their own displays. While we relied entirely on paper charts for our Mediterranean/Atlantic/Caribbean cruise, in the Pacific, we gradually shifted toward electronic charts. We used an old laptop running OpenCPN (a popular open source charting software) and interfaced to our GPS' NMEA output as a chart plotter. Still, it wasn't until Fiji that we started using electronic charts for coastal navigation, and even then, we always carried paper charts as a backup.

In Panama, we came across a wonderful (and free) computer operating system called Navigatrix, created and maintained by sailors for sailors. Navigatrix includes a comprehensive compilation of electronic tools for navigation, communication, information and security, ideally suited for use on a boat (including OpenCPN Chartplotter, zyGrib GRIB file viewer, Airmail for HAM and Sailmail, GPS interfacing, MS Office compatible word processor and spreadsheet, and more). It is extremely robust and can be installed on the hard drive alongside your current operating system or run from a 4 gigabyte USB stick (hence it works even if your hard drive doesn't). Navigatrix comes fully preconfigured and can be downloaded for free at navigatrix.net.

With Navigatrix we could remove the hard disk from our navigation laptop and run the entire operating system plus software from an SD card. This reduced the laptop's current draw to about 1 Ampere – a lot less than a typical marine chart plotter. This is something to keep in mind when considering electronics and computers for a Pacific crossing. You should also remember that you'll be without Internet connectivity for long stretches, which means you can't always keep up with automatic downloads for software patches and security updates. This was another advantage of Navigatrix: it works out of the box without the need for constant updates.

## Sails

One of the advantages of buying a used boat is the wardrobe of sails that often come included. Our Dufour had already been equipped with a removable inner forestay and two staysails (including a tiny storm jib). We rarely used these sails, but were glad to have them the few times we did encounter a gale. In fact, we used the "baby" staysail several times but never used the storm trysail we carried.

When we left North America, we also carried a triple-reef point mainsail, a lightweight 130% genoa, and an innovative new head sail we call a twin genoa. It consists of two lightweight genoas sewn onto the same luff tape that can be flown wing on wing downwind or lying against each other on other points of sail. On long downwind passages, we always flew the twin genoa at night since one person could roller-furl it quickly from the cockpit in case of a squall. By day, we switched over to our Parasailor: a spinnaker-like sail with an air slot and a lifting "wing" that makes it ridiculously easy to set and fly. We loved this sail not only for its efficiency, but also for the dampening effect it had on the boat's roll.

## Anchor Rode

From our first trip, we knew we could count on our twenty-kilogram Rocna anchor for holding in just about any kind of conditions. However, the one hundred feet of 10mm stainless steel chain that served us well in the Mediterranean and Caribbean would not be adequate for many deep-water Pacific anchorages. Therefore, we swapped the chain for 200-plus feet of 8mm galvanized chain. That's one of the many trade-offs of cruising: weight versus length and price. We packed an additional one hundred feet of line to extend the overall rode length. In a stern locker, we carried two Danforth anchors and another thirty feet of chain and line for the rare instances when we anchored bow-to-stern. One good snubber and a second back-up line worked wonders, even when we sat out several gales at anchor.

# Power

Power is another subject that merits an entire chapter, especially since different crews have vastly different power needs. Some crews rely heavily on generator power, which seems illogical given the abundance of wind and solar energy, not to mention high fuel prices and distances between fueling points. Their decks are typically cluttered with jerry cans which can reduce mobility on deck and pose a hazard in rough conditions.

For us, it made more sense to minimize our power consumption and make the most of available space by using a flexible arrangement of renewable energy sources. Our sloop carried four solar panels (for a total peak output of about 150 Watts), of which two were permanently mounted on the dodger. The other two could be set up either on the bow, atop the bimini, or amidships. We also carried a dual tow/wind generator: on passages, we towed it off the stern rail, and at anchor, we converted it to wind mode and hoisted it on the inner forestay. With this arrangement, we could meet all our power needs at anchor or underway, by day and by night, and on cloudy or windless days. It was a rare occasion when we had to run the engine to power our batteries.

We managed very well on these power sources because we do not rely heavily on amp-hungry equipment such as a watermaker or autopilot. Our Hydrovane self-steering worked extremely well throughout three years of near-constant use. The auxiliary rudder also gave us a secondary means of steering should our main rudder sustain damage.

We only ran our ancient refrigerator for basic cooling purposes when power permitted. With good insulation, we found that running it for a few hours at night was sufficient to keep staple items cool all day. This worked perfectly for cheese and beer but not for fresh meat, which we generally did without (instead, we relied on canned chicken, eggs, and quality canned hams). In a similar vein, our only source of warm water was a solar shower which was very effective when the sun was out. (When it wasn't, we used the stove to heat water.) Solar showers come in various models: check for one with a sturdy nozzle that's easy to turn on and off.

Using a foot pump to bring fresh water to the galley sink helped us reduce our power needs, too. The foot pump also gave us the ability to draw very small amounts of water – say, for brushing teeth. Similarly, we used simple solar garden lights as additional anchor lights in crowded harbors. Resource-conscious as we were, we never felt like we were roughing it. On the contrary, we reveled in the simplicity of it all and had correspondingly fewer electronics to maintain or repair.

## On Deck

On hot tropical days, it's vital to shade the deck from the sun. We created a large deck awning for days spent at anchor from an old sail and used smaller hatch covers underway. As for cockpit shade, we like having a system that folds back easily for those glorious nights under a starry sky. The biggest improvement we made to it came when we paid a New Zealand canvas maker to replace and redesign our aging bimini. She added an infill flap that zipped into the open slot between the dodger and the bimini – a simple addition that made a huge difference to perceived space on board. We used it at anchor on rainy days to create a protected space in the cockpit. The new bimini also came with a rain-catcher fitting which helped us augment our fresh water supply.

Many sources recommend carrying a hard-sided dinghy for the coral shores of the Pacific, but this wasn't an option given our deck space. We used a mid-sized inflatable Zodiac throughout the trip, and though the dinghy floor was heavily patched by the time we arrived in Australia, the outer shell never suffered a puncture. It was small enough to fit on deck for short day trips in good weather, but for longer passages, we always deflated and lashed it at the foot of the mast (for lack of locker space). The outboard sat on a bracket on the stern rail and we used a pulley system to lower it with relative ease. Sounds complicated, but we could have the dinghy and outboard stowed very quickly once we got the hang of it.

A small cruising boat doesn't have much room for fun extras, like the kayak I always dreamed of. I finally got my wish in a sturdy inflatable model that could be bundled into a relatively small space in the cockpit locker. My fears that the kayak would meet an early demise against the coral of the Pacific were for naught, and it performed well in all but the strongest cross-winds thanks to an attachable skeg. The kayak served several functions: as a secondary dinghy, so our crew could go to two different places at the same time, as a vehicle for shallow-water exploration, and finally, as a playtime platform for the kids while at anchor.

## Gas and Water

Like many crews, we used LPG gas for cooking and consequently had to deal with different systems and standards as we crossed the Pacific. Standard North American propane bottles are handy since they can also be filled with butane provided you have the right adapter. However, local businesses in French territories are only permitted to fill blue butane bottles (the type used in Europe). A typical way around this is for several crews to buy one large butane bottle together and gravity feed their propane bottles, then return the blue bottle to recover the deposit. In most other islands of the Pacific, you could practically show up with a plastic bag and find someone willing to fill it with the local LPG mix. New Zealand requires that gas bottles be locally inspected and stamped for a fee. North American steel propane bottles will meet local standards but lighter weight fiberglass or aluminum models may not.

Remember, there aren't many marinas in the Pacific, and it's often necessary to jerry-jug water from ashore. Rather than carrying large jerry cans for transporting water, we kept a large supply of five liter bottles which were much easier to carry and hoist from the dinghy to deck. We found outstanding water quality on many of the islands we visited, with few exceptions (the Galapagos Islands, Hiva Oa, and several dry atolls). Using our 70 gallon supply sparingly, we were able to stretch our fresh water for over six weeks at a time.

## Clothing

In our three-year trip, the coldest temperatures we experienced came when we left the US East Coast for the Caribbean in November, and in leaving New Zealand for Fiji at the end of May. I was happy to have a few layers of warm clothes, though I kept the selection small since they would only be used for a week or so at most. In terms of foul weather gear, look for a jacket with a fleece liner at the collar and forehead; otherwise, you'll soon feel chafe. Given the warm temperatures, I didn't invest in quality pants. Instead, I used inexpensive fisherman's overalls over polypropylene long underwear the few times I needed protection against cold and damp (perhaps ten times over three years).

Most of time, we wore light summertime clothing: T-shirts, bikini tops and lightweight, quick-dry running shorts (these are comfortable, have a built-in liner that eliminates the need for another layer, and dry quickly). Finally, a wide-brimmed sun hat is a must for any sailor. Look for a hat that cinches under the chin and can also be tightened around the crown of the head to help it stay put in a blow.

## Miscellaneous Gear

Another important piece of equipment is a sturdy bucket with a reinforced handle and line to scoop salt water for various uses. We also carried a three-foot wide inflatable child's wading pool that fit into the floor space of our cockpit. The original idea was to have a safe, on-board recreation option for a three-year-old. Soon the pool was serving double duty as an inflatable laundromat, either in a marina or at anchor – a very practical accessory!

After our first sailing trip, I learned the value of nesting tupperware: it takes up a fraction of the space a mismatched set of containers does. Plastic egg cartons are worth their weight in gold, as is a selection of Zip-loc bags in all sizes.

As for reading material, we became Kindle converts during our sailing time. Much as we love the feel of a real book in our hands, there's nothing like the huge capacity and convenience of an e-reader. I'll never forget the time I was pining for a new title off a remote Fijian island and found just enough of a signal to download exactly the book I wished for. Bliss! In e-readers as in any other portable devices, it pays to consider battery life and power consumption. Our basic models could run for days, even weeks, before recharging. Newer models with extra features consume much more power. No matter what devices you choose to carry, make sure you can plug them in on board. Twelve-volt chargers for almost any small device (including camera batteries and e-readers) can be found on the Internet.

For the most part, we didn't miss what we didn't have, since the Pacific made up for it all with a thousand other prizes. If we could have somehow fit more on board, I would have liked a portable printer to print photos for the friendly islanders we met along the way. A printer would also have allowed us to print notices for enterprising locals who offer their services to boaters. A watermaker would come in handy for extended stays in lonely atolls with no reliable fresh water source, though the cost, space, and power trade-offs ultimately struck this item off our list.

Ultimately, every crew will create a unique list of equipment they deem critical. Some crews carry SCUBA gear and compressors to make the most of diving opportunities in remote locations. Others bring all the comforts of home along for the ride and have the space to accommodate them. If this style of cruising is for you, go ahead and enjoy. If, however, your budget or tastes run to the more spartan end of the spectrum, don't worry: your Pacific experience will be every bit as rich and comfortable as theirs. A voyage of a lifetime isn't defined by discretionary gear but by balmy days, fresh breezes, and a constantly stimulating environment at sea and ashore – all of which the Pacific provides in generous supply.

# Chapter 4

# The Costs of Cruising

The most difficult question to answer is how much cruising costs, because every sailor has his or her own definition of "necessity" and "comfort." The best answer may be Bernadette Bernon's "it costs what you've got."

We know sailors who have crossed the Pacific on an average of US$500 per month and others who might multiply that number by five, ten, or even more. A frugal crew with an older vessel that never ties up at a marina, goes out for a meal, or hires help for repairs will be able to go on a long way on a tight budget. Their principal expenses will be boat parts, food, cruising permits, fuel, and insurance (if they purchase insurance at all). Of these, the latter two are highly discretionary. Given fair conditions, we often chose to drift along for days instead of motoring through hundreds of dollars of diesel just to make landfall sooner.

Similarly, the costs of outfitting a boat vary widely. Some crews spend top dollar for safety gadgets, electronics, and creature comforts, while others are happy with a back-to-basics approach. All in all, most cruisers report that they spend a fraction of what they do back home since transportation and accommodation costs are essentially zero. After all, anchoring is free, wind is our primary source of propulsion, and deserted atolls offer limited opportunities to spend money.

We consider ourselves cost-conscious sailors. We pay for boat and health insurance and treat ourselves to the occasional meal out while making our own repairs and otherwise watching our wallets closely. We cruised the Pacific from 2011-2014 for an average of US$90 per day – which included everything but the cost of the boat itself: food, fuel, insurance pro-rated by day, cruising fees, and parts/repairs. (We paid approximately US$1700 per year for boat insurance and US$1500 per person per year in health insurance.) Our normal daily operating expenses were much lower than that $90 average, but the overall average is skewed by periodic investments in the boat: new rigging, haulouts and bottom paint, new engine mounts, plus one-time costs such as transiting the Panama Canal. We saved a great deal of money by cruising on a sturdy older vessel: our 1981 sloop (loaded with many extras) cost €50,000 in 2006 and sold for the equivalent of €44,000 in 2014.

That's us. You can compare the cruising costs of various crews on Bill Dietrich's website.[1] Just remember, it doesn't have to cost a king's ransom to cruise the Pacific – unless you want it to!

---

[1] http://www.billdietrich.me/Costs.html

# Chapter 5

# Follow the Sun:
# A Migrant's View of Solar Power

"But tomorrow may rain, so I'll follow the sun..." Paul McCartney sang in the 1964 *Beatles for Sale* album. That's also what we hoped to do aboard *Namani*: to follow the sun by leaving temperate latitudes for the tropics in fall, dropping out of the tropics with the onset of hurricane/cyclone season, and repeating the pattern the next season.

With that itinerary in mind we felt confident that our solar panels would have no trouble keeping up with our power consumption. They seemed a bit out of place in Maine, our home base in the US, but surely they would deliver ample power in the sunny tropics, right?

"Yes, but..." would be our answer, and the 'but' is a strong one. With the experience of three seasons in the tropics behind us now (first in the Caribbean, then in the South Pacific), we suggest that sailors look at the data before jumping to conclusions. You might be surprised to find that the same solar panel that delivers 100 Watt-hours (Wh) of electric energy per summer day in the Chesapeake Bay will only provide 60Wh per day around Christmastime in the Virgin Islands.

So let's look at how the numbers that define effectiveness of photovoltaic solar panels play out for cruising sailors. The data that follows will provide some helpful bench-marks for getting the most out of your on-board power plant, whether you're outfitting a boat for extended cruising or sitting in an exotic anchorage, trying to squeeze out a few more Amps to keep the beer cold.

We'll start with a basic example to understand the variables at play for a boat spending the northern hemisphere summer in the Chesapeake Bay (between 37° and 38° North) then migrating to the Virgin Islands in November. After spending the winter months at about 18° north latitude, it returns to the Chesapeake Bay at the onset of hurricane season in May. Figure 1 shows the key variables for this example, plotted along a one-year timeline.

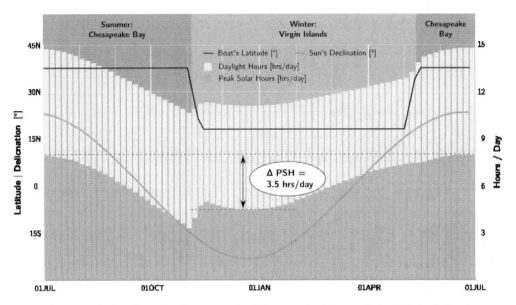

Figure 1: Solar situation between the Chesapeake Bay and the Virgin Islands

If we ignore the impact of clouds for the moment, the parameters that will determine daily solar power output at a boat's location are the length of the day and the sun's altitude above the horizon. Solar panels receive maximum light energy when the sun is directly overhead (altitude = 90°). The light energy received by the panels drops as the sun's position in the sky approaches the horizon. This drop is caused by light beams spreading over a larger area and by increased atmospheric absorption as the altitude of the sun decreases. The *Post Script: Sun Altitude and Solar Power* (page 34) at the end of this chapter illustrates how these two effects reduce the power output we receive from solar panels.

Figure 1 shows that we actually lose on both counts as we move into the tropics. The number of daylight hours drops from a peak of almost fifteen hours during summer in the Chesapeake Bay to an average of about 11.5 hours while we're in the tropics. At the same time, the gap between our latitude and the sun's declination widens as the sun crosses the equator on the way to its mid-winter position above 23° south. As a result, the sun will be significantly lower in the tropics than we are used to from our summers in the Chesapeake Bay.

To evaluate the combined impact of these two effects on our solar power situation, we use a quantity that is sometimes referred to as "Peak Solar Hours" (PSH). PSH tell us how many hours of direct overhead sunlight would provide the same solar energy as the slowly rising and setting sun at our location over the course of a day. PSH neatly boil down our solar situation to a single number. For example, in January in the Virgin Islands, we have the sun above the horizon for about eleven hours. As the sun moves across the sky during these eleven hours, it delivers the same amount of solar energy that a theoretical stationary sun directly overhead our position would provide in just over five hours – five PSH in this case.[1]

It is this "sun vertically overhead" scenario that most of us have in mind when we talk about "how many amps" our solar panels deliver. It is also the scenario assumed in manufacturers' output specifications for solar panels. With this in mind, PSH is what we should be looking at in order to realistically estimate the energy we can reap from our solar panels each day along our cruising itinerary. This can be a bit sobering: if I see my solar panels delivering a charge current of 10A during the height of summer in the Chesapeake Bay around noon time, I can assume only 5.3 PSH of that output over Christmas in the Virgin Islands.[2] Take off another 20% to 30% for cloud cover and I'm at 4 PSH – on a sunny day and assuming no obstruction from rigging or shore structures.[3]

Figure 2 shows daily PSH values over the year across a range of latitudes. If you know your energy needs over a twenty-four hour period at anchor, you can use the data from Figure 2 as a starting point for sizing your solar capacity. For example, let's assume a moderate energy consumption of 720Wh (60Ah at 12V) per day that we hope to recover from solar panels. Given the PSH data from above (4 PSH per day in the tropics after adjusting for cloud cover), we would need 720Wh / 4h = 180W of power output from our solar panel(s). Manufacturers provide "Maximum Power Ratings" for their solar panels but these are based on a maximum voltage higher than the typical battery charging voltage (about 13V on average). To account for this difference, we have to reduce the published Maximum Power Rating by about 20% to make it comparable

---

[1] In many publications, PSH are erroneously used to denote an energy quantity. You might find a "PSH of 10 kWh" which is equivalent to saying that something "weighs 3 feet". The confusion is due to the fact that peak solar irradiation (the light power received from the sun) is about 1 kW/sqm at sea level in the mid-latitudes. In this case, the numerical value of PSH is roughly equal to the number of kWh of daily irradiation per square meter. This can be misleading since actual peak solar irradiation varies significantly with latitude and the time of year as discussed in this chapter.

[2] At mid-summer solar noon in the Chesapeake Bay, the sun will be at an altitude of 76° rather than directly overhead. However, the solar output at that altitude is about 97% of that of a sun directly overhead – close enough for the rough calculation in our example.

[3] Going back over our log books, I see "cloud cover" entries of "2/8" for most of our sunny days in the tropics. There are of course also fully overcast days, but we would size our solar capacity for the typical rather than the worst case.

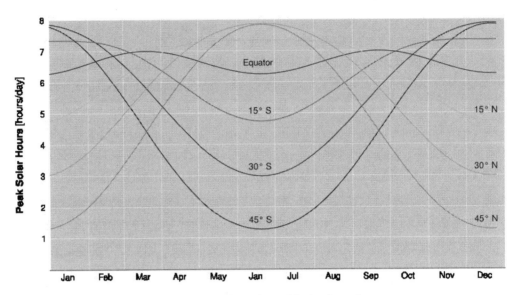

Figure 2: PSH as a function of latitude and season

to our calculated power requirement. Conversely, we can divide our calculated power requirement by 0.8 to compare it to the number in the panel specifications: 180W / 0.8 = 225W.

That is a sizable footprint for a relatively modest daily energy consumption. It also assumes that we can mount the entire panel area free of obstructions from rigging and other above-deck equipment – a challenge, especially on smaller boats. By way of comparison: we could get away with about 150W of panel power during summer in the Chesapeake Bay, reducing our footprint requirement by one-third (based on a typical PSH value of eight hours before cloud cover adjustments).

## Angling for Position

On a small boat it can be difficult to mount that much panel area free of obstructions. Any obstruction of direct sunlight markedly reduces a solar panel's electrical current output. This would drive up our rated power requirement, further compounding the problem. What we can do is use the available area more efficiently by making the solar panels adjustable, allowing them to follow the sun during the day.

Figure 3 looks at the effect of flexible mounting during January in the tropics and July in the Chesapeake Bay. Let's assume we can adjust the solar panels' angle by up to 15° from a horizontal position. Many mounting options will actually allow a bigger adjustment. However, we're unlikely to adjust the panel's angle continuously during the day and most mechanisms will only allow adjustment around one axis. Therefore, we'll stick with the conservative assumption of 15°.

The graphs in Figure 3 show a significant increase in the PSH value with flexible mounting: an adjustment of up to 15° can boost our sun intake by more than one-third (37%) in the tropics in January and by more than one-quarter (27%) in the Chesapeake during July. Rather than adding another panel in a suboptimal position, we will often be better off putting our existing solar capacity (or at least a portion of it) on some kind of adjustable mount. Some boats have panels mounted port and starboard on the stern pushpit where they can be gradually lowered from a horizontal position. Others have a stern arch construction that allows rotation of the panels around an axis that runs athwartships. On smaller boats, the best option might be a free "mobile" panel that can be moved around the deck and easily tied into an optimal position. Of course, the wind may decide to turn this into a sport, turning the boat in circles until you give up the chase.

## What About Wind Power?

The lack of moving parts makes solar panels a very attractive solution for cruisers – one less item that can incur mechanical failure in a remote location, and a silent one at that. Thanks to small but steady improvements, commercially available monocrystalline solar panels now approach 20% efficiency (the percentage of light energy hitting the panel that is actually converted into electrical energy). However, it seems the majority of cruising sailors still struggle to recover their on-board energy consumption exclusively from solar panels. Logically, one turns to wind to supplement solar power. Wind generators are still a common feature on many cruising sailboats and may become the sole source of green energy during cloudy days.

As with solar power, one has to be realistic about what can be expected from an on-board wind generator. For example, in 2012, the NOAA weather station in Lime Tree Bay (St. Croix) recorded over sixty days during which the sustained wind speed never got above ten knots during the November to April cruising season. Even Fajardo on Puerto Rico's exposed east coast had more than forty of those 'low-wind' days, when wind generators would have struggled to produce any meaningful output. While wind generators are great power producers when it blows, they are not a cure-all for our solar power woes. Sizing our solar capacity under realistic assumptions remains key if we want to reliably cover our on-board electricity needs without burning diesel.

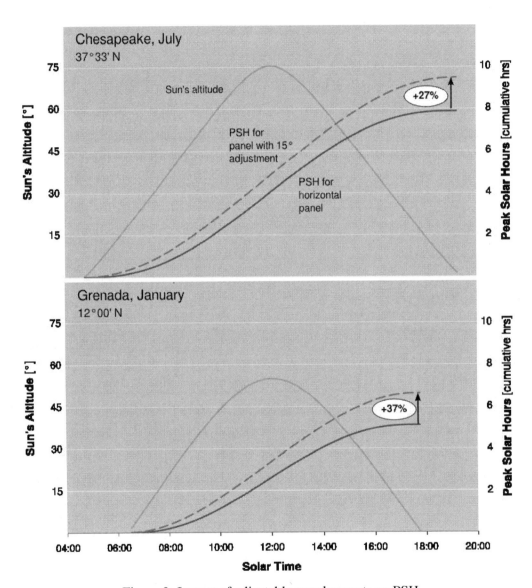

Figure 3: Impact of adjustable panel mounts on PSH

# A Real Life Example

Our sloop is probably a "low energy" boat by modern standards. We consume less than 700Wh per day at anchor without restricting ourselves. We recover this consumption through a combination of solar panels and a convertible wind/tow generator. Our total solar capacity is about 150W rated power output from four panels. Of these four, two are permanently mounted above the dodger. The other two are movable around the deck so that we can keep them free of obstructions and angled towards the sun as the boat swings at anchor. Waterproof sockets at the bow and stern allow us to plug in these two mobile panels where we need them. This configuration allows us to fold back our bimini at night to enjoy a starry sky and also avoids the weight of a permanent stern arch aloft. For us, it's an ideal solution.

Underway, the effectiveness of both solar panels and wind generators is greatly reduced. Sails will often shade the solar panels while apparent wind speeds on trade wind routes are too low to drive significant wind-powered output. That's when we convert our Aquair wind/tow generator to its tow mode. It's the perfect alternative for us on passages. The tow generator provides in excess of 1kWh per day at our typical cruising speed (5kn on average), plenty to cover our modest power requirements underway. At anchor, we convert the unit to wind mode and hoist it on the inner forestay. We have considered installing a permanently mounted wind generator on a stern post but eventually decided against it to avoid weight aloft as well as the expense. Now that our young son can do the conversion from tow to wind mode and back, we don't mind the extra effort.

To pick up the "follow the sun" theme, Figure 4 shows our solar journey over the course of two and a half years. Starting from Portland, Maine in September of 2011, we sailed down the US East Coast to Charleston, South Carolina, and then went offshore to Panama, with stopovers in the eastern Bahamas and Jamaica. In 2012 we followed the Coconut Milk Run via the Galapagos, French Polynesia, the northern Cook Islands, Niue, and Tonga. We spent the South Pacific cyclone season in New Zealand at about 35° South. Our second season in the South Pacific had us visit Fiji, Vanuatu, and New Caledonia before dropping out of the tropics again in November 2013 to spend the southern summer on Australia's east coast.

Our experience along this route confirms the data from the theoretical example above: the times of abundant solar power for us were indeed outside the tropics – that is, in New Zealand and southeastern Australia during the southern hemisphere summer. While in the tropics, we were glad that we did have our trusty Aquair generator set up in wind mode to augment the solar panels' output.

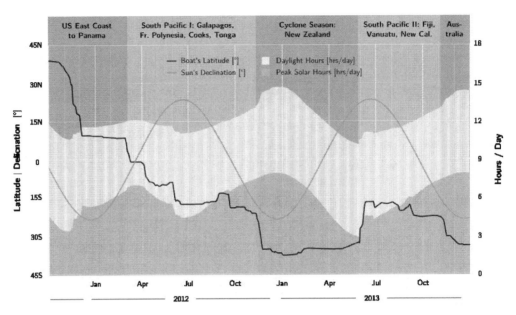

Figure 4: *Namani's* solar journey

Ultimately, what's true on land also applies on a boat: your best source of energy is conserving it. With realistic expectations as to what your green on-board power plant can deliver, you should take a critical look at what's draining the Amps on your boat. After all, part of the reason we're on the boat is that we want to get away from all those shore-side gadgets and gizmos. And once they're out of reach, you'll find you won't miss them much.

## Post Script: Sun Altitude and Solar Power

As mentioned earlier, any deviation of the sun's position from directly overhead will reduce its power input to your solar panels in two ways:

1. As the sun drops from its zenith to the horizon, a given cross-section of a solar light beam will be spread over a larger area as the light hits at an increasingly lower angle. For example, at a sun altitude of 60° above the horizon, this effect reduces the power produced by your solar panels by approximately 15% vis-à-vis their output with the sun directly overhead. With the sun at an altitude of 30° above the horizon the output will be reduced by 50%, and at 15° by about 75%. Figure A1 shows how a given quantity of incoming light is "diluted" over a greater surface area as the sun's altitude drops.

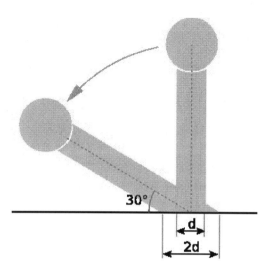

Figure A1: Impact of sun's altitude on energy density

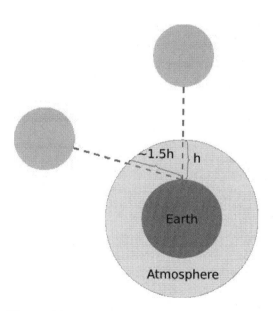

Figure A2: Impact of atmospheric absorption

2. Atmospheric absorption: A portion of the sun's light that is directed towards the earth is absorbed by water vapor and other gases in the atmosphere. The lower the sun in the sky, the longer the path light has to travel through the atmosphere and the stronger the resulting absorption. At an altitude of 60°, increased atmospheric absorption will reduce the solar power that reaches your solar panel by about 4% compared to the sun being directly overhead. At an altitude of 30° this effect is approximately 20% and at 15°, the reduction reaches 40%. Figure A2 shows an illustration of this effect.

## Sources

All data underlying the graphics in this chapter was computed by a Python script nomad.py, developed by the author. Nomad uses PyEphem to calculate sun ephemeris data.[4] The source code of the script is available at the author's homepage.[5]

The 2012 wind data was taken from NOAA's National Buoy Data Center website.[6] The source data lists wind speeds averaged over eight minutes at six-minute intervals. Intermittent gusts are higher than the speeds listed at those intervals, but they will also increase air turbulence which significantly reduces wind generator efficiency.

Solar panel efficiencies: National Renewable Energy Laboratory,[7] Fraunhofer Institute for Solar Energy Systems.[8]

---

[4]http://rhodesmill.org/pyephem/index.html
[5]http://tinyurl.com/ogzlxwj
[6]http://www.ndbc.noaa.gov/
[7]http://www.nrel.gov/solar/
[8]http://phys.org/news/2013-09-world-solar-cell-efficiency.html

# Chapter 6

# A Cruiser's Library

Given limited space on a cruising sailboat, we were very selective about the books we "allowed" on board *Namani*. The following are our top picks for a Pacific-bound sailor's cruising library.

**Technical**

- *Boatowner's Mechanical and Electrical Manual* (Nigel Calder): The cruiser's boat bible. If we had to throw books overboard to keep the boat afloat, this would be the last one to go. Although we referred to it less often as we became increasingly and intimately familiar with our boat's systems, this book remains an invaluable resource.

- *Celestial Navigation in the GPS Age* (John Karl): An excellent book that effortlessly introduces the theory behind celestial navigation without ever losing track of the application.

- *Modern Marine Weather* (David Burch): The most comprehensive, profound and accessible coverage of the subject that we have come across.

- *Offshore Sailing* (Bill Seiffert): An unusual book in that it simply offers "200 Tips" for offshore sailors, most of them relating to outfitting and equipment modifications. It will make you look at your own set-up with fresh eyes and includes a wealth of useful pointers. After four years aboard *Namani*, we still pick up the book from time to time and continue to find new thoughts and ideas.

- *Instant Weather Forecasting* (Alan Watts): This flip-through book provides great visual references thanks to its pictures and concise text.

### Field Guides

- Smithsonian Handbooks: An excellent series of compact, well-illustrated guides. Our favorites are Ian Ridpath's *Stars and Planets*, Mark Carwardine's *Whales, Dolphins, and Porpoises*, and Peter Dance's *Shells*.

- *Birds of New Zealand and the Central and West Pacific*, a Princeton Illustrated Checklist (Ber van Perlo): This book filled the only gap we found in the Smithsonian series. It is a well-illustrated, easy-to-use identification guide.

### Other

- *The Cruising Chef's Cookbook* (Michael Greenwald): While we're usually not fans of cookbooks, this one is different. Written by an avid sailor and Paris-trained chef, it's practical, relevant, and fun.

- *The Journals of Captain Cook* (Philip Edwards, editor): we pulled this book out and read in snippets, both for the inspiration and to consider how the places we visited had appeared to European explorers once upon a time.

- *Lesson Plans Ahoy* (Nadine Slavinski): This book discusses approaches to home schooling on a boat and details ten hands-on learning units in science, mathematics, history, writing, navigation, and even physical education.

# Part II

# Safety

# Safety

Landlubbers tend to view ocean sailing as danger distilled, but the truth is, our family usually felt safer on the water than on the highway. At home, friends often focus their questions on the horrible storms or tropical diseases they imagine we've survived. Much to their disappointment, we have to scratch our heads and think past the countless good memories to come up with anything negative.

It's important to remember that cruising is a special kind of sailing. If racing is about being in the right place at the right time, cruising is about not being in the wrong place at the wrong time. Given forethought and a conservative approach, it's usually possible to avoid that wrong place and time. With a sturdy boat and good seamanship, you can go a long way toward keeping "luck" on your side.

We were certainly healthier out on the sea than during the average working year, when the shared germs of school and office had our immune systems constantly weathering a different kind of storm. As for exotic diseases, we faced more mosquitoes in Maine than we did in Vanuatu. Theoretically, we could have left the heavy drugs at home, since we ended up giving or throwing 99% of them away at the end of our trip.

Of course, there is an element of uncertainty in anything you do, whether it's walking down a city street or taking to the open sea. Sailors can greatly stack the odds in their favor by using the power of prevention. That means cruising well-charted routes, avoiding cyclone season, and keeping an eye on weather developments at all times. It also means choosing anchorages with an eye on tomorrow's weather, not today's, and avoiding firm schedule commitments. Taking care of the boat falls into the same category: sailors who conduct regular boat checks to nip problems in the bud rarely have to scale the mast in mid-ocean to jury-rig a repair. Of course, there are those who thirst for thrills, but the way we see it, just crossing the Pacific is adventure enough. Why create our own obstacles?

This section discusses how to stack the odds in terms of safety and health on board. It begins with an interview we gave *Ocean Navigator* magazine about our approach to safety, and goes on to discuss life rafts (selection and installation), grab bags, and other safety measures, as well as health on board. While there's no magic recipe to guarantee safety, be assured: in cruising as in much of life, a little prevention goes a long way.

# Chapter 7

# Offshore Safety: An Interview with *Ocean Navigator* Magazine

Q: *How do you approach the subject of safety? Has your experience sailing offshore affected your thinking on safety?*

A: Having a young child on board makes us especially safety conscious. For us, prevention is more important than any single piece of expensive rescue equipment. This starts with a cockpit jack line that we can clip in to before leaving the shelter of the cabin and extends to deck jack lines and safety netting. We take a conservative approach to every passage by waiting for a favorable forecast and trying not to allow ourselves to be driven by a firm schedule. Even if other crews are heading out of port, we may stay behind and wait for a better weather window to avoid trouble. We have learned to turn a deaf ear to well-meaning advice at times and trust our own judgment about what we are comfortable heading out in. On the other hand, having lived aboard for four years and crossed both the Atlantic and Pacific Oceans, I am amazed at how infrequently we have encountered truly uncomfortable weather at sea by cruising within safe seasons. (Knock on wood!)

We think of safety equipment in three categories: First, there are the things that should minimize the chances of getting into a distress situation. This includes standard equipment that should be on any boat such as jack lines, suitable storm sails, radar, and most importantly, sound practices and routines on board. I guess you call that good seamanship. Secondly, there is the equipment that helps to communicate a distress situation: EPIRB, radio, flares and the like. Third, there are the things that increase your chances of survival in a distress situation: the ability to deal with injuries; to conduct emergency repairs on the boat to keep water out and the vessel under control; and a life raft, grab

Dressed for the occasion

bag and its contents. The farther you move offshore and away from major shipping routes, the more important the third category becomes. You may be able to get a distress call out, but you will likely be far away from help and cannot expect others to endanger themselves to come to your aid.

Our nightmare scenario has always been hitting a submerged object such as a stray shipping container, resulting in the boat sinking quickly. That has influenced our choice of life raft and the way we have installed it on deck. The other less threatening but equally uncontrollable event would be a lightning strike that fries all electrical equipment on board (including water pumps and handheld GPS). Hence we need to be confident that we can make a safe landfall in a complete and lasting "power down" scenario.

Q: *How do you plan for possible medical emergencies? Did you receive any medical training before you began voyaging?*

A: We carry a well-stocked first aid kit and many prescription medicines (in both children's and adult doses), from antibiotics to eye medication and malaria treatment. I found our doctors at home very helpful in writing prescriptions and dispensing advice. Similarly, our local pharmacies proved very understanding in providing medicine with the longest possible shelf life. Nadine's training as a Red Cross First Aid Instructor made us feel reasonably well-equipped to handle basic first aid issues. Luckily, we have suffered very few accidents or illnesses. The only two hospital trips in four years of cruising were for a broken collarbone sustained at the local playground in Cairns,

Australia, in the very last week of our cruise, and a hospital trip in Saint Lucia when little Nicky, then four, pushed a piece of Lego up his nose! Both those incidents had nothing to do with the perceived dangers of a life at sea. Generally, we feel much healthier and even safer at sea than we did in our land lives, when we were often in enclosed spaces full of germs or driving at what now seem to be breakneck speeds.

Q: *What type of life raft do you have? How often do you have it serviced?*

A: We now carry a Viking RescYou six-person life raft which must be serviced every three years. We chose this model in part because we knew it could be serviced relatively easily in places along our planned cruising route (for example, Tahiti, New Zealand, or Australia). We had a perfectly good BFA life raft before, but decided to replace it with the Viking because the BFA required annual service at considerable cost and inconvenience. We specifically chose a self-righting life raft in order to have one less potential obstacle to clear in this worst-case scenario. The life raft is mounted on the coach roof in a hard case.

It pays to carefully examine the contents of your life raft's survival gear. Most provide only limited quantities of drinking water, for example. This concerned us, especially since we would be heading into the Pacific where even in the best case, rescue operations run over long distances and therefore long time frames. We had the option to have extra items packed into the life raft; ideally, we would have liked to add a manual (hand pump) water maker. However, the cost was prohibitive. Instead we settled for an emergency desalinator which is part of our grab bag.

Q: *What do you have in your abandon ship / grab bag?*

A: Our grab bag is a red waterproof bag that is always in reach by the chart table. It contains flares, a handheld GPS, handheld VHF, lithium batteries for both those devices, foil blankets, a compass, paper and pencil, fishing gear with knife and small cutting board, energy bars, a hand-crank flashlight, and copies of key documents such as passports. All these items are sealed in individual Zip-loc bags. We also have an abandon ship list above the chart table to remind us to take the EPIRB with us, as well as the sat phone, the extra water container we keep handy, plus the spear gun if we have time.

Recent additions to our grab bag are several emergency desalinators made by SeaPack at a relatively affordable price. These are one-use, forward osmosis membrane filters that provide an extra (though small) water reserve. The advantage of these filters are price; the disadvantages are the bulk and finite quantity of water produced (one 3.2 pound package produces four liters – a little more than one gallon – of water).

Q: *Do you have an EPIRB?*

45

A: We have an ACR Global Fix unit mounted near the companionway. Having initially purchased and registered the EPIRB for an earlier trip, we were careful to check that the registration and battery were renewed before we set off on our Pacific cruise.

It is our understanding that due to the relatively high number of false EPIRB alarms, many maritime rescue services will only act on an alarm if they can confirm that the boat in question could plausibly be at the transmitted distress position. For this reason, we make sure that the emergency contact data registered with the EPIRB is up to date. We also keep our contacts abreast of our cruising plans. In addition, we have spread these across time zones, with one contact in North America, one in Germany, and one in New Zealand. Lastly, we exchange EPIRB ID Codes with other boats on our route. This is a 15-digit alphanumeric code that is printed on the EPIRB. This is the code that is actually transmitted by the EPIRB when armed and received by shore stations within the GMDSS. It is different from the MMSI, which is a virtual number assigned to the boat against which the EPIRB is registered. By making other boats in our vicinity aware of our EPIRB ID, these boats can also confirm the plausibility of a distress call without having to rely on someone making a cross border database lookup for our MMSI and emergency contacts. They would likely learn of the distress via one of the SSB nets such as the Pacific Seafarers' Net. We found that news travels very fast and effectively across the various radio nets.

Q: *Do you have an AIS unit? If so, what class unit?*

A: We have a simple stand-alone AIS receiver that gets its signal from a VHF antenna splitter. We found it useful in the North Atlantic, particularly in being able to hail ships by name on the VHF rather than the vague "vessel in approximate position ..." Overall, the AIS was far less useful to us in the Pacific, where the few freighters or fishing boats we saw did not have operating AIS units.

We do not use our AIS as a means to detect ships. Instead, we rely on visual watch on deck and radar in restricted visibility. For one thing, we are sure our simple unit can miss targets by alternating reception between A and B channels. In addition, we encountered very few large commercial vessels in the Pacific once we left Panama behind. Since we cannot rely on AIS detection for smaller fishing boats (or larger vessels fishing illegally without transmitting an AIS signal), we use it only as a source of additional information once we notice another vessel via other means. AIS only really came back into play as a useful tool along the east coast of Australia.

Q: *What types of weather services do you use when making an offshore passage? How do you gather weather info?*

A: We basically use three sources for our weather information. First, we try to get synoptic charts (surface analysis and forecast) via radio fax (or the Internet before departing for a passage). These provide us with a good idea of the "big picture" and relevant meteorological details such as fronts, troughs, and convergence zones. Especially before longer passages, we try to follow these charts consistently over one to two weeks to get a feel for the rhythm of weather patterns and how well the forecast matches reality.

Second, we use the output from NOAA's GFS model via Saildoc's email service in two forms. One is a moving spot forecast three or four days out with wind and wave data. The other is a longer term outlook (seven to ten days) on surface pressure via GRIB files over the same large area covered by the synoptic charts. This gives us an idea of what the computer model thinks will happen beyond the forecast horizon of the synoptic charts (typically seventy-two hours). We take the GFS data with a grain of salt, given that it is "raw output" from a computer model. Still, it helps us to spot potential issues early on.

Our third source of information is satellite images which we can also receive via radio fax. We find these very useful for getting an idea of the intensity of fronts and convergence zones. The synoptic charts are a "daily must" for us. GFS data and the satellite images, on the other hand, we may only receive every few days or when weather developments require more stringent tracking.

Q: *Do you use a weather routing service?*

A: We subscribed to Chris Parker's services in the Caribbean and found his service especially helpful when weather windows were very narrow such as when late or early season tropical storms posed a significant threat. In the tropical Pacific outside cyclone season, on the other hand, we don't see the need for a weather router. The passage from Tonga to New Zealand was a bit more challenging with respect to finding a suitable weather window. We were lucky to get help and sound advice from a veteran cruiser (and amateur weatherman) who had sailed this route many times before. In the end, his advice turned out to be better than the guidance other boats received from professional routers, and we had a very relaxed passage.

There is always a learning effect from listening to someone with more experience and knowledge, so the need for a weather routing service diminishes over time. I would still consider some form of experienced outside support whenever there is a risk of a tropical system developing during a passage and/or if very narrow weather windows are concerned. This could be a professional weather router or a knowledgeable friend ashore with access to relevant data sources who can do some healthy second-guessing. In either case, I would want someone with actual sailing experience in the relevant sea area whom I could talk to over SSB rather than simply receiving emailed forecasts from sources without firsthand knowledge. Unless emailed forecasts are very detailed and highly customized, I feel you miss a lot by not being able to interact with the weatherman, to ask questions and understand their reasoning. Simply providing the current conditions at our position to the weather router may influence his or her evaluation of the forecast data she/he is looking at. In the end, it's always your own judgment and your own decision what to do with the advice, and that becomes more difficult the less you understand the rationale behind the advice. Besides, you're missing out on a learning opportunity.

Q: *What types of safety equipment did you purchase and why?*

A: While we have invested in some essential pieces of gear (notably, a life raft, EPIRB, and rarely-used radar), we don't feel that safety can be purchased and ticked off a to-do list. Our most important safety gear are our eyes, ears, and common sense. For example, we keep a constant lookout on deck. We are always surprised to hear of crews who spend most of their night watch time below decks (some even watching DVDs). We stay clipped on in the cockpit and only pop below to check the chart, get a snack, etc. Of course, we read or listen to music during night watches, but we constantly scan the horizon and feel the wind on our faces rather than simply monitoring the displays of AIS, radar, or any other equipment. This way we feel more in tune with the conditions around us, rather than cocooning ourselves away from them.

Similarly, we try to avoid trouble by tracking weather carefully. Even when we can't avoid a system, at least we can prepare for it. We reef early and switch to our smaller staysail when conditions call for it. Finally, we also try to avoid dramatic emergency operations by checking the rigging, steering, and other vital systems before every passage. That way, we lessen the chances of having to leave the safety of the cockpit in rough conditions to repair something that should not have been overlooked in the first place. That said, we know that the sea and our boat will always keep a few surprises in store for us, and strive to keep spares and appropriate safety gear on board for different eventualities.

With a small boat and limited budget, we feel we get the most effective protection through the simplest of systems: things like safety harnesses, equipment checks, and maintaining a good look-out. The same really should hold true for crews on bigger boats with bigger budgets.

# Chapter 8

# Installing a Life Raft on the Coach Roof

A life raft is a must for any cruiser planning to go offshore. While many people invest great effort into choosing the right raft, weighing considerations such as performance and budget, fewer think ahead to the actual installation. Whether you're buying your first life raft or upgrading to a new one, make sure that proper installation is as high a priority as choice of equipment. With some helpful pointers from our boat yard (Yankee Marina in Yarmouth, Maine), we were able to install a new life raft ourselves and now have the peace of mind of a job well done. It is a project of about two days that can be managed with basic tools and know-how.

## The Small Boat Conundrum

The ideal place to mount a life raft is on the stern rail, which has the advantage of easy deployment and good attachment points for the painter. However, many smaller monohulls simply lack stern space, especially once a self-steering device and swim ladder have been mounted. The only feasible option on many boats is a horizontally mounted cradle placed just forward of the dodger. There, the crew still has access to the life raft and the painter can be secured on a deck cleat. The main challenge would be heaving the raft across the life lines, but given the raised center section of the deck, this should not be a major hurdle.

However, there are a few challenges in installing a life raft in this location. One is that the coach roof is typically a relatively soft section of sandwiched deck. It is not constructed to absorb significant loads, such as a wave sweeping over the deck and pulling at the life raft. A second problem is that most coach roofs have a slightly convex curvature that will not be flush with a straight cradle. Finally, there is the issue of achieving a neat installation without marring the interior cabin ceiling with through-bolts. The approach we used in installing our life raft resolved each of these problems, as described in the steps below.

Installation consists of four steps: (A) making mounts that will distribute the load of the life raft over the coach roof, (B) preparing the deck for the mounts, (C) fitting the mounts to the deck, and (D) attaching the cradle to the mounts.

**Tools and supplies needed to complete this project**:

- Life raft, cradle, and 3/8" cradle bolts

- Handheld drill with 2 ½ and 3" hole drills and sanding mounts

- Screwdriver, masking tape, plastic wrap, acetone, plastic gloves, cutting tool

- 5cl syringe (can often be obtained at pharmacies for free)

- Rotating hand sander, 100-220 grit sandpaper

- ¼" structural fiberglass sheet glass to construct mounts

- Epoxy (such as West System 105 Resin with 206 Fast Cure Hardener, plus filler such as West System 406)

- Bedding Compound (such as 3M 4000 UV)

- Paint that matches deck color

## Step A: Making Mounts

The very first step in this process is to determine the exact position for the cradle by placing it in the desired location and marking drill holes. Then determine how thick the coach roof is by carefully probing with a drill at one of the marked mount points. In a sandwich composite construction, the goal is to cut through the top layer of fiberglass and the balsa core, but not all the way through to the interior fiberglass liner. In our case, these two layers of the coach roof were two inches thick, and therefore we knew our mounts would be two inches tall.

With this preliminary information established, you can begin to prepare four mounts that will support the cradle. These can be made by stacking discs cut from sheet glass to create a mushroom-shaped mount. Eventually, the mounts will be fitted into four wells in the coach roof, establishing solid attachment points for the life raft.

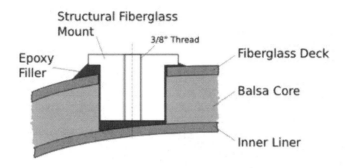

Schematic of the mounts bedded into the coach roof

To construct a mount, you will need to stack a number of discs cut from ¼ inch structural fiberglass sheet, with a disc diameter of 2 ½ inches. The number of discs depends on the thickness of your deck: for example, our two inch thick coach roof called for eight ¼ inch discs. Top off the stack with one wider disc (three inches in diameter) to achieve the mushroom shape. The discs can be cut using a hole saw with 2 ½ and three inch fittings. The hole saw will also drill a narrow hole through the center of each disc. You will need four mushroom-shaped mounts all together. For a two inch thick mount, that means cutting a total of thirty-two narrow discs plus four wider tops.

Next, sand each disc with 100 grit sandpaper and then bond each stack of discs with epoxy (such as West System 105 Resin with 206 Fast Cure Hardener). To keep the layers aligned, put a temporary bolt through the center holes and tighten against a washer and nut. A layer of plastic wrap can be put around the bolt to prevent it from sticking to any epoxy.

After the epoxy has hardened, sand the rough edges of each mount. An easy way to do this is to put the protruding part of the temporary bolt into an electric drill and let it spin while you hold sand paper against it. Once the bolt has served its purpose, it can be removed and the hole widened slightly in preparation for the last stage: tapping a 3/8" thread into each mount. These will accommodate the stainless steel machine screws that will eventually fix the cradle to the mounts. In our case, the screws were 3/8" x 2"; a thinner coach roof might take a 3/8" x 1½" screw. At the conclusion of Step A, you will have prepared four mushroom-shaped mounts, each with a hole through the center.

## Step B: Preparing the Deck

The next step is to drill holes (or "wells") into the coach roof as counterparts for the cradle mounts. Be careful only to drill to the depth you have determined. Use the same hole saw fitting to cut 2½" wide wells into the coach roof. To prevent the central drill bit from penetrating the inner liner, re-adjust it so that it is flush with the outer saw after cutting through the first ¼" of fiberglass and wood.

Mounts and cut out wells

Once you've made the cuts, carefully lever out the fiberglass/balsa plugs. All that remains now in terms of deck preparation is to sand and clean the inside walls of each well. Make sure the wells are completely dry. You must also sand the surface of the coach roof a half inch around each well; that's where the wider head of the mushroom-shaped mount will eventually sit. Check that everything fits by temporarily bolting the four mounts to the cradle and placing it into position. This is the time to remedy any tight spots (either by sanding the mounts or using a Dremel tool to widen the well).

When you're satisfied with the fit, clean all contact surfaces of the wells and mounts with acetone. Then generously mask off the areas around the wells to catch the inevitable epoxy run-off.

Masking off the wells

## Step C: Fitting the Mounts

In this step of the process, you will fit the mounts into the coach roof wells. Once you begin working with epoxy, things will move quickly, so be sure you have everything at hand. At this point, the mounts should still be temporarily fitted to the cradle, so you will be handling the cradle as a whole.

It is important to protect the bolts running through the center of each mount from epoxy overflow, because they will be removed one more time before installation is complete. Stuff the lower end of the bolt holes with a small amount of plastic wrap and place a small piece of masking tape over the top of each bolt. This will prevent epoxy from being squeezed up through the hole and sticking to the bolt.

Now you're ready to connect the matching pieces in earnest. Mix a batch of epoxy (such as West System 105 Resin with 205 Fast Cure Hardener). Cover both contact surfaces with a layer of clear epoxy: first, all surfaces of the mounts, and second, the insides of the wells (including the extra ½" ring around the top of each well). Once these sections have a layer of epoxy, add some adhesive filler to the same batch of epoxy (such as West System 406) and partially fill each well with the thickened mixture. This epoxy will fill any void beneath the mounts and will be squeezed up along the walls of each well. Use enough epoxy for some to be squeezed out the top when the mounts are pushed into place. Now place the cradle with its protruding mounts into position and press firmly.

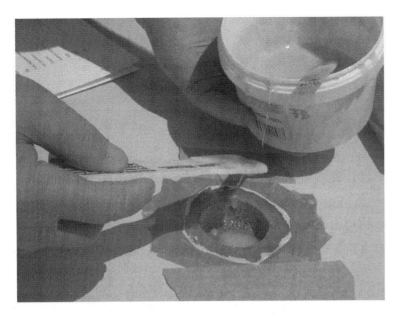

Filling the wells with epoxy

Then weigh the cradle down until the epoxy starts to set (for example, by standing on the cradle or putting the life raft on the cradle).

A curved coach roof will still have a small gap between the underside of the flat mount top and the downward curving deck. Use a surgical syringe (5 cl size works best) to apply thickened epoxy into these gaps. Then trim any excess epoxy from the top edge of the mounts. We use out-of-date credit cards or other plastic cards for this purpose; they have just the right stiffness and their corners can be trimmed to the right radius.

After the epoxy has dried, you can complete this step of the installation by painting the mounts so that they match the coach roof. To do so, unbolt the cradle from the mounts and move it aside. Use a soft disc sander to fair the exposed epoxy around the top of the mounts and follow up by hand, using 220 grit sand paper. This prepares the surface for painting: ideally, use two coats of a two-part polyurethane paint (such as Awlgrip), mixed to match the color of the deck.

## Step D: Bedding the Cradle

Once the paint is completely dry, you can move on to the final step. Bedding compound can make a mess, so be sure to mask off the area around the wells in addition to the

Filling the gap under the mount

sections of cradle that might get smudged. Carefully clean all contact surfaces (including the bolts) with acetone. Then apply bedding compound (3M 4000 UV works well) to the undersides of the cradle at each mount point and along the length of every bolt. Excess bedding compound will be squeezed out when you screw in the bolts; this can be trimmed away after it has set. The final step will be to remove the masking tape and mount the life raft onto the cradle. Now you can step back and admire a job well done!

Taken step by step, this process requires more patience than expertise. The result is a neat, secure life raft that can stand up to the forces it may be exposed to. It's unusual to feel so much satisfaction in installing a piece of equipment you hope never to use, but it's well worth the effort.

## Post Script: Choosing a Life Raft

There are many life raft models available, with prices ranging from US$2,000 and up for a new unit. By no means should you save a buck and rely on an out-of-date, second-hand life raft. As you compare life rafts, check that the cradle or valise will fit in the space you have, and remember to include the price of the container in your budget calculations.

Bedding the cradle

Be aware that some life rafts are designed for near-shore use; features such as insulated floors and multi-day water rations are not a given. While it is reasonably easy to right an inverted life raft, we decided to pay a premium for a self-righting model since we have a young son and did not want to risk having an extra step in a real emergency. Short-handed or older cruisers might want to make the same investment. Other factors that can guide your decision are the service intervals of each model (three years is optimal) and ease of re-servicing (we planned a cruise across the Pacific and therefore decided on a Viking since it can be serviced around the world).

Size is another important factor. In theory, a four-person life raft should be sufficient for four people. Having climbed into a four-person raft during a sea-survival course some years ago, however, it was immediately clear to us that this would be too small if we ever needed to spend more than twenty-four hours adrift. Therefore, the decision to step up to a six-person raft was an easy one, although it came at slightly higher cost and a larger space requirement.

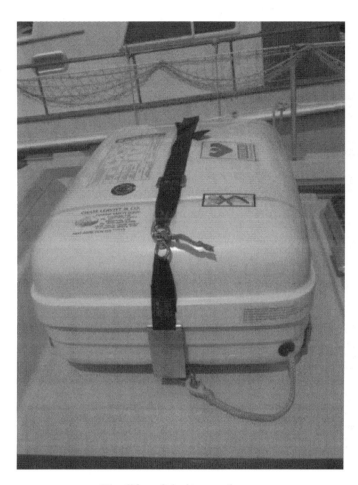

The life raft in its new home

# Chapter 9

# Simulating Life Raft Entry

Any sailor contemplating a blue water passage should look for the opportunity to actually deploy and enter a life raft. A number of sailing schools offer half-day or weekend safety courses that do exactly this. In our case, we had a used life raft that was impossible to sell, so we could use it for our own simulation. We were careful to notify the marina staff in our location and to use a discreet area lest any passers-by become alarmed. Although a simulation in quiet, in-shore waters is not ideal, it did provide a calm run-through that did not frighten our young son.

A (not so) dry run with our old life raft

What did we learn? To begin with, it took a surprising number of hard jerks on the deployment line to fire the CO2 cylinder and inflate the raft. On the other hand, righting and entering the life raft was relatively straightforward. The strongest crew member should enter first to help the others in. The boarding ladder can swing awkwardly under the raft as weight is put on it, but the hand-ladder inside the raft gave us the extra grip needed to climb in. We discovered that the raft lurches as each person enters, so we were careful to distribute our weight for balance.

The next step – separating from a potentially sinking vessel – proved awkward. For starters, the knife provided in the raft for this purpose was so firmly affixed that it was difficult to free. The painter was difficult to access from the main entry since it attached at the opposite end of the life raft (the idea being to keep the main entry away from breaking seas). We learned that the painter should be accessed through the smaller lookout hatch on the windward side of the raft. Details like these are important and vary between different manufacturers, so it is important to go through your owner's manual carefully.

Finally, we familiarized ourselves with drogue deployment and the survival pack contents. It is possible to have extra equipment (such as a handheld water maker) packed into the raft on request. Every captain should also prepare a grab bag with additional equipment. The first thing to reach for, however, is your EPIRB, which should be tied outside the life raft to transmit your position. Hopefully, you will never have to resort to such measures, but it pays to be prepared.

# Chapter 10

# Other Safety Considerations

## Cockpit Safety

One of the most important pieces of safety equipment we cruise with is a simple cockpit jack line. Cheap and easy to install, the three-foot long jack line allows us to clip in before we leave the companionway or before switching over to the deck jack lines. It only took a day's work to splice a rope and mount two U bolts (with suitable backing plates) in the cockpit. Now we remain safely clipped in during night watches or in foul weather. Many cruisers invest in far more complicated and expensive gear, yet overlook this critical first point of safety on board.

## Grab Bag Contents

In addition to an EPIRB, your grab bag should always be packed and ready to go. Use a brightly colored, waterproof bag that is marked with reflective tape and fitted with a lanyard. Our grab bag carries the following equipment to supplement the life raft survival pack, most of it in individual Zip-lock bags:

- Flares (hand held, floating, and rocket flares)

- Handheld GPS

- Handheld VHF

- Lithium batteries for both the above (non-rechargeable)

- Foil blanket

- Handheld compass

- Copies of ship's papers and passports

- Flashlight (hand-crank type)

- Energy bars

- Paper and pencil

- Small knife and cutting board

If we had the time, we would also bring the 5-liter water container we keep next to the companionway (half-filled for floatation). Above the chart table, we keep a list of what to do in an abandon ship situation, from making a mayday call to packing essential equipment.

*Namani's* grab bag

# Chapter 11

# Family Health in the Pacific

Both our sailing trips have been magical times that we wouldn't trade for anything – not just for the travel and the sailing, but most of all for the family time we have enjoyed. Many cruising families we met along the way agree. It's too bad the countless happy stories don't get the same kind of attention that the few negative ones do. In this chapter, we offer an example of how easily a potentially serious child's health issue was resolved by the cruising community in the Pacific.

We were anchored off the island of Taveuni in Fiji along with friends on another boat who sailed from Europe with their two young sons, ages four and seven at that time. One morning, their son Niclas awoke with badly swollen tonsils. Although the family had a variety of medicines aboard, they were dismayed when they read the fine print of the children's antibiotic their pediatrician gave them to take aboard. It listed swollen tonsils as one of the few ailments that antibiotic was not recommended for. Since they knew we also carry children's medication, they called us on the VHF. Happily, our children's antibiotic did cover tonsil infections, so all we had to do was row it over to them. Easy.

Meanwhile, another boat in the same anchorage had listened in to our VHF conversation. They knew of a retired doctor aboard yet another vessel in an anchorage a few miles away. Although the doctor wasn't listening to the VHF at that time, other boats nearby were. Within an hour, the doctor had been found and put in touch with the parents. She assured them that the antibiotic we provided was fine. The doctor also recommended that the family not set off for the remote Lau group as planned, in the small chance that the infection became acute. Thus the parents were able to treat their child and rest easy, not only in the knowledge that a doctor was nearby, but also that staying back was the right thing to do. In the end, they had a lovely time cruising islands they had all to themselves because the bulk of the fleet had gone on to the Lau group.

Not a very spectacular story, but it illustrates several important things. First, a well-stocked medical kit is a must, and attention must be paid to details such as an antibiotic's spectrum of coverage. Second, there's a vast pool of resources within the Pacific cruising community. There are a huge number of boats out there (we rarely had an anchorage to ourselves), and everybody gets to know just about everybody, if not directly then in the second degree. Third, with communications systems like VHF and SSB radio, you're never alone. (We believe an SSB is an absolute must despite the cost; with it we were able to have twice-daily check-ins with other boats even on our passages. Had anything cropped up then, we could have easily talked to a doctor.)

Finally, it's a fallacy that remote island communities in the Pacific lack medical facilities. In this day and age, many islands have some sort of regional clinic that sailors can tap into as needed. You'd be surprised how much help is out there. Case in point: in the sparsely populated Yasawa group of Fiji, there's a centrally located clinic that friends used when a stomach bug persisted for over a week (for mother and child). They hired a local skiff to take them there (twice the speed, plus local knowledge of the reefs) and saw a UK-trained doctor within an hour. Again, easy. Much easier than you would have thought. In Suwarrow, an uninhabited Cook Island popular with cruisers, one man hurt his foot and promptly got stitches from the doctor aboard another boat anchored there. Again, easy.

I can add many more cruising success stories, but I'll leave it at that for now. The three years we spent cruising the Pacific were among the healthiest and happiest of our lives. We were sick far less often than at home, where the germ breeding grounds of school keep us in constant contact with contagious illnesses. We suffered very few injuries because we were careful. We knew the potential for risk, and we acted accordingly. I'd say that far more injuries occur on your average neighborhood playground (not to mention the average highway) than out in the cruising grounds of the world, especially if you sail aboard a well-found vessel along prime cruising routes in favorable seasons. In fact, Markus sustained the worst injury of our Pacific trip when he fell in an Australian urban playground and broke his collarbone!

Yes, there's always a chance that something sometime might go wrong. But given good preparation and care, that chance is no greater than the chance of a freak mishap at home. When I was in grade school, a childhood friend nearly died of a ruptured appendix because her parents didn't take her complaints seriously – they were too busy playing tennis! Luckily, all was well in the end. The point is, you don't need to be in the middle of the Pacific for bad luck to strike. And you don't have to hope for good luck – you can make your own luck by taking sensible precautions.

Every family must make their own decision about taking children cruising, but whatever you do, don't let paranoia hold you back.

Cruising kids enjoying a low boil in Vanuatu

## Post Script: What About Sharks?

Sharks are a danger I've learned to put in the same category as rogue waves or out-of-control eighteen-wheelers on the highway – horrible to imagine but incredibly unlikely. The two times I've come eye to eye with a shark, the shark was at least as spooked as I was and immediately darted away.

Generally, you're safe swimming in shallow, reef-protected waters because the bigger, more dangerous sharks are ocean dwellers. Reef sharks look intimidating but pose little danger – unless you're spear-fishing, when it's prudent to get out of the water or switch to a different location as soon as you land a fish.

We swam worry-free in anchorages throughout the Pacific with only two exceptions. In the Marquesas, where there are no fringing reefs, we couldn't resist the water, but swam with caution – especially after the time a large shark fin appeared off the beach, stalking the children wading in ankle-deep water. Having said that, we swam in the same bay dozens of times to see the manta rays; sharks seem to be rare visitors. In Australia, we rarely ventured in the water – as much out of deference to the jellyfish as the sharks.

Otherwise, we made the most of our South Pacific experience – swimming, snorkeling, and playing in the water to our hearts' delight.

Shark warning on Suwarrow

# Part III

# Underway

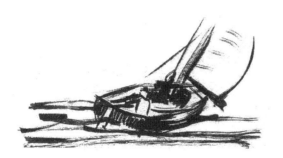

# Underway

What was it Mark Twain said? "Twenty years from now you will be more disappointed by the things that you didn't do than by the ones you did do. So throw off the bowlines. Sail away from the safe harbor... Explore. Dream. Discover." Setting off can be both intimidating and exhilarating. Life aboard a moving, heeling home takes some getting used to, but once you've settled in, you may never want to head back to land. While there's a lot to learn and consider, there's also something supremely satisfying about a life lived in touch with nature, the elements, and the cycle of seasons.

We start with a chapter on Radio Nets for both safety and companionship on the high seas. Then we continue on to weather and forecasting resources, celestial navigation, and managing solar power. Then we'll move from the deck into the galley and suggest convenience foods for the offshore sailor. Finally, we have a chapter on working while sailing to provide examples of people whose professions support all or part of the cruising lifestyle. Read it to judge whether working pays off – in more ways than one!

# Chapter 12

# Do-It-Yourself Radio Nets for Blue Water Passage-Making

Long blue water passages can be daunting for seasoned hands as well as for sailors venturing into their first major offshore adventure. Safety is one cause for concern, and potential loneliness is another. But you don't have to go it alone, even on the open sea. With single side band radio, you can reach across the ocean to communicate with sailors thousands of miles away. It isn't necessary to join an organized sailing rally or tap into a tightly regulated net: we cobbled together our very own radio net for our Pacific crossing and found the result an unqualified success. This "home-made" radio net enhanced our ocean crossing experience in every way – with weather information, advice on fixing gear, and a healthy dose of comic relief during a month-long Pacific passage.

Creating your own radio net can be easy, especially if you're following the seasons along cruising routes where sailors congregate in stepping off points such as the Chesapeake Bay, the Canary Islands, or Panama. We found a crowded anchorage full of cruisers in the Galapagos Islands in March, most of them equipped with SSB and, like us, looking for "company" heading west. All it takes is an agreed-upon time and frequency. Of course, sailors can also tap into established venues such as the Pacific Seafarer's Net, but some of these nets are quite formal or longwinded and require participants to hold ham radio licenses (unlike informal nets operating on marine frequencies). For this reason, a small yet robust net of five to twelve boats offers the perfect combination of safety in numbers without being overly rigid.

Our radio net was initiated by two crews, ourselves aboard *Namani* and our friends on forty-two foot *Astarte*. Early on, there were only three boats underway, so checking in

71

was an easy-going, unstructured affair. As more boats set off and joined us, we moved to a more formal structure, with Markus of *Namani* and Michael of *Astarte* alternating net control duties. Some of the late-comers were crews we had recruited before setting off, but several were sailors who just happened to stumble across our fledging net on the air. Our choice of frequency proved fortuitous in this regard, since we used 8143 kHz on the upper side band two hours after the fading Pan Pacific Net that was familiar to many cruisers. Soon we had a dozen boats in our international group, all thirty-five to fifty foot monohulls that set sail within a three-week period. Every good team needs a name; one early proposal was "The Close Reachers," reflecting the frustrating conditions encountered by the first to depart, but we eventually settled on the "POST" net (an acronym for Pacific Ocean Sailing Tribe, a gang that soon developed clan-like characteristics). Most were heading for the Marquesas, while a few set a more southerly course for Easter and Pitcairn Islands.

Markus taking a turn as net controller

## Spanning an Ocean

The 8 MHz frequency served us well throughout most of the passage, but when the POST net boats spanned the entire 3,000 miles between the Galapagos and Polynesia, we turned to an alternate 12 MHz frequency. Invariably, some boats have better SSB transmission than others, so relays were necessary to compile the entire group's information. This was another time we were thankful for the relatively small size of our group, since relays can quickly grow monotonous, not to mention energy-consuming for short-handed crews in the midst of never-ending watch schedules. We met for about thirty minutes each morning, with the net stretching a little longer in its most sociable and humorous late editions.

What if a yacht failed to call in one morning? In our group, each vessel put forward an individual request as to whether the Coast Guard should be notified with a message of concern should they fail to report for two successive days. This would corroborate a possible EPIRB signal without creating waves of panic in case of a more innocent loss of power or transmission ability.

## Fringe Benefits

Our initial aim in creating a net was to be able to report our position to an outside source daily so that we wouldn't disappear unnoticed into the depths of the Pacific in the event of some disaster. However, we soon discovered a number of practical advantages to our net, such as hearing local weather and sea conditions observed by other boats. For example, when the first crews to depart ran into a powerful contrary current, those behind knew to follow a more southerly course. It proved extremely valuable to have a real-time picture of what might be developing ahead or behind throughout the passage. Similarly, the first boats could also inform the others about what to expect once they had made landfall.

Another advantage of the net was the ability to solicit technical advice. *Astarte's* steering problem was discussed and correctly diagnosed, and *Mary Madeleine's* seemingly serious gearbox problem was resolved by advice from *Adventure Bound*. This extended to discussions about sail configurations, both for immediate need and for future reference. How were those under twizzle rig coping with the rolling swell, in comparison with a prevented main and poled-out genoa? Was the money invested in a pricey lightweight sail paying off?

Members of the net also pooled resources: when *Adventure Bound* couldn't make contact with a radio ham on Pitcairn Island, *Astarte* stepped in to help, using on-board SailMail to contact the islander. Another instance concerned the guessing game among Marquesas-bound cruisers about arrival procedures: would there be dire consequences to visiting spectacular Fatu Hiva before officially clearing in on Hiva Oa? Several boats emailed ahead for the latest update, which they then shared through the net.

Several members tuned into one of several other radio nets as well, creating a tangled web of cross-alliances. We on *Namani* had two appointments each day, including the POST net and a German-speaking "Funkrunde." Greg and Danielle, Francophone Canadians aboard *Mary Madeleine*, also tuned in to the evening French-speaking net.

73

Several of our members likewise reported to the Pacific Seafarer's Net. By connecting with a variety of nets, each crew could filter and pass on pertinent information to our small group, thus keeping us connected to a much wider network – a global village, if you will, united by the sea and bouncing radio waves. Once, a mysterious flare was reported on a different net; This information was passed on to us, and thus twelve more crews were alerted to a potential vessel in distress (happily, it turned out to be a false alarm). As Barbara of *Astarte* aptly put it, our net was like Facebook on the ocean.

Above all, we enjoyed the social aspect of the net, especially as the long passage stretched into week three and then four. Crews tallied fishing scores, commiserated over poor conditions, and shared many a laugh thanks to good-humored sailors who revealed their funny, funnier, and funniest sides. In fact, when we offered *Katydid's* Robin, the only single-hander in our group, to move to first in the roll call to shorten his time, he replied with a vehement, "No! This is my social time!"

## The Cast of Characters

Our radio net quickly developed a two-part rhythm. The first ten to fifteen minutes of radio time were dedicated to position and weather reports, followed by a sociable second section of advice, banter, and jokes. On the open sea, days can be rich in overall impressions but generally uneventful, and the net let us glimpse life beyond our own limited horizons. It was a little like watching TV, and we had the choice of several channels.

It all started innocently, with *Darramy's* fishing success drawing calls for advice on lures. This led to a few episodes of the Cooking Channel, featuring *Adventure Bound's* recipes for all those tasty fish. The latter crew also spun off an Adventure Channel, chronicling Zimbabwean Bruce's antics in the deep blue sea. Going overboard to clean the hull in a calm, he ended up spearing two mahi mahi! The father-son team aboard *Sophie* issued a Race Report, racking up consistent daily runs of 160 to 180 miles. Meanwhile, the Dutch couple aboard *Happy Bird* offered a Home Improvement program shortly after Roderick sent Yvonne (grandmother of two) up the mast in a heavy swell to recover a parted halyard. Ever-upbeat Michael of *Astarte* ran the Weather Channel, with Brian of *Darramy* reporting painstakingly exact measurements from his "wavometer" (2.3 meter swells on every sixth wave) and "cloudometer" (37% cloudy skies). Brian also directed the Comedy Network, starring his imaginary crew member, Roger the cabin boy, who would be sent off on errands up the mast and even to other boats with various complaints. We laughed ourselves silly and knew that our friends were all doing the same in their not-so-solitary stretches of ocean beyond our horizon.

Since few of the POST net members had met in person before setting off, it was great fun forming a mental image of each person over the air. Even more fun was actually meeting many of our cohort in French Polynesia. As it turned out, a number of other boats (equipped with SSB receivers only) had been tuning in, too. We discovered this when perfect strangers greeted us in the Marquesas and said they had been tracking our progress all along!

## A Contrast

The POST net and our German-speaking "Funkrunde" make for an interesting comparison. Both consisted of approximately twelve boats exchanging positions and local conditions over roughly half an hour. However, each went about this in a different way. While the POST net operated via established net controllers, the German Funkrunde subsisted for two weeks in a much looser (and decidedly un-Teutonic) system. Rita of *Aninad* would simply come on the air, hail a friend, report the basics, and exchange a few pleasantries. The friend would then call on another vessel and initiate the next two-way chat, while the rest of the group patiently listened in and noted each vessel's information. Each boat would eventually draw in another, in no established order. This seemingly haphazard method worked because the crews were already familiar with each other from a group dinner in the Galapagos, and if someone was left out, well, they could be counted on to pipe up at the end.

Eventually, the German fleet spread out and transmission clarity faded, so they also shifted to a designated net controller. The task fell to Heike aboard *Victoria*, who not only possessed strong transmission capability but also had a clear voice and perky radio personality fit for professional broadcasting. Interestingly, most calls on the German net were made by the female members of each crew (most of whom were couples, plus three families with young children), with Corinna of *Moin* handling much of the relay work. To keep things interesting, Heike pulled her six-year-old son, Niclas, into the fray, allowing him to hail each boat on the roll in turn. Who couldn't resist a smile when his sweet, tiny voice came on the air? This kind of personal touch is only possible within a small-scale net, allowing a scattered, faceless group to become a community, no matter how far-flung.

The main challenge for both nets was accommodating the last crews after the majority had made landfall. Ideally, a team of net controllers should stay on duty until the last boat arrives safely in port. Poor SSB transmission within the mountain-ringed Marquesas made it difficult for those at anchor to communicate with vessels still underway, though email progress reports via SailMail could still get through. In addition, the last three POST boats were able to sidestep to another informal net and thus maintained direct outside contact throughout the entire crossing.

Our experience shows that informal radio nets can be great fun and bring many advantages. With a few like-minded crews and a decent SSB set, sailors can cross oceans with a feeling of safety and camaraderie, regardless of the region they explore. In fact, many of the crews remained friends throughout their Pacific travels – on and off the air.

Nicky at *Namani's* nav station

## Lessons Learned

What did our experiences teach us? For one thing, we were glad to have kept an unchanging UTC meeting time (1600) for our net rather than attempting to keep up with time zone changes across the Pacific. This is especially true for boats of vastly different speeds and staggered departure dates. We were also careful to start with a late enough time slot so as to prevent the net meeting time from drifting into the wee hours of the morning once we made westward progress and the appointed hour became earlier and earlier in terms of local time.

Having two net controllers share the burden also worked well on the POST net. Ideally, the two controllers will also be fairly far apart, the better to receive other members of a far-flung group. In general, 6 MHz would have been a better choice than 8 MHz given the timing of our net and the great range between boats. 8 MHz also seems to create more interference with other on-board electronics (such as autopilots) on many boats, but one of our members could not receive this frequency on their SSB set. It also pays to check for overlaps before publicizing your net and to set an alternative frequency. We encountered a hiccup when our net started to overlap with chitchat from a nearby fishing fleet on 12 MHz later in the passage.

Finally, small radio nets allow each crew to put forward individual wishes, such as what to do in case of a repeated "no-show." On the other hand, members should reach some consensus on which weather conditions to report and how exactly to measure them (for example, true or apparent wind direction, and how to measure wave height) before these become subjects of wearisome (or entertaining) discussion over the air.

## Post Script: Some Single Side Band Radio Basics

As far as SSB equipment is concerned, you will have a choice between marine and amateur transceivers. Marine transceivers typically have a more rugged and fool-proof design. For example, they lack many of the filtering and fine-tuning capabilities of amateur units. A modern marine SSB will also be able to transmit and receive on non-marine frequencies. Marine units have nominally higher maximum output power than amateur units (150W rather than 100W). In practice, this won't matter much: 100W is plenty and the limiting factors will be installation details such as antenna connection or the effectiveness of a counterpoise.

The biggest difference between marine and amateur ("ham") units may be price: marine units may cost two to three times as much as amateur units. If you decide on an amateur device, be aware that the transmit capability for marine frequencies will have been disabled. Many cruisers modify their ham sets so that they can also transmit over marine frequencies. While this modification is illegal in some countries (including the United States) it is straightforward for many ham models and you can find instructions on the Web. Typically, it is a simple matter of disconnecting a diode on the circuit board. Aside from the legal aspect, this will definitely void any warranty – proceed at your own risk. The Sailnet forum has an informative thread on the legal aspect.[1]

Check the licensing requirements of the country that issues your Ship Station License for communication equipment. An internationally recognized Long Range Certificate is relatively easy to obtain and will license you for communication on the short wave frequencies reserved for marine use. To legally transmit on the short wave frequencies

---

[1] http://www.sailnet.com/forums/cruising-liveaboard-forum/50351-hf-radio-modified-marine-modified-ham.html

used by radio amateurs (and some of the popular radio nets such as the Pacific Seafarers' Net), you will need an additional Amateur Radio License (a "ham" license). Of course, in a distress situation, it is legal to use any form of communication independent of licensing requirements.

Installing a shortwave radio on a sailboat is a subject that has been extensively covered on cruisers' Internet forums. It requires setting up the transceiver plus an antenna (typically an insulated backstay) and antenna tuner. A unit installed on a non-metal hull will need some form of counterpoise (often copper foil or bronze plates). The Communications section on the Seven Seas Cruising Association's discussion board is a good place to start researching the matter.[2] Another good resource is Bill Dietrich's page which compiles a wealth of information about communications from a boat in general.[3]

[2] http://www.ssca.org/forum/viewforum.php?f=5
[3] http://www.billdietrich.me/Radio.html

# Chapter 13

# Weather Notes

Good literature on "how weather works" in the South Pacific abounds. Jim Corenman's *Letters from the South Pacific* have an excellent section about weather (page 17 onwards) that provides an entertaining yet insightful introduction.[1] If you want to dive deeper into the subject, David Sapiene's *Weather for the Yachtsman* is a good source written by an experienced New Zealand sailor and forecaster.[2] His weather-related presentations at Pangolin are also worth checking out.[3] These documents are available for download. Last but not least, there is Bob McDavitt's *Mariner's Metpack*.[4] Written by another New Zealand meteorologist, it also provides a good introduction to South Pacific weather, albeit with a more specific focus on New Zealand and the NZ Metservice's forecast products. McDavitt's Metpack is only available in print.

In this chapter, we'll first outline what to expect in terms of weather as you're moving west through the South Pacific. We'll follow with a description of how we approached weather forecasting aboard *Namani* and finish with a peek at ocean currents along the way.

## Moving West – What to Expect

Assuming you're traveling outside the South Pacific Cyclone season (which typically runs from November to April), what follows is a very brief summary of weather patterns you're likely to encounter along the Coconut Milk Run. A good overview of the

---

[1] http://svsoggypaws.com/files/JimCorenman-SouthPacificLetters.pdf

[2] http://www.pangolin.co.nz/downloads/weather_for_the_yachtsman_2008.pdf

[3] http://www.pangolin.co.nz/jetsam-index

[4] http://boatbooks.co.nz/weather.html#23104

various sources for weather forecast data along this route available in "Coconut Milk Run Weather", an article in the April 2012 issue of *Ocean Navigator* magazine.[5]

You can typically leave Panama for the Galapagos Islands with the help of easterly trade winds spilling over from the Caribbean but will likely have to deal with light and fickle winds as you get closer to the equator. There may be an opportunity to take advantage of favorable currents along the way (see *A Word About Currents* on page 85).

Once you move south of the Galapagos Islands to pick up the trades, you should be all set – as long as those trades are established. If they're not, it will be a game of patience while keeping an eye on the NOAA surface forecasts and streamline analysis for big picture developments.[6] None of the available forecast products will pick up the small scale details that cause fickle winds in these latitudes.

As you move from the Marquesas (at about 9° south) to the Tuamotus and on to Tahiti and the Iles Sous le Vent (at about 17° south), you leave the zone of "carefree" weather. You will have to pay some attention to systems approaching from Australia via New Zealand and tracking east at about 30° to 40° south. These systems typically do not pose any danger in French Polynesia during the sailing season and you won't cross any of their associated fronts at your latitude. However, they can disturb the trade winds and cause squally conditions and wind shifts – possibly by working in concert with segments of the South Pacific Convergence Zone (SPCZ). The chapters *Atoll Cruising 101: The Tuamotus* (page 199) and *Post Script: Weather and Tide Resources for the Tuamotus* (page 204) have more information on how this may affect you.

As you progress west, the impact of the SPCZ and the fronts and troughs off New Zealand becomes stronger and you must pay attention to the weather again, especially when planning longer passages. Most boats cover the 1,000 NM between the tropics and the temperate latitudes in either New Zealand or Australia at the front and tail ends of the South Pacific cyclone season. Looking for a weather window during these inherently unstable times can be a bit of a challenge or a fun pastime depending on your taste. *Playing the Weather to New Zealand*, an article in the April 2014 issue of *Ocean Navigator* magazine, looks at general strategies and weather forecast sources for sailing from the tropics to New Zealand with the approach of the cyclone season (see also *Picking a Weather Window for a Tonga-to-New Zealand Passage* on page 251).[7]

Moving back into the tropics during the southern hemisphere fall, you will again be looking for a suitable weather window. We noticed that seasoned cruisers who have

---

[5] http://www.oceannavigator.com/Ocean-Voyager-2012/Coconut-Milk-Run-weather/

[6] http://weather.noaa.gov/fax/marine.shtml

[7] http://www.oceannavigator.com/March-April-2014/Weather-to-New-Zealand/

Getting ready for foul weather between New Zealand and Fiji

been "commuting" between New Zealand and the tropics for many years were invariably at the back of the pack, waiting patiently for their chance to avoid late season tropical depressions along the route (see also *New Zealand to Fiji: the Long Way Around* on page 269).

Along the southwestern rim of the Pacific (Fiji, Vanuatu and New Caledonia), the antics of the SPCZ may cause squally conditions. In addition, systems moving eastwards to the south will periodically disturb the trades in the by-now-familiar pattern. This is not necessarily a bad thing, though. Some popular passages in this stretch of ocean can be challenging in strong southeasterly trade winds (for example, sailing to the southern end of Fiji's Lau Group from the bigger islands in the north) and a passing trough over New Zealand may just give you that favorable wind shift.

As you sail towards Australia, you will be on the lookout for lows that stall and deepen in the Tasman Sea. Even if their strong winds don't reach you farther north, they can cause ugly seas. You also want to watch for lows that come off the coast of New South Wales. These typically form out of troughs farther inland and can be quite ferocious. These lows are typically smaller in scale and fast-moving.

81

Steering through the passage of a squall

## Weather Forecasting on *Namani*

On *Namani* we had two different routines for receiving and interpreting forecast data, depending on whether we were underway or somewhere with shoreside Internet access.

Underway, we relied on weather fax and email via SSB and a Pactor modem plus laptop combination. Bandwidth is very limited underway, forcing us to restrict data volume to a minimum.

We would use weather fax to get surface pressure forecasts (NOAA,[8] NZ MetService,[9] or "BOM", the Australia Bureau of Meteorology,[10] depending on location) as well as NOAA's Streamline Analysis. The surface forecasts were our "bread and butter" in understanding the big weather picture up to seventy-two hours out. The Streamline Analysis helped to identify convergence zones and other tropical trouble spots. Occasionally, we would also receive NOAA's satellite image for the West Pacific (a grayscale version is available via weather fax).

We also used the GRIB ("Gridded Binary") forecast data available from NOAA's GFS

---

[8] http://weather.noaa.gov/fax/marine.shtml

[9] http://www.metservice.com/maps-radar/maps/southwest-pacific

[10] http://www.bom.gov.au/marine/

model output. Many crews download GRIB forecasts with wind data (typically displayed as barbed wind arrows) only for grid points in their immediate vicinity because bandwidth is at a premium. The problem here is that wind data across a latitude/longitude grid greatly inflates the size of GRIB files (two vector components for each grid point and time step, stored at full floating point precision). Instead of wind forecast GRIB, we would get two separate files via email:

1. A GRIB file over a relatively large area with only surface pressure (plus rain if tropical convergence zones are a concern). With twenty-four hour intervals and a 2° x 2° grid size, a ten-day forecast over the entire southwest Pacific will still be under 10KB in file size. For example, an email to query@saildocs.com with the following line in the message body will provide isobars and precipitation in twenty-four hour intervals up to ten days out from central Australia to west of New Zealand between 5° and 45° south:

```
send GFS:05S,45S,140E,170W|2,2|24,48..240|PRMSL,RAIN
```

2. A Spot Forecast that lists a set of forecast parameters for a specific position in a tabular text format. While underway, we would request a "moving forecast" for our average course and speed. A file with a few days' worth of forecast data will be small (<2KB) even at six or three-hour intervals.

The large scale overview (point 1, above) provides the big picture. In most cases the wind can be estimated accurately enough from isobar contours – with all the usual warnings that this is raw computer model output. We used this data to complement the surface forecasts and get an idea of what might happen beyond seventy-two hours in the future. Obviously, there is a great deal of uncertainty the more you advance the forecast horizon. Nevertheless, the longer-range model predictions help alert us to potential trouble. Continuity between subsequent forecasts is often a good indicator of how confident the models are in their prediction.

The short-term detailed data (point 2, above) is helpful at a micro-level: for example to pick out changes in wind direction along our route (or at anchor without Internet access). We would send an email to query@saildocs.com with one line in the message body:

```
send Spot:18.3S,168.5E|3,3|PRMSL,WIND,WAVES,RAIN,LFTX,CAPE
```

This means "send me surface pressure, wind speed and direction, wave height and direction, precipitation, Lifted Index and CAPE [11] for position 18°18'S 168°30'E over

---

[11]Lifted Index is an indicator of the stability of the atmosphere's layering. A positive value indicates stable conditions, while negative values indicate instability. CAPE is an indicator for available convective

the coming three days in three-hour intervals." The ensuing email response would look like this:

```
Data extracted from file gfs150117-06z.grb dated   ...
Data extracted from file ww3-20150117-06z.grb dated ...
request code: Spot:18.3S,168.5E|4,3|PRMSL,WIND, ...


Forecast for 18°18S 168°30E (see notes below)
Date   Time   PRESS  WIND DIR WAVES DIR  PER RAIN LFTX CAPE
       utc    hPa    kts  deg mtrs  deg  sec mm/h  °C
---------- ------ ----- --- ----- --- ---- ---- ---- ----
01-17 06:00 1009.5  6.9 232   0.9 139 8.1       0.1 49.2
01-17 09:00 1010.8  4.4 215   0.9 144 8.3 0.0 -0.4 53.2
01-17 12:00 1010.6  2.6 209   0.9 149 8.4 0.0 -1.1 76.0
01-17 15:00 1009.7  2.4 219   0.8 135 8.6 0.0 -1.4  101
01-17 18:00 1009.6  1.1 206   0.8 146 8.8 0.0 -1.2  108
01-17 21:00 1010.3  0.8 052   0.8  75 9.0 0.0 -0.9 68.8
...
```

When looking at this GFS forecast, we assumed that actual sustained winds would vary by plus or minus five knots from the forecast, plus 40% in gusts. A forecast wind speed of less than ten knots typically meant "light and variable." For a moving forecast, we would add boat speed in knots and true course over ground in degrees to the request (note the 5.5,215 at the end of the line):

```
send Spot:18.3S,168.5E|3,3|PRMSL,WIND,WAVES,RAIN,CAPE|5.5,215
```

When we have shoreside Internet access, things are easier because bandwidth becomes less of a restriction. We would still look at surface charts and satellite images and also use the GFS GRIB data.

In addition, we found the following two sources of weather forecast data very useful, especially when looking for longer weather windows between the tropics and New Zealand or Australia:

1. MetVUW,[12] the University of Wellington (New Zealand) Meteorology Department. They compare US, Euro and UK model outputs and either pick and chose or blend them into their own seven-day forecasts for the Southwest Pacific.

2. ECMWF,[13] the European Center for Medium Range Weather Forecasting. This

---

energy in the atmosphere. High CAPE ($>2000$ Joule/kg) in combination with a negative Lifted Index points towards heavy thunderstorms with very squally conditions which may not be reflected in the wind speed forecast.

[12] http://metvuw.com/forecast/forecast.php?type=rain&region=spacific&noofdays=7

[13] http://tinyurl.com/o6sa7fk

is the European version of the US GFS model and provides a surface pressure forecast for ten days. For longer-range forecasts, we found it very useful to check whether the ECMWF and GFS models disagreed significantly. If so, we knew that anything might happen. Otherwise, we would have reasonable confidence in the basic longer-term outlook beyond seventy-two hours.

## A Word About Currents

Along some stretches of the Coconut Milk Run, currents can have a significant impact on your passage times. The East Australian Current is one prominent example. Currents can also make a big difference on a passage between Panama and the Galapagos Islands. Reports from fellow boaters leaving the Galapagos Islands for the Marquesas indicated that the generally west-setting current south of Isabela Island seemed to reverse every seven to ten days for about forty-eight hours. We learned that lesson too late and spent one twenty-four hour period tacking 100 NM only to end up a mere 10 NM from the previous day's position.

Pilot Charts that show the average historic wind conditions on the world's oceans also provide a good representation of steady, large scale current phenomena like the Equatorial Current.[14] However, they lack the resolution (both in space and time) for smaller and more dynamic features.

One of the few sources of current prediction data that is accessible underway is Meteo France's global prediction model of ocean currents. Its output can be obtained as GRIB files via an email interface. Some popular GRIB file viewer applications have trouble displaying the data but OpenCPN's GRIB plug-in works well (see graphic on page 86).[15]

To get Meteo France current forecasts, send an email to `navimail@meteo.fr`, with the subject `Requete` (request) and the following text in the message body:

```
@mto@reqt@grib@
A 1
Z 154.750 −30.250 6.500 7.500
M 0.5
D 10
P courant
G 24 48 72 96 120 144 168 192 216 240
C bzip2
```

---

[14] http://tinyurl.com/ozuhbdt

[15] http://opencpn.org/ocpn/grib_weather_plugin

```
s 2.1.3
@mto@reqt@fin@
```

This will result in a response email that contains a compressed GRIB file with current forecast data. The file can be opened and displayed by OpenCPN's GRIB Viewer plug-in, indicating current strength by color and direction by arrows.

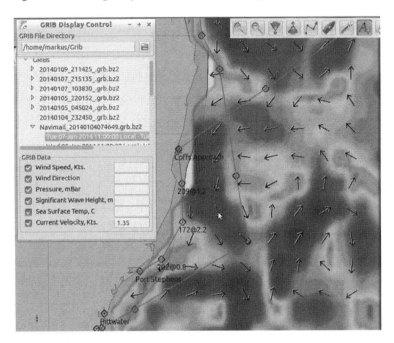

The meaning of each of the lines in the email request above is as follows:

- `@mto@reqt@grib@`: remains the same for every request

- `A 1`: remains the same for every request

- `Z 154.750 -30.250 6.500 7.500`: The rectangle for the forecast, given as longitude and latitude of the center point of the rectangle (with west longitude and south latitude represented by negative values), followed by its width and height in degrees

- `M 0.5`: Grid spacing in degrees; valid values are 0.25, 0.5, 0.75, 1.0, 1.25, 2.5

- `D 10`: remains the same for every request

- `P courant`: remains the same for every request

- `G 24 48 72 96 120 144 168 192 216 240`: forecast times in hours

- `C bzip2`: file compression method

- `s 2.1.3`: remains the same for every request

- `@mto@reqt@fin@`: always the same

The model outputs seem to be updated once a week. Depending when you send your request in that weekly cycle, you may receive a note in the response: "incomplete extraction/extraction partielle." You will, however, still receive the data for the remaining portion of the forecast period.

We found the model surprisingly accurate in the South Pacific. The accuracy does seem to degrade toward the end of the weekly forecast horizon (at least in areas where eddies and currents move significantly over a week). However, the first seventy-two to ninety-six hours were often strikingly accurate.

# Chapter 14

# Celestial Navigation for the Recreational Practitioner: Adapting an Old Art for Today's Cruisers

There are few things quite as satisfying as fixing your position by measuring the altitude of a few heavenly bodies. With no other landmarks around, stars and planets help to put a face on an otherwise featureless expanse of ocean – they become our friends at sea during the night. Even though there's no longer a practical need to use celestial navigation in the age of GPS, it seems a good way to stay in touch with our "friends."

For the recreational navigator, the fun and beauty of celestial navigation often becomes obscured by a maze of numbers and a lack of confidence. In this chapter, we introduce pragmatic tweaks to the traditional way in which celestial navigation is taught, putting the focus back on those friendly stars and our sextant. Why not get more fun and insight out of practicing celestial navigation on board while mastering an old art with confidence?

The approach we outline below can be applied to any celestial sight. It's particularly useful for fixing your position by observing multiple stars or planets at twilight. While the good old sun sight certainly has its value, there's a special reward in the instant gratification of finding your position without the uncertainties of a running fix.

## Setting the Focus

What takes practice to perfect on a rolling boat is actual altitude measurements with a sextant. The more of these measurements we can take and evaluate, the better. We therefore want to minimize the time spent on sight reduction (Figure 1, step 3) and instead focus on taking and evaluating sights (steps 2 and 5).

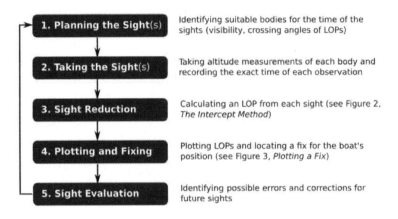

Figure 1: Celestial navigation cycle

In the early days of GPS, continuing the practice of celestial sights was motivated chiefly by the need for an emergency backup navigation method. Consequently, the focus was on a minimalistic procedure, using only pencil and paper for the sight reduction step. As a result, the recreational navigator spent most of his time on tedious computations, consulting logarithmic tables and filling in forms in a process that – without daily practice – can be as error-prone and frustrating as filling in your 1040 tax return.

Today, however, it's much more likely that grab bags contain a functioning handheld GPS rather than a sextant, nautical almanac, sight reduction tables, and a timepiece with known offset and rate of deviation from UTC. We no longer need to restrict ourselves to a tedious barebones procedure for safety reasons. Instead, we're free to use one of the countless electronic calculators that reduces sight reduction to a few keystrokes and to focus our attention on taking and evaluating sights instead (see *Useful Tools for Celestial Navigation* on page 99). Many of these tools also feature an electronic ephemeris which can replace the Nautical Almanac. Alternatively, the Nautical Almanac includes detailed instructions for programming sight reduction on a calculator or computer. If, on the other hand, you'd rather stick with the old pencil and paper method – there's nothing wrong with that, just don't let it deter you from practicing and evaluating your sights.

## Changing the Game

Now that we're no longer bogged down by tedious sight reduction work, we can think about how to best spend our precious time at twilight. Figure 2 introduces some of the terminology referred to in the text below.

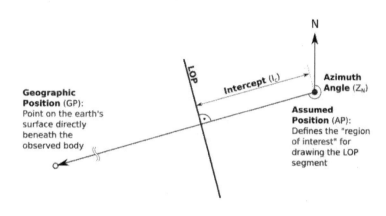

Figure 2: The Intercept Method – some terminology

According to traditional lore, you should have at least three, but preferably four or more, LOPs from different stars or planets. The more LOPs you have, the better you can box in your position, or so the argument goes.

That approach works well for seasoned navigators with a few thousand sights under their belts and with strong confidence in the accuracy of their sights. For recreational practitioners, however, taking single sights of many different bodies is perhaps the least effective use of our limited time at twilight.

For us, the accuracy of each altitude measurement will typically be uncertain. Adding more measurements of doubtful quality is more likely to increase ambiguity than to improve accuracy (see Figure 3, *Plotting a Fix*). Fixing our position inside (and in some cases outside) the cocked hat ends up being mere guesswork and makes it difficult to systematically identify and learn from our mistakes.

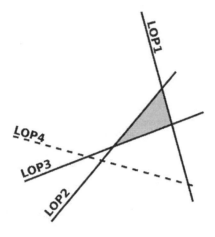

Figure 3: Plotting a fix

So let's accept that our sights will not be perfect. They will include an unknown random error; some will be too high, others too low. For a single measurement it will be impossible to tell which and by how much. However, if we had a series of altitude measurements of the same body, we could obtain a better estimate of the true altitude value (and therefore a high quality LOP) by applying simple statistical methods. So why waste those precious minutes of twilight by taking individual sights of uncertain quality of many different bodies? Instead, let's focus on only two bodies but aim to make their LOPs as accurate as possible by taking multiple sights of each body.

That leaves the question of how to best estimate the true altitude value from a series of sights. Intuitively, we think of the average (arithmetic mean) as a way to cancel out errors in a series of measurements. However, this is not the best method for sextant sights taken on a small boat. For the average to be the best estimator of the true value, the errors in our sextant altitude measurements must possess certain statistical properties: they must be statistically independent, equally distributed, and conform to a certain type of statistical distribution. Our sextant sights will fail to meet at least two (if not all three) of these requirements. They will be neither independent nor identically distributed. In fact, we have no idea what type of distribution our measurements will conform to.

In our case, a much better – and simpler – estimator of the true altitude value is the median (the middle value out of a sorted series of measurements). The median is a robust estimator, good for situations where we cannot make assumptions about the statistical properties of our measurements – precisely what we need.

With this in mind, the approach we propose is straightforward:

**Step 1**: Identify two bodies (stars, planets, moon) that will be visible at twilight, with their azimuth angles separated by 45° to 135° (90°±45°). A difference in azimuths outside this range will lead to an LOP crossing angle that is either too acute or too obtuse, which may amplify any error in the altitude measurement when later plotting the fix.

For example, one June evening found us sailing between Fiji's Lau islands (see Figure 4, *Picking the right stars*). Looking for suitable candidates among the fifty-seven navigational stars, we selected bright stars that would be visible above the horizon. This left us with the eight stars shown in Figure 4. Of these eight, only four were not obscured by sails, rigging, and gear off the stern, and only Arcturus and Antares provided a robust crossing angle – another very good reason to focus on only two bodies.

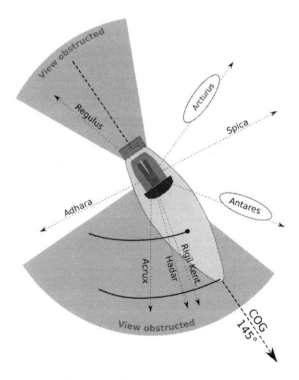

Figure 4: Picking the right stars

**Step 2**: At twilight, take an uneven number of sights for each of the two bodies in quick succession. Five sights each work very well. We have found little improvement by taking seven or more sights.

**Step 3**: Use your preferred method for calculating the intercept for each sight (ten intercept values if you took five sights of each of the two bodies). An electronic sight reduction tool will help do this quickly and easily.

Then, for each body, sort the intercept values and take the sight with the median (middle) intercept value to plot the LOP. For example, if the sights of one of our two observed bodies yielded a sorted intercept series of:

```
4.2 away

3.9 away

1.2 away

0.3 toward

2.8 toward
```

we would take the middle value of 1.2 away and its associated azimuth angle to plot the LOP for this body.

**Step 4**: Plot the two LOPs to determine the fix latitude and longitude (some electronic calculators will do this automatically).

**Step 5**: Evaluate your fix against your GPS position, looking for ways to improve your sights by reducing any systematic error in your measurements (more on that later).

In addition to providing robust estimates of the observed bodies' true altitudes (and thus high-quality LOPs), this approach also allows us to collect a comprehensive set of sight data. We can later analyze this data to help us improve the quality of our sights.

Five sights each for two bodies may sound like a lot, but it is actually quite quick and easy. Since we stick with the same star or planet for each sight series, we don't have to reset the sextant and bring the body all the way down to the horizon every time. Nor do we have to change our orientation or our position on the boat. And the software eliminates the headache of manually reducing the ten sights.

# Putting It All Together

For a complete example, let's go back to that June evening in Fiji: an overnight passage, the sun setting to the west, and a mostly cloudless sky. Beam reaching on a course of 145° at evening twilight, we were lucky to have Venus available for a sight. Figure 5, *A sample sight* shows the five sights we took of Venus, sorted by intercept.

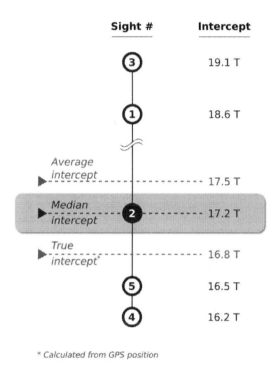

Figure 5: A sample sight

Our second sight landed on the median position with an intercept of 17.2T. Since we had a GPS position to later check our fix, we could also calculate the theoretically correct intercept of 16.8T. This made our median sight 0.4' too high but significantly better than sights 1, 3, and 4. As it turned out, sight number 5 was even closer to the true value, although we would have had no way of knowing that without peeking at the GPS. Our objective here is not to identify the best sight in our series (impossible without GPS), but to have a method that will reliably produce a good estimate of the true altitude value. Most importantly, it will eliminate outliers such as sights 1 and 3. Had we only taken one sight, our LOP would have been off by 1.8 NM (sight number 1) rather than 0.4 NM and – without knowledge of our GPS position – we would have had no way of judging the quality of that single sight.

The example above also demonstrates that sights number 1 and 3 skew the mean (average) intercept (as opposed to the median intercept) upwards to 17.5 NM. Scenarios like this, where the outliers are distributed asymmetrically around the true value, are quite common with waves rolling the boat and obscuring the horizon. In these cases taking the median sight will produce better results than using the mean of a series.

The complete fix from our example is shown in Figure 6, with the second LOP derived from a five-sight series of Arcturus.

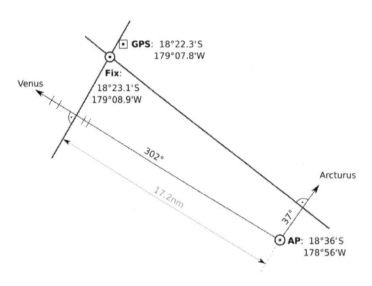

Figure 6: The completed fix

## Some Fine-Tuning

As recreational practitioners of celestial navigation, we could stop here and already have a robust and pragmatic method for producing reliable fixes. But while we're at it, we may as well push the idea a little further.

One thing to keep in mind when applying the above procedure is that our position changes over the course of the sights, effectively producing a running fix over a short distance. In most cases, we will not be concerned about the small error this introduces. For example, if our first and our last sights were taken twenty minutes apart at a boat speed of six knots, the resulting intercept error for a star that was observed 60° forward or aft of the beam would be 1.7 nautical miles at most – unlikely to bother us on the open ocean. The error will be less for bodies that lie closer to the beam. Swifter work will reduce this error; twenty minutes is a generous allowance for completing the two-sight series.

If we need to eliminate this error, we can borrow a page from aviators for whom this is a more substantial issue. The Sight Reduction Tables for Air Navigation (Pub. No. 249 Volume 1)[1] include a handy table to correct a calculated intercept for "Motion of the Observer." The navigator enters the table with Speed Over Ground (SOG) and the relative angle that a bearing line to the observed body forms with the ship's Course Over Ground. Given these two arguments, the table provides the correction to be applied to our calculated intercept per minute of elapsed time. At fifty to nine-hundred knots, the SOG for which these corrections are tabulated are more representative of aircraft than of cruising sailboats. We can, however, simply divide the SOG values and the resulting corrections by ten or one hundred to match our earthbound realities (look for "Alternative Table 1" at the end of the publication).

Some electronic sight reduction calculators (such as the CelNav package detailed in *Useful Tools for Celestial Navigation* on page 99) will automatically correct for this error. We also find this correction convenient to advance or retard our celestial fixes to fall on the half hour, making them easier to reconcile with the ship's dead reckoning plot.

Another aspect to keep in mind is systematic error. Possible causes for systematic error include a misaligned sextant, misjudging the horizon in a big swell, or failing to swing the sextant correctly to measure the exact shortest distance between the observed body and the horizon. Picking the median intercept will help reduce random error in our sights but not a systematic error. While our method cannot compensate for such systematic errors, the data we collect in the process can help us identify and remedy them.

Assuming we are practicing celestial navigation for our own enjoyment and still have access to GPS data, we can use our GPS position at the time of the fix as our Assumed Position (AP) for the sight reduction calculation. If our sights were perfect, our intercepts would come out at zero, resulting in an LOP that runs through our GPS position. We can then tell immediately from our intercept values whether our sight series appear

---

[1] http://tinyurl.com/kb7lyaz

to be shifted consistently above or below zero rather than being scattered around this central value. If we spot such a bias, we can track down the root cause and start to correct for it, successively perfecting our technique.

Early into a four-week passage between the Galapagos Islands and the Marquesas, we found our sights to be high by one to two arc minutes on average. After carefully checking the sextant and eliminating misalignment as a possible error source, the problem was eventually tracked down to gripping the sextant too tightly, resulting in a skewed swinging motion. This in turn led to systematically overstated altitude readings. Loosening the grip (after adding a wrist-loop to allay our fear of losing the precious piece overboard) showed an immediate and permanent improvement in sight accuracy. Sometimes simple solutions are the best. The ability to easily spot these biases is also the main reason why we use a sorted series of intercepts rather than simply picking the median among fully corrected sextant altitudes (which would save us eight subtractions in the process).

Another valuable exercise is to mark the best perceived sight in each series and then check the actual accuracy based on the GPS position. It took us a while to figure out what makes a "good sight," but in the process we learned to judge the quality of our sights as we take them. This becomes particularly valuable when we have to make do with a single sight, snuck in between the clouds, without the luxury of a full five-sight series.

## Wrapping Up

To recap: we focus on the essence of celestial navigation by letting electronic tools automate the tedious sight reduction procedure. Then we turn the traditional approach of using LOPs from many different bodies on its head by taking a short series of sights of only two bodies. Applying the median estimator to the resulting data improves our fix accuracy by reducing random error and the impact of outliers. It also provides valuable feedback for improving our technique by identifying and eliminating systematic errors.

With this approach, we recreational navigators get about 80% of our fixes within four nautical miles of our GPS position and 97% within ten nautical miles. The method proves particularly useful in higher seas with a pronounced rolling of the boat. While the spread of the intercept values increases in higher seas, the median remains surprisingly robust.

Perhaps the biggest benefit has been the confidence we developed in our sight taking and our ability to judge the quality of our sights. As a result, a sometimes frustrating trial-and-error experience has become a fun pastime in which we can actually see our progress.

The ultimate reward comes when we can switch off the GPS and experience the satisfaction of practicing an old art on our small boat. And who knows? Now that we've got the important parts down, we may even turn purist and dig out those logarithmic sight reduction tables again. . .

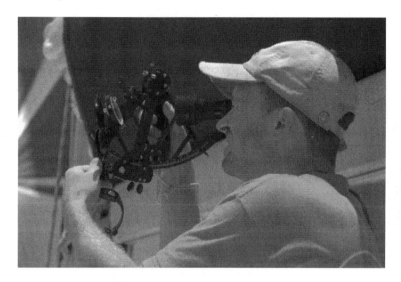

Taking a sun sight en route to the Galapagos Islands

## Post Script: Useful Tools for Celestial Navigation

A Google search for "navigation calculators" will bring up many freely available sight reduction software programs.[2]

OpenCPN, a popular chart plotter software for Linux, Mac OS X, and Windows, offers a celestial navigation plug-in which offers ephemeris calculation, sight reduction, and automatically plots LOPs.[3]

CelNav, a free software application developed aboard *Namani* by Markus, was designed to specifically support the method described in this chapter. In addition to automating sight reduction, it includes an electronic almanac and the ability to log sight data in a

---

[2] See, for example, www.celnav.de and www.navigation-spreadsheets.com
[3] http://tinyurl.com/kpqrw6g

spreadsheet format for later analysis.[4] CelNav is also available as part of Navigatrix, a complete operating system and software tool-set for use on a boat.[5]

An invaluable tool for anyone involved in celestial navigation is Stellarium, an electronic planetarium that makes it very easy to identify suitable stars and planets for a fix.[6]

For those who want to learn more about celestial navigation, there are numerous tutorials available on the Internet.[7] If you are not afraid of a bit of math, Henning Umland's *A Short Guide to Celestial Navigation* is an excellent source, well suited to complement some of the more "how-to" oriented guides.[8]

An excellent book that effortlessly introduces the theory without falling short on the practical application is John Karl's *Celestial Navigation in the GPS Age*, Paradise Cay Publications, 2011.

---

[4] http://tinyurl.com/lokg3pb

[5] http://navigatrix.net

[6] http://www.stellarium.org

[7] http://celestialnavigation.net/resources

[8] http://celnav.de/astro.zip

# Chapter 15

# Quick, Easy, and Good: Convenience Foods for the Offshore Sailor

Of course, we'd all like to be accomplished galley chefs, amazing and delighting the crew by whipping up delicious meals regardless of the boat's angle of heel. But let's face it: sometimes, just being in the galley while underway is a monumental effort, and often, the crew will be satisfied with a simple but hearty meal. This is particularly true if you are a short-handed crew with little enthusiasm for elaborate meal preparation between round-the-clock watches.

What follows are our tried and true tips for tasty, convenient meals during offshore passages. Don't worry – we're not talking ramen noodles here! Nowadays, there are many high quality foods available in well-stocked supermarkets in North America and abroad. Compact and long-lasting, these supplies make fine meals or snacks in their own right, and can be downright delicious when enhanced with a fresh ingredient or two.

I usually start by exploring the exotic food aisle of a large supermarket. Our favorites are the boxed kits made by Simply Asia, such as Thai Peanut or Sesame Teriyaki dinners. These come with soy noodles and sauce, feed two to three people, and can be embellished with vegetables and chicken (fresh or canned). Cooking time is a mere eight minutes. What else can the crew (and the cook) wish for the first night out on passage? Simply Asia, Kikkoman, and other brands also produce small pouches of sauce mixes that will spice up any meal with minimum effort.

Another convenience food I stock is a quality powdered soup mix made by Cugino's. We love their "Chicken Noodle Knockout," with "Chicken Enchilada" and "Baked Burgundy French Onion" soups running close second and thirds (all are sold in midsize pouches). The mixes provide a great meal, especially with extra vegetables or canned chicken. Compared to other soup mixes, this brand can seem a little pricey, but considering that one pouch feeds four adults with leftovers, it's a good deal. To conserve propane, I cut the suggested fifteen minute cooking time down to ten with another five minutes standing covered with a lid. If you can't find Cugino's, look for any up-market powdered soup mix, such as Bear Creek Country Kitchens. For variety, we make clam chowder by mixing a potato soup package with powdered milk and a can of clams (try Laurie's Bistro potato soup as a base).

Nadine in *Namani's* galley

Pizza is yet another easy and satisfying passage-making meal. Of course, you can make your own dough, but I use pre-made pizza bases and a jar of pizza sauce for an easy meal. My son goes so far as to call the result the best pizza he's ever tasted (it must have something to do with being offshore). You can add your favorite toppings (long-life salami is one option) or simplify things by buying pre-grated cheese. We don't have refrigeration on board our sloop, but sealed blocks of cheese survive in the bilge for up to three weeks, even in the tropics, and blocks of cheese preserved in jars of oil last even longer. When shopping for pizza bases, check for short cooking times since different brands vary from seven minutes to as much as twenty. Second, make sure the pizza will actually fit into your stove. For this reason, I usually choose small size pizza bases that can be easily personalized and served.

For special surprises between meals, I stock a few mixes to treat the crew (and myself) to occasional goodies such as muffins or brownies. Any mix will do, but make sure you have the necessary additives on hand (usually eggs and oil). To simplify things further, I use Betty Crocker "Simply Add Water" Muffin Mix. I won't claim that the result would win a prize at the county fair, but these muffins are ridiculously easy to make, and they sure do get gobbled down quickly. On a rocking platform, every extra ingredient endangers your galley balancing act and increases the potential for a mess, so the water-only mixes are particularly handy. If you're feeling ambitious, on the other hand, you can also add oil and eggs for the "home style" version of the same mix.

As a confessed chocoholic, I also stock lots of brownie mix and find the small, half-size boxes especially handy. These bake quickly and make the perfect amount for our small family (I can also reliably bake them in my solar cooker when at anchor). There are few pleasures as great as enjoying a brownie at sundown! In the past, I shied away from quick mixes that called for eggs since we don't have refrigeration, but I have since learned that eggs will keep for several weeks as long they are turned regularly, and brownie mixes that use fresh eggs do taste better.

When a special occasion approaches, I plan ahead with the right ingredients. For example, knowing that Thanksgiving would fall sometime during our November passage across the central Caribbean, I bought a can of pumpkin pie filling and the condensed milk needed to complete that simple recipe. If a birthday is coming up, I will keep candles, icing, and a special cake mix in the larder. Often, the more expensive name brands found in up-market supermarkets really are tastier.

For the things that I do make entirely from scratch, I save a lot of trouble by preparing before our departure. For example, I pre-mix the ingredients for my own bread dough in Zip-loc bags so that when the time comes to bake, I only have to add yeast and water to the blend of flours and dash of salt I have already measured out (see *Bread Recipe* on page 104). This makes bread making quick and easy; the result is a healthy, hearty pleasure.

The key to good offshore eating is preparation, so stash a good supply of long-lasting convenience foods before you get out of range of large supermarkets. If you aren't sure whether a mix will tickle your taste buds, sample a few before setting off. For example, Trader Joe sells a variety of quick Indian meals that might be just the thing for your crew. Be sure to check the food's shelf life before setting off for remote cruising grounds. Finally, look for meals with the shortest cooking times – but don't make the mistake of reading microwave instead of stovetop directions!

All your preparation will be for naught if you don't stow these convenience foods where they will be close at hand. Otherwise, you will find yourself excavating an entire locker to find what you need, thereby killing the prospect of an easy meal. Keep supplemental ingredients near each mix – for example, dried berries with the muffin mix, a can of corn or chicken near the soup, and so on.

I'm not suggesting that you subsist entirely on these foods, but sometimes art must be sacrificed for the sake of a quick, one-pot meal that can be whipped up in the most uncomfortable offshore conditions. These ideas will serve you especially well in the first days of a long passage. Once you settle in to life offshore, you might be inspired to pull out the cookbook and exotic spices. On the other hand, you might like some of the suggestions here so much, you'll be turning to them for quick, easy, and tasty meals no matter where you are!

## Bread Recipe

This is our adaptation of Chris Doyle's "No-Knead Bread" recipe. It is incredibly easy and provides us with nice, healthy bread whether we are offshore for an extended period or at a secluded anchorage.

- 6 cups flour (3 cups white, 1.5 cups whole wheat, 1 cup rye, 0.5 cup flax meal)
- 2 tsp yeast
- 1 tsp salt
- 3 cups warm water
- Cornmeal

In the evening, prepare the dough. First dissolve the yeast in warm water, and mix the flour and salt thoroughly before combining them with the yeast liquid. Leave the dough covered overnight in an airtight container. By morning, the dough will have risen all by itself. Flop it onto a board sprinkled with cornmeal and leave to rise for two hours in a closed oven (no heat). Then heat a pot with lid (or a loaf pan covered with aluminum foil) in the oven for ten minutes at 450°F (230°C). Sprinkle the pot with more cornmeal and add the dough. Bake for thirty minutes, turn and take off the lid, then bake for another fifteen minutes. The result is a delicious, hearty loaf of bread.

# Chapter 16

# Working While Cruising: Can the Two Mix?

Sounds good, doesn't it: working as you cruise around the globe. Many sailors fantasize about such an arrangement, but just how viable is it to work while you cruise? What are the risks and the limitations? What are the rewards?

Many sailors really do manage to combine work and pleasure, financing their dreams in whole or in part by working as they go. Some are self-employed, while others use modern technology to communicate with an employer or business back home. But working afloat has its headaches and compromises, just as real-life cruising does. The responsibilities of work can impact cruising plans and demand the support of fellow crew. Working requires self-discipline, organization, and in some cases, considerable investment. Sometimes, the freedom of cruising is sacrificed in favor of the job. On the other hand, the income earned allows sailors to stretch their time out cruising by seasons or even years. Many working cruisers report that their occupations also enrich their overall experience: connecting them to communities, helping others, and keeping their professional skills sharp.

What types of work are compatible with cruising? A wide variety, it seems. There are writers, financial planners, graphic artists, musicians, management consultants, and resourceful jacks-of-all-trades. I spoke with a number of working sailors who shared their insights, advice, and warnings so that others thinking of following their lead may do so with a realistic frame of reference.

## SCUBA Instructor

Helena Traksel of *Merilelu*, a 1998 Dehler 40, may well have one of the more glamorous-sounding jobs afloat. The Dutch sailor left behind a career in architecture to turn her SCUBA diving hobby into a means to bring in cash while cruising the world. But it's not all play under the sea. In fact, hers is a demanding job that requires the full partnership of her husband, Kari, who prepares gear, fills tanks, and stands by each dive. "He does as many hours as I do," Helena says. By teaching an average of four students a month, their combined efforts bring in enough cash to pay about a quarter of their modest cruising expenses. However, it's a high-investment profession when one considers the costs of PADI instructor training (upwards of $2,000) and equipment. *Merilelu* carries a compressor and four sets of SCUBA gear, which in turn require copious amounts of fuel and fresh water, not to mention precious space. The rewards of the working-cruising lifestyle, on the other hand, are many. "An architect is about stress, being in an office. I'm blessed with two good professions, and opposite ones," says Helena.

Helena's choice of work was carefully planned. "I had been sailing before and I saw the market – almost a need – in remote places like the Marquesas." She keeps her "business" small, using word-of-mouth advertising among fellow cruisers. In fact, she could earn more, but the Dutch diver strives to maintain a balance: "The idea is to see the world and work on the side, and not the opposite. The main thing is to enjoy a different lifestyle than you did before." Dive instruction is a good example of a job that doesn't usually restrict one's cruising schedule, since interesting anchorages and good diving often have much in common. Helena has taught fellow cruisers in some of the world's most remote and pristine dive locations, such as the lesser-known Tuamotus or the Cook Island atoll of Suwarrow. Not a bad arrangement!

## Office Afloat

Not everyone plans to work and sail. For some, opportunity knocks, and they don't turn a deaf ear. Alex Kleeman of *Saltbreaker*, a 1979 Valiant 32, was ready to quit his job as a programmer to go sailing, but his San Francisco-based company just wasn't ready to let him go. Instead, they asked him to take on smaller, less urgent projects that could be worked on independently. After leaving California in September, 2011, Alex worked roughly ten hours a week on the way south through Mexico, Nicaragua, and Costa Rica, but did less while crossing the Pacific. As he says, "The opportunities I kept seeing around me seemed to trump work a lot. When the boat is floating over an impressive coral reef, you just have to go snorkeling!" Once in New Zealand, however, Alex went back to working twenty to thirty hours a week to top up the cruising kitty.

"If I didn't work on the way over, I probably would have been flat broke when I showed up in New Zealand. With the work, I came out a little bit ahead. I kept thinking of it like bonus money. At this point, it's very much replenishing."

In Alex's case, working remotely requires only a laptop and the occasional Internet connection. Though Alex admits that he got lucky with his work situation, it's important to note that his "luck" might have turned out differently had he not established a solid, long-time working relationship with his company, proving his abilities and his reliability. He advises others seeking a similar arrangement to be flexible, accepting a pay cut or less interesting projects in exchange for the freedom they gain.

Alex at work aboard *Saltbreaker*

While Alex generally finds that work is compatible with cruising, he adds, "There are definitely times when I could not work – on passage or underway, unless it's really calm. Like, not moving!" He adds, "I can think all day and formulate what I want, but in the end I need to set aside a chunk of time to get it done." Internet access is another restriction, but Alex found that he could work around that by preparing a queue of information to look up when the opportunity arose. On the whole, he says, "Cruising and working tends to imply you're going slowly or spending more time in each place." As in everything with sailing, flexibility is key. Alex finds that "People spend too much time sitting around saving up enough money." He suggests leaving home with just enough savings to reach a given destination, then working more intensely to be able to extend the cruise by another season. Thus far, it's been his recipe for success.

## Diesel Mechanic

Like Alex, a number of working cruisers maintain some ties to their former employers, such as Robert DeLong of *Cricket*, a 1967 Alberg 37. Periodically throughout his trip from British Columbia to Panama, the mechanic would fly home for a few months of work, then pick up where he left off. Once he set out across the Pacific, though, he was able to work exclusively from his boat. Once word spread through the cruising fleet that there was a qualified marine diesel mechanic in their midst, he had plenty of offers of work. Enough so that if he wanted to, Robert could cover all of his cruising expenses (approximately $500 a month). But like other working cruisers, Robert limits his working hours to better enjoy the locations he visits. For him, the income allows luxuries such as restaurant meals and moorings that his modest budget wouldn't normally permit.

Surprisingly, his line of work is light on equipment. "My toolbox weighs about 600 pounds! I can't bring it on board," he explains. Since different engines require different tools, he relies heavily on the boat owner's tools along with his own basic kit. On the other hand, the work calls for a highly specialized skill set. Robert is an experienced marine diesel mechanic, not "just" a general repair man. "Time and time again, I'm repairing things that are done by 'professionals.' Boat engines are amazingly complicated systems and very unforgiving," Robert warns. His qualifications are one reason Robert is in such high demand. Another is his generous approach. "For every hour I can charge, I spend two to three hours giving free advice," he admits. But, as he says, "It's my community and I'm helping them out."

Work often impacts Robert's cruising schedule. "It affects my freedom because you make commitments. There's been a couple of times when I've stayed behind because I had another two to three days of work to finish. You're suddenly responsible for two boats making their weather window." On the other hand, because he often stays longer in one place, Robert finds that he gets to know the local scene better than many cruisers who breeze through more quickly.

Because Robert is a singlehander, work provides a social avenue. He enjoys meeting other sailors and encouraging them to do their own repairs. In doing so, he says, "I'm helping somebody become more proficient at living their dream." The satisfaction this brings has become an important aspect of Robert's cruising experience. Like Helena, the SCUBA instructor, Robert is careful not to tread on the toes of local business people. Much of the work he does is in out of the way places. Just try calling a mechanic in Fatu Hiva or Minerva Reef! His advice to others? "If you want to make a living making your way across the Pacific, develop a skill in electronics (radar, autopilots, AIS) because no one has it!"

## Professional Crew

Another way of earning money is to use your sailing skills as a means to finance adventures afloat. When Maine-based sailors Bob and Maggie Daigle returned from a world circumnavigation aboard a friend's yacht, they weren't ready to swallow the hook. Instead of returning to their careers, they moved into charter work, a step facilitated by the contacts they had made during their circumnavigation. Now the licensed captains run a privately-owned charter catamaran in the Virgin Islands. However, the couple agrees that "it's a totally different mindset from cruising," more work than play.

This line of work requires multiple certifications, from captain's licenses recognized in the United States and the BVIs to special endorsements required to operate a charter yacht. And there's no underestimating the amount of work involved, Bob reports. "Both Maggie and I have been very very hard workers throughout our professional lives, but both of us agree we've never worked quite so hard before. During the charter we're literally on from 6 a.m. until 9 p.m. – with half an eye open in the night as well. The boat is heavily used, so we have probably ten to fifteen items to fix, replace, or install during our twenty-four hours between the end of one charter and the beginning of the next. This job may seem glamorous – but I don't think I have a T-shirt left that is free of oil stains!" Their schedule is centered on guest bookings, which usually prevent family visits during holiday periods.

So why bother? For one thing, it allows the couple to do what they love in a beautiful region, in addition to making interesting new acquaintances – even deep friendships – with guests. The couple enjoy working as a team, too. "This crewed charter business is taking full advantage of each of our skill sets, and stretching both of us continually to learn new things. This is a very physically demanding type of work, so it keeps us both quite fit, which we really like," Bob explains. One perk is the eight-month-on / four-month-off schedule, which allows the couple to relax and recuperate during the summer.

Another positive is that they essentially pocket all their earnings (a fifty-fifty mix of tips and payment per charter from the boat owner), since their expenses during the season are virtually nil. It did take a season to establish themselves in the business, but since then, bookings have kept this crew bustling. But the job is not for everyone, Maggie cautions. "This is definitely not a job for a couple who want to 'live the dream' for the first time." Bob suggests that sailors "take a year or two and go cruising to make sure you really like this lifestyle. After confirming this, you can introduce guests into the picture." That said, the couple positively glows with satisfaction at their overall work "package." All in all, working as professional crew is an enticing prospect for those with the right resolve and qualifications and doesn't necessarily require boat ownership.

## Writing

Full-time cruising provides an abundance of time and inspiration, a perfect foundation for aspiring writers. Some sailor-authors write for periodicals; others pen entire books, from novels to nonfiction. For most, writing is an enjoyable hobby that brings in the occasional bonus rather than a means of underwriting the lifestyle. Personally, writing helps cement vivid impressions in my mind, and it inspires me to observe people, places, and situations more closely than I might have otherwise. It's a low-investment, flexible line of work (in terms of equipment if not time) that puts few demands on your fellow crew and rarely impacts cruising plans. However, like many other working cruisers report, it can be difficult to churn out quality writing when the boat is in motion. Most writers carve out quiet time at anchor to further their literary aspirations. This, in turn, makes it a challenge to balance the amount of time devoted to "work" with time spent enjoying the surroundings, a conundrum faced by all working cruisers.

Given the vast range of possibilities in working while cruising, what are the commonalities? All the working cruisers I spoke with have mastered valuable skill sets; they are flexible, disciplined people; and they cruise on modest budgets. For most, hitting their stride in terms of work took some time. Finally, most agree that it can be difficult to use time underway productively. Rather, it is down time at anchor that falls victim to work. Like everything else about sailing, there are compromises to be made, though the parameters are largely of one's own making.

Is working while cruising for you? With reasonable qualifications and modest expectations, it certainly is worth a try. After all, success stories always begin with some level of risk-taking. If working is a way to make cruising possible, why not give it a try? Ultimately, most cruisers who work agree that their efforts pay off – in more than one way.

# Part IV

# US East Coast to the Caribbean

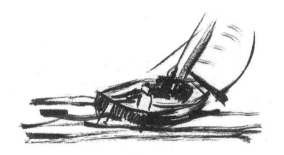

# US East Coast to the Caribbean

This section serves as bonus material for East Coast sailors heading for the Panama Canal. Chapters cover the facts and flavors of a shakedown cruise down the eastern seaboard, a "longcut" through one section of the Intracoastal Waterway, and a passage from Charleston to Panama via the Bahamas and Jamaica.

In many ways, sailing from the East Coast to the Caribbean can be the most challenging passage of the entire voyage to Australia due to tricky weather windows, the challenge of the Gulf Stream, and a potentially long windward beat to the tropics. We only met an equivalent challenge much later on our passages from the tropics to New Zealand and back. The East Coast to Caribbean passage is one to treat with great respect, and one from which you'll learn a great deal. On the far side of that trip lies an enticing reward: tropical Panama, along with the promise of another ocean just on the other side of that narrow neck of land.

# Chapter 17

# A Shakedown Cruise Along the US East Coast

The dream part of every cruise is exhilarating sailing and the anticipation of interesting places to visit. The down side, on the other hand, is never-ending maintenance work and equipment failure, a constant stream of problems that demand solutions. Somewhere in between is the reality: a balance of pleasure and effort to truly earn the privilege of the sailing life. After a long hiatus from cruising, we were reminded of this when setting off for a cruise along the northeast United States aboard *Namani*.

The idea was to move south while shaking out any kinks in our boat systems before eventually stepping up to offshore passages. Even after devoting several seasons to a full refit and a final six weeks to getting the final touches ready for an extended sabbatical at sea, a few projects remained unfinished. Just as the boat needed a warm-up cruise, so, too, could we use the opportunity to ease back into full-time living aboard. Over the course of the following month, we would sample several distinct cruising grounds between Maine and the Chesapeake Bay. In the end, though, it wasn't the navigational challenges of each region that defined the theme of our cruise, but the time devoted to completing projects underway. It's safe to say we read more manuals than novels as we moved south with the seasons.

## Departure

Our jumping off point was lovely Portland, Maine, a city rising in brick layers above the stone fortifications of Casco Bay. The harbor is protected by a ring of islands so closely huddled that anti-submarine nets could be strung between them during the dangerous days of World War II. Nowadays, the only thing that will snare a sailor are the lobster pots strewn everywhere. Using the last rays of the setting sun to dodge them, we departed on the first leg of our trip, an overnight sail to the Isles of Shoals.

One by one, winking navigation buoys and the bright beam of Portland Head Light faded as we headed out to sea and crossed the Rum Line. Not the rhumb line, but the Rum Line: the term goes back to prohibition days, when smugglers ducked through gaps between patrols three miles offshore. Hand steering through a night of light winds in seemingly endless three-hour shifts quickly helped us prioritize the to-do list: repairing the autopilot and testing our new Hydrovane wind vane self-steering were bumped to the top, as soon as daylight permitted. In the meantime, however, we devoted part of the moonlit night to calibrating our new radar. This was achieved by setting a direct course for fishing boats or buoys – a disconcerting exercise to say the least! So it came as some relief when dawn lit the low, rocky shores of the Isles of Shoals fifty miles later.

Gosport Harbor, a sheltered pocket ringed by the Isles of Shoals, is a natural stopping point for yachts transiting New England: from here, they are poised to make an overnight run to the Cape Cod Canal or a series of day-trips along the coast of Massachusetts. We spent a quiet day in Gosport, dividing our time between catch-up naps, reviving a corroded contact in the autopilot, and exploring the peaceful islands. This menu of activities provided a sample of what would ultimately fill out our shakedown cruise.

## The To-Do List

When it was time to push off again, we opted for the inshore route and immediately experimented with the Hydrovane, which can steer the boat with wind power alone. Once we had *Namani's* new sails trimmed and balanced, this turned out to be a smooth operation, and we could put our hands to other tasks. It was September, and high time for Nicky and me to get serious about home schooling, for starters. Meanwhile, Markus repaired the cockpit speaker so that we could hear the VHF clearly instead of only a faint squawk from below. However, we also uncovered a new problem: a minor but persistent leak through a low-set porthole. Prospective cruisers, beware of this law of boating: scarcely is one item crossed off the to-do list before another is added to the bottom. In fact, it's better to imagine a boat's chore list as an endless scroll rather than a single sheet of paper with a deceiving end point!

Over the course of the afternoon, the innocent morning haze gradually morphed into menacing storm clouds that gained height from one hour to the next and sent us scurrying into Gloucester harbor. There we waited out a strong cold front and addressed the leaking porthole. The exercise reminded us of another law of boating: each do-it-yourself job starts with at least a day of locating parts and supplies. In the end, we could only find an inferior sealant and settling for a temporary fix until our planned work period (as distinguished from the unplanned ones) in the Chesapeake Bay. Still, we were happy to spend time in Gloucester, a friendly working harbor with an interesting history. Joshua Slocum set off on his circumnavigation from this very port in 1895, and generations of fishermen have worked the waters of New England from its docks.

Underway again under a cold, blue sky, we bundled up in thick layers of clothing. *Namani* left the imposing twin lighthouses of Cape Ann behind and gradually passed Boston's glittering skyline. Timing our arrival at the Cape Cod Canal to coincide with a favorable current, we shot through the seven-mile slot at a speed of eight knots and ended a long day in pleasant Onset. Fall colors on land blended with the setting sun to wash the anchorage in red, orange, and pink hues: a living postcard of autumn in New England.

## Moving with the Seasons

Making our home on the water and following the seasons, we felt like part of a natural cycle, moving in step with flocks of geese who settled on the ground each evening and rose aflutter each morning, heading south, ever south. Now in Buzzard's Bay, we could ride fifteen to twenty knot following winds to intriguing places like little Cuttyhunk, with its handful of year-round residents and World War II lookout stations; legendary Newport, where we were more impressed by the lovely colonial houses in the historic district than the famous mansions; and Block Island, the smallest city in the smallest state, according to tourist literature. This was coastal cruising at its best, blessed with Indian summer weather and a mini adventure in every port – a winding hike, a foggy bike ride, a meander along brick-paved side streets. Except for an afternoon devoted to re-connecting the SSB transceiver, the ever-present job list was pushed to the back burner while we built memories from the sights (historic lighthouses), sounds (honking geese), and flavors (ice cream) of each day. Anchorages were void of summer crowds and temperatures were back up over 60°F, making a dip in the sea a pleasure rather than a major act of willpower.

The only thing marring our enjoyment of these quintessential New England pleasures was anxiety over our upcoming leg to New York City. We penciled out a precise schedule to run the gauntlet of strong currents ahead: a foggy 10 a.m. departure from Block Island to catch slack tide at The Race, the western entry point to Long Island Sound, followed by a current-enhanced westward run throughout the shower-swept afternoon. Just as predicted, *Namani's* speed dipped at night when the tide turned, and true to the forecast, rows of dark clouds drenched us in a series of wet onslaughts.

A bigger challenge than the weather was keeping track of commercial boat traffic. In open water, it's quite effective to light up a ship like a city block: less so when a ship is moving against a background of city blocks! A steady stream of tugs silently pushed their loads, east or westbound, throughout the night. I was also caught off guard by a buoy that suddenly switched from blinking red to green – until I realized it was a traffic light in a Long Island suburb. At long last, the rising sun lit the first of New York City's bridges. *Namani* was spot on schedule at infamous Hell Gate, which, I was relieved to discover, was a tame beast indeed during its brief slack water slumber. When the tide is running, on the other hand, this confluence point of two rivers is notorious for powerful, swirling currents. Sliding through unharmed, we felt we had passed another test of our shakedown cruise: Passage Planning 101.

Timing our arrival at Hell Gate

The worst behind us, we ticked off city sights from our cockpit like first-time tourists, even though we know New York well. I snapped wildly away at the Empire State Building and Ellis Island, wondering how travelers managed before the age of the digital camera. *Namani* was one of a handful of sailboats transiting the East River, watching the city stir to life with the rising sun. Soon we were engulfed by the noise of buzzing helicopters, zipping ferries, and lumbering trucks on the riverside highways: just another morning in the big city. It occurred to me that weather reports are to sailors what traffic reports are to city commuters, and I felt lucky to belong to the first group.

Cruising is as much about taking care of your boat as it is visiting interesting places, so our first order of business was to locate more gear, including sealant, charts for Central America, and a new stereo. Our bargain mooring at the 79th Street Boat Basin was just a dinghy ride and three blocks away from the subway. In contrast to bucolic New England, everything in New York seemed large and loud, its bustling streets lined with restaurants, shows, and shops in all sizes and flavors. Still, the New England connection was there: many of the imposing public buildings are built of Maine granite, delivered once upon a time by hardy Down East sailors.

## Goodbye, New York

After three days of buzzing city impressions, it was something of a relief to depart. The main hazards on the way to the Verrazano Narrows were barges moored smack in the middle of New York harbor. From the foam at their bows, I could have sworn they were making way, but it was only the three-knot Hudson current at work. The Statue of Liberty raised her torch in farewell as New York gradually slid out of view. Another remarkable port was behind us, and we looked forward to quieter landfalls from that point forward – and quieter water, after being thoroughly shaken and stirred by the wind-against-tide combination in the Ambrose Channel.

After the superlatives of the preceding weeks, we weren't too impressed by New Jersey's low-lying coast and sprawling settlements. More interesting was the combination of coastal sailing and Atlantic waters: the open ocean to port, land to starboard. Buoys moaned, gonged, and whistled in succession as we broke through the line of 40° north at last. A series of heavy squalls struck in the early morning, accelerating moderate winds into a series of short-lived roars and making the term "shakedown" a literal expression. Each such episode, however wet and intense, had the positive effect of making us feel ever more ready for the long passages we had planned for later in the season.

Cape May earned New Jersey many bonus points with its beautifully detailed Victorian houses and nearly deserted beach. These captured our attention while we waited for favorable conditions to enter potentially bumpy Delaware Bay. Well, we didn't exactly wait: Markus installed the new stereo – mainly to give us the pleasure of listening to music while completing future projects. Meanwhile, we observed the ebb and flow of boaters arriving, resting, and departing the anchorage, one batch after another, all intent on reaching warmer climes.

Finally, *Namani* took a shortcut through the Cape May Canal to the Delaware Bay, slipping through without incident despite her six-foot draft. Once again, we had our timing right: our current-enhanced speed rose while seas diminished and we flew up the Delaware Bay at up to nine knots over ground (until, that is, a trimaran passed and showed us the meaning of "flying"). Forty miles from Cape May, we furled the sails and entered the sheltered, fourteen-mile-long Chesapeake and Delaware Canal.

Resting at anchor in Chesapeake City's tight basin that night, we felt tired but excited to have reached another milestone: the Chesapeake Bay, a sheltered expanse over 150 miles long. Just two short days later, *Namani* was breezing along on a close reach to Annapolis: "a quaint drinking town with a sailing problem." Picking up a mooring just a stone's throw from the historic town, we toasted our progress to date: one thousand miles, nine states, and three canals since setting off from Maine a month earlier. We had weathered three overnight runs (literally, given the numerous downpours) and felt as if we were again in the swing of the cruising life. Now we were poised to explore Chesapeake Bay while preparing for a passage to Panama. Later, near Norfolk, we observed several crews making hasty departure preparations for the Caribbean without the benefit of a shakedown cruise to get to know their vessels, crew, or even their toolboxes, making us doubly value our East Coast experience.

In hindsight, we discovered that the swift currents we were warned of (near Cape Cod, around New York, and in the Delaware Bay) were quite manageable when timed carefully. Fall cruising was chilly at times, but the absence of summer crowds was a definite plus. Throughout our cruise, we were reminded that good times must be earned through ongoing maintenance and repairs, especially when sailing an older vessel. Most of all, our experience taught us the importance of simply getting a cruise started, even if some secondary projects remain unfinished. Quite simply, all the work will never be done. If we'd waited for that elusive time, we would still be in Maine (lovely as it is) instead of reflecting upon our experiences from the tropics.

Finally, it's fair to say that no cruise is ever long enough. Any of the interesting areas we visited would make a fine destination for leisurely exploration in itself. Did we have a clear favorite? At the risk of sounding like an elementary school teacher ("you're all winners"), I would avoid picking a single favorite. The real winner is the cruiser who draws from the lessons of a shakedown cruise and heads for ever new horizons.

120

## Lessons Learned

The moral of our story is not to underestimate the amount of time and effort it takes to get a boat truly ship-shape. We were sailing a boat we knew well and had already spent six weeks preparing; nevertheless, each cruising day ended in one project or another. Prospective cruisers beware: don't even think about setting off on your dream cruise without a thorough shake-down!

When planning each leg of a trip, it pays to research three possible end points for each day: an ambitious stretch if conditions allow, an intermediate destination, and a nearby port to pull into if you discover a problem underway. It's a mental game: with all three possibilities fleshed out, we feel good about making our ambitious end points, but if something goes awry, we don't have to scramble for alternative ports.

Since this trip was the beginning of a two-year cruise, we kept a close eye on expenses. Although we had to pay for more moorings than we had anticipated, we were able to keep our costs within a budget of $70 per day. Half of this went toward mooring fees and food; the rest covered insurance, hardware and repairs, fuel, public transportation, entertainment (bike rental, museum entry), and so on. We treated ourselves to two inexpensive meals out and consumed many an ice cream along the way.

# Chapter 18

# The Intracoastal Waterway:
# Not Just the Means to an End

Heading south from the Chesapeake Bay to Panama and ultimately, the Pacific, our minds were very much on blue horizons. When ugly weather denied us an offshore run around Cape Hatteras, it took some attitude adjustment to follow the Intracoastal Waterway for four days instead. At first, following 200 miles of shallow, narrow waterways – a combination of rivers, canals, and open sounds – took some getting used to. By day two, however, the ICW had become more than just a means to an end as we began to appreciate a completely different cruising experience.

From mile zero off Norfolk, the first section of the ICW is all "hurry up and wait" to catch the opening times of nine different bridges and one lock. At peak fall season, we found ourselves traveling in a tight pack of eight sail and five powerboats, all drawn by the lure of a warm winter in southern climes. But the flavor and pace of the ICW gradually change after the first twenty-mile stretch. Boat traffic spreads out, each vessel following its own pace, and the surrounding landscape becomes ever more peaceful and wild.

From ICW mile 40 to 125, sailors are miles away from any sign of human habitation. The shore is a wild tangle of trees, vines, and bushes. Small brown deer emerge, silently sipping fresh water in the morning mist. Osprey wheel high overhead in search of prey, and a keen lookout may even spot an eagle peering regally down from her nest. Smaller birds flit over the surface of the water, spinning and diving in pursuit of insects, while long-legged wading birds step purposefully through the shallows. We had not delighted in the likes of beautiful, secluded anchorages like Buck Island (mile 56) and the Alligator River (mile 101) since leaving Maine weeks earlier.

Watch your mast top...

Just as the novelty of following straight canal edges wears thin, the waterway opens into the next winding river, with markers to help boats remain in the main channel. In and around broad expanses like the Albemarle Sound, you can hoist the sails and shut off the engine for up to forty miles at a time. Making way through this landlocked system, we imagined what a relief it must have been for crews of cargo ships in the dangerous days of World War II to be able to follow these secure waterways, out of the reach of lurking offshore U-boats. Today's visitor can visit a number of interesting small towns along the ICW (some with free dock space), although you might find yourself shying away from civilization, as we did.

No, the ICW isn't for everyone – and it automatically excludes any boat over sixty-four feet in height and a draft exceeding six feet. And no, I wouldn't want to follow it any farther than I had to. It was a great relief to finally take my eyes off the depth sounder when at last we reached Beaufort and headed out into the Atlantic. After all, that's what our sloop is made for. But four days of seeing coastline from the "inside" was an interlude we will remember fondly – even after we pointed the bow for the deep blue ocean.

# Chapter 19

# To Panama in a Hop, Skip, and a Jump: from Charleston to the Caribbean

To me, it seemed a bold and promising plan: to depart the US East Coast as soon as a November weather window allowed and head for Panama in a hop (800 miles from the Carolinas to the eastern Bahamas), a skip (300 miles to Jamaica), and a jump (600 miles to Panama). Then we'd have the entire winter to cruise Panama's fascinating coasts – both of them – before heading off across the Pacific. Brilliant, yes?

Strangely, other sailors we met while moving south along the East Coast of the United States disagreed. Jamaica? They grimaced. Too dangerous. Panama's San Blas Islands? Too quiet. Better to spend time getting acquainted with Saint Augustine or the Abacos, they advised, launching into detailed descriptions of the comfortable marinas we might visit along the way. Nice destinations, to be sure, but I was determined to reach more distant parts, fascinated by blue horizons.

Luckily, Markus agreed with the plan, and our son, Nicky – well, he can be talked into just about any family venture aboard *Namani*. The tricky part would be reaching Panama in a narrow window of opportunity: after the end of hurricane season in November but before the Christmas Winds set in to give small boats a wild ride in the central Caribbean. We like an exciting sail, but not too exciting, and were determined to get across the Caribbean early.

It's one thing to make a brilliant plan and another to actually realize it. The days of early November slipped away while late season tropical storm Sean raged offshore. It was a

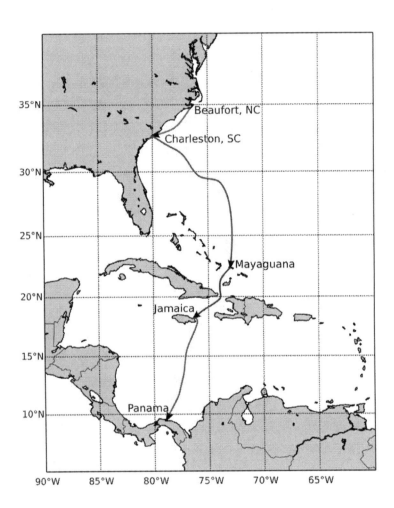

good time to be tucked into the safe harbor of Beaufort, North Carolina. Another week passed, but northerly winds would not let up enough to allow us to cross the Gulf Stream in reasonable conditions. Itching for action, we moved on to lovely Charleston, South Carolina, positioning ourselves directly west of a narrow section of the Gulf Stream. Finally, we got the green light from our weatherman, Chris Parker, and set off, full of anticipation – and some trepidation – of what might lie ahead.

## Charleston to Mayaguana: Six Days / 801 NM

Months of preparations and worry about this passage eventually climaxed in... well, an anticlimax, because the thirty-mile Gulf Stream crossing proved to be a non-event. *Namani* motored over smooth seas marked only by a few stray clumps of Sargasso weed, accelerated at times by a favorable eddy, then suddenly fighting a different offshoot of the Gulf Stream. According to the forecast, the real challenge would come a few days later, with southeasterly winds and an increasing swell that made it critical to make our easting now.

The first two days at sea were our quietest, with modest gains of about 120 miles each day and some hours of fiddling with the sails before resorting back to the engine for a better upwind course. By day three, we shut off the engine for good, moving nicely under sail but still fighting to maintain course against the east-southeast wind. Undeterred by pesky details of heading or speed made good, Nicky marveled in the clear night sky; he even insisted on sleeping in the cockpit rather than his pilot berth. Markus and I took turns standing three-hour night watches, clipped in beside Nicky with a watchful eye on the compass. The steering was left to our Hydrovane, our trusty fourth hand that faithfully maintained the best course to windward – a meager 175°.

*Namani* was making a strong six knots, but wind on the nose and a sloppy leftover swell on the beam made her motion very uncomfortable for the next three days. Our world was one of heaving, splashing, and the occasional bashing as the hull fell into troughs between waves. This had the unfortunate side effect of swamping the bilge, since we hadn't sealed the hawse pipe properly: a foolish oversight that cost us time at the pump and a good drenching on the bow.

Soon we were thoroughly tired of our windward slog exacerbated by the cross swell: there was too much motion to read, play games, or do anything much more than watch the horizon. We consoled ourselves with respectable twenty-four hour runs of 132, 152, and 140 miles – and fantasized about the next two legs of our passage, which would theoretically be easier downwind runs. The good news was, we were holding up well

Nicky, unfazed by the bumpy ride

with our two-handed watch schedule. Still, I felt a nagging uncertainty about my master plan: what if the central Caribbean turned rough before we could get across?

Each night, the waning moon rose a little later, and each day, we shed another layer of clothing, now down to shorts and T-shirts for good. With the wind peaking at thirty knots at night, we reefed the mainsail and struck the genoa in favor of a smaller staysail that flies on *Namani's* removable baby stay. Despite the decrease in canvas, *Namani* still streamed along at six knots with a slightly more comfortable motion, an indication that we had reefed at the right time. Waves continued to splash over the bow and port side, penetrating *Namani's* normally dry cockpit. Never had we had such a salty passage!

The ceaseless commotion made the sight of Mayaguana on our sixth morning out a welcome sight. In this area of the southeast Bahamas, depth contours squeeze together like tight isobars on a messy weather chart. We didn't come into soundings until the very entrance to Abraham's Bay, a five-mile-long refuge strewn with coral heads. Proceeding cautiously at tick-over speed, we guided *Namani* through until she came to rest at last, the lone boat in a vast anchorage.

In short order, we took a refreshing dip, pumped the dinghy, and cleared customs ashore. At anchor for a long weekend layover, the essence of our days changed completely. We settled back into a diurnal rhythm, trading the slate-colored ocean for an aquamarine paradise and substituting the music of Jimmy Buffett for the voice of the weatherman.

A change we could get used to! But not yet. In the Bahamas, we were poised at the "wrong" edge of the Caribbean and wanted to get across fast. Having toured the sleepy island and restored order to the boat, we were off once again.

## Mayaguana to Jamaica: Three Days / 338 NM

If our passage to Mayaguana was something of a tedious ordeal to be endured, the three-day downwind run to Jamaica was a gentle walk in the park. Any misgivings about the master passage plan now gave way to satisfaction. An ominous-looking series of squalls turned out to be relatively benign, especially with an ENE wind abaft the beam and only a minor swell. Gone were the days of hanging from handholds and clinging to every inch of easting by the skin of our teeth; this was the kind of Caribbean passage-making we had hoped for! The main challenge came on the second night, when we nervously tiptoed an invisible line between mountainous Cuba, tinted orange-red by the setting sun, and the Windward Passage shipping lane, dotted with the lights of freighters. To my relief, it was a night of little action on both fronts.

Cuba's low mountains remained in view for most of the next morning, and we even caught a glimpse of Haiti's lofty Massif de la Hotte far to the east. These impressive heights were a welcome sight after months along the relatively low-lying U.S. East Coast. At the same time, I imagined the three-dimensional world invisible beneath us: the sea floor rising and falling in mountains, plateaus, and dramatic valleys. Although it seemed as if *Namani* was barely crawling along, a look at the speed log revealed five to six knot progress under poled out genoa alone. It was Thanksgiving Day at sea, and the setting sun colored the scattered white crests of waves with its red hues: yet another beautiful sight to be grateful for on a long, full list.

Our third dawn at sea lit the breathtaking sight of Jamaica's aptly named Blue Mountains ahead. As *Namani* closed with the coast, we were enveloped by the exotic scent of a rich and humid forest. While wind and seas came to a crashing halt on Jamaica's north shore, we ducked through a narrow side entrance into the perfectly protected inner harbor of Port Antonio.

If Mayaguana was our solitude interlude, Port Antonio was our taste of city bustle on a small, walkable scale. Nowhere did we find evidence of the dire warnings we had received about Jamaica, only friendly and helpful people in what is known as the safest (if rainiest) corner of the island nation. From the accommodating customs officials and staff of comfortable Errol Flynn Marina, to the street vendors and local populace, we felt warmly welcomed. The town was a bustle of activity and reggae music, and the rooftop "Tip Top Restaurant" was the perfect perch from which to take it all in.

Two helpful street vendors in Port Antonio

The town is worn down, and not only around the edges, but the genuine people and the scenery quickly won us over. Cruisers can tie up at the easygoing marina or anchor out in the perfectly protected inner bay, then explore with peace of mind. Port Antonio is the gateway to the surrounding Blue Mountains, a rugged expanse carpeted by lush jungle and dotted with red flowers, aptly named Flame of the Forest. We spent a day rafting down the Rio Grande with the amiable Captain Debbo, who not only taught us how to pole his thirty-foot bamboo raft, but even indulged us with an hour-long swim call in the deliciously cool, fresh water. It's a memorable day trip that supports local enterprises in an environmentally friendly way.

## Jamaica to Panama: Five Days / 590 NM

Port Antonio proved to be a practical and easy place to complete all our business, not to mention indulge ourselves in some fun. Still, we did feel like the odd man out again. In the southeast United States, everyone seemed headed for the Bahamas; here, the cruisers were all staying within a triangle formed by Jamaica, Cuba, and the Dominican Republic. Sometimes, forging your own path can mean a struggle with creeping doubts, but every sailor has to heed their own ambitions, time frame, and interests. Ours stood up to the test and pointed us steadfastly south.

After five short days in Jamaica, a fair weather window offered the promising opportunity to reach Panama in relatively comfortable conditions. Our previous passages were only stepping stones to this decisive leg across the central Caribbean. It was still early December and we hoped the statistics would bear themselves out in our favor: according to pilot charts, the wind and waves would build significantly over the coming weeks as the trade winds started to fill in, but by then we should be in Panama – or so we hoped!

*Namani* rounded the east end of Jamaica on an easy beam reach, but the rest of our 600-mile trip to Panama was a broad reach under foresail alone. We enjoyed steady northeast or east-northeast winds the entire way, with only a gradually building cross-swell to put on a short "complaints" list. The lightest winds came on our first full day out of Jamaica, giving us a chance to fly our new Parasailor with satisfying results. *Namani's* roll evened out thanks to the lifting force of the sail's "wing," and we made good time while keeping the shallows of Morant Cay safely to port.

Our friend Bill had flown in to join us in Jamaica, hoping for some memorable offshore sailing. Having a third watch-keeper aboard brought us a curious new phenomenon: free time. On the first two legs of our trip, I was either standing watch or sleeping: there was no in-between. On this passage, I would go off watch and straight to my bunk out of habit, only to find that I wasn't actually sleep deprived. Now what? I quickly re-discovered the pleasant pastimes of reading, playing games, and working on home schooling with Nicky.

Soon, we had all settled in to the new rhythm, hiding under the shade of the bimini by day and reveling in the stars at night. For a time, we ran downwind with our twin genoa (two symmetrical headsails sewn onto one luff tape) opened wing-on-wing. Later, with a growing swell on the beam, we poled both parts of the genoa out to one side and gybed from one broad reach to another for a somewhat more comfortable motion. The main excitement of day three was the visit of an American drug-enforcement plane that circled *Namani*. I tried to demonstrate our innocent intentions by waving a friendly hello together with young Nicky. Otherwise, our attention turned to a series of mild squalls and passing freighters (about five each day) shuttling between Panama and the Windward Passage.

*Namani* ticked off the miles, slowly rolling along. Compared to the featureless horizon, the night sky was the most memorable part of this passage. As *Namani* headed ever farther south, familiar constellations hung at angles like paintings gone askew with time. At this latitude, the waxing gibbous moon bulged at the bottom rather than from the side, casting a pale light that turned everything grayscale, like a black and white film classic.

Sometimes I tackle night watches with a good read or a travel guide, anticipating the

131

Bill enjoying a broad reach under the Parasailor

landfall ahead; at others, I'm content to simply sit and think. Occasionally, I play host to my anxieties, as was the case on the third night out, when the wind and swell were expected to increase significantly. Was the lightning on the eastern horizon a harbinger of worse to come? Would the increasingly agitated seas intensify? As usual, I feared the worst and was ultimately relieved when nothing more drastic than an eight-foot swell with a bearable eight-second interval materialized. As it turned out, our timing was just right: an Australian crew who sailed the same route two weeks later reported more onerous thirty knot winds and twelve foot seas.

Fifty miles from the coast of Panama, we put several rolls in the genoa to slow down enough for a dawn arrival. Excited at the prospect of landfall, all hands came on deck to watch the unmistakable green hill of Punta San Blas take shape over the horizon. Soon after, we could pick out low, palm-lined islands like El Porvenir, where we could clear into Panama. Once that was complete, we could officially declare the blue water passage-making section of our trip over, and balance it out with coastal cruising along the gorgeous San Blas islands.

## Looking Back

Sitting at leisure in *Namani's* shaded cockpit in a picture-perfect tropical anchorage, we could reflect on three weeks filled with impressions: vast seascapes, the small world of our boat, and memorable landfalls. We could enjoy the bounty of our efforts, with nearly three quiet months in which to arrange our Panama Canal transit and enjoy varied cruising grounds on both sides of the isthmus: a long breather before heading into the vast Pacific.

Above all, we felt the satisfaction of a plan come to fruition. Our route was not an especially treacherous or bold one, but it often seemed out of step with other sailors. We had heard and carefully considered much contrary advice along the way, reevaluating but ultimately sticking with our original plan. Lessons learned? Be flexible, make informed decisions, and dare to be different.

# Part V

# Panama

# Panama

Panama is a bridge between two worlds, a small country with incredible diversity and vibrant indigenous cultures. On a boat, you're perfectly poised to experience much of it up close and personal – from traditional Kuna in the San Blas to the urbanites and skyscrapers of Panama City, not to mention the engineering marvel that is the Panama Canal and a jungle rich in its own scents, sounds, and textures.

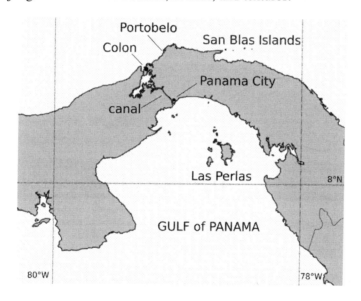

For Pacific-bound sailors, though, the practical aspects of Panama are just as significant as the cultural value. It's the last place to stock up on supplies before heading into seven-thousand miles of open water. From oil filters to anchor rode and brownie mix – Panama has it all, and at the best prices you'll see until... well, until you're back in the Americas.

This section of *Pacific Crossing Notes* touches on each of those subjects, including tips for organizing a canal transit, a list of our favorite chandlers and suppliers in Panama

City, as well as a look at historic Portobelo, a taste of Kuna Yala (San Blas), and an overview of a "working cruise" in the lesser-known Las Perlas archipelago.

To be sure, Panama can be gritty (and in some cases, corrupt), but we found that the pros vastly outweighed the cons (pun intended). For us, Panama marked the beginning of a great adventure – and the beginning of many friendships that carried on as we all sailed westward over the horizon.

# Chapter 20

# The San Blas Islands: Practical Tips and Responsible Cruising

No longer off the beaten track, the Kuna Yala – better known as the San Blas islands – are now a well established cruising ground in Panama's coast. What's the big attraction? Idyllic anchorages protected by palm-lined islets; hurricane-free, year-round sailing; plus the fascinating indigenous culture of the Kuna people. This chapter will help you maximize your enjoyment of the San Blas area and minimize any inconvenient surprises.

A few words of precaution. First of all, the secret is out: popular anchorages in the western San Blas islands shelter a dozen or more yachts at a time. We gaped upon finding thirty-seven boat clustered just in the West Lemmon Cays, a well-protected anchorage close to the region's administrative center on the island of El Porvenir. Some sailors are just passing through, while many others are passing time: lots of it! It's not uncommon to find cruisers who remain in this island paradise for months, or even years. It's an interesting, international bunch, with an active and helpful SSB cruiser's net that "meets" each morning with a weather report, position check-ins, and news (tune in to 8107 at 08:30).

We were a little overwhelmed by the social aspect of the net (announcing yoga sessions, book swaps, and barbeques), but grateful for the practical information the experienced cruisers could share: where to find supplies, procedures for the Panama Canal, and so on. If you want solitude, head for the eastern San Blas, an area less frequented by outsiders, or avoid the main draws of the western San Blas (Chicime, East and West Lemmon Cays, Cayos Holandes, and the Coco Banderos). These popular places draw so many visitors because they offer idyllic conditions and crystal-clear water, while the reefs of the eastern San Blas can be trickier to navigate in more limited visibility.

## Money, Charts, and Trash

Panama uses the US dollar as its official currency, but there are no ATMs in the region, so bring lots of cash in small bills. Paying the Panama cruising permit fee of $193 (in cash only) will take a big bite out of your reserves. The good news is that cruising permits are now valid for one year and issued on the spot in El Porvenir. You can also expect to pay an immigration fee ($30 for a crew of four) and a fee to the autonomous Kuna government ($20 per yacht and $2 per person). All these offices share one building on El Porvenir. In addition, you can expect to pay a $10 monthly charge in the most popular anchorages. This fee is periodically collected by a local Kuna representative. It's a well-regulated system: the collector will show you an official document confirming his authority to charge the fee, and give you an official receipt as proof of payment.

In addition to bringing lots of cash, you should also come prepared with charts of the region and the outstanding *Panama Cruising Guide* by Eric Bauhaus (including detailed charts and reliable way points). You should also come stuffed to the gills with provisions. There are only three places to buy supplies in the western portion of the island group: Wichubhuala (just a dinghy ride away from El Porvenir), Carti, and Nargana (the latter two are islands immediately off the mainland). These towns have bakeries and small shops that stock a very limited selection of canned goods and bottled water. Finding fresh produce or meat can be difficult.

Local fishermen will come around with their catch ($2 bought us a good-sized tuna), and a fresh produce boat also visits popular anchorages periodically. However, their schedule is unreliable and the pickings are sometimes slim (the entire selection one week was potatoes and eggs; at best, the vendor will carry a variety of vegetables as well as fresh chicken). Many cruisers monitor channel 72 and will announce a sighting of the elusive produce man with the excitement of an old-time whaler hailing a distant spout.

Trash is a major problem, so think ahead when provisioning and establish a way to compact your trash on board until you can properly dispose of it. There are no reliable places to deposit trash in the Kuna Yala. Never give your trash to locals who promise to dispose of it properly, only to dump it into the sea around the next corner. There's nothing sadder than the sight of wrappers and plastic bottles floating through the otherwise pristine waters of this stunning archipelago. Much of the debris comes from the mainland, where the sea is seen as a fair dumping ground (and it was, back in the days when the only trash generated was coconut husks and fish bones). Long-term cruisers dump cans and glass into deep water, where they will eventually corrode, and either burn plastics (do so only with permission from the local Kuna) or collect plastics until they visit a place outside the region with established trash-handling procedures. Even then, the "best" to hope for is that your trash ends up incinerated or in landfill. It's a sobering, world-wide issue.

## Generous Hosts: the Kuna

There are many beautiful cruising grounds around the globe, but this area is unique thanks to the presence of the indigenous Kuna people. The Kuna are a folk under pressure of outside influences: this means you. The *Congreso*, their well-organized, self-governing body, seeks to protect Kuna culture with a number of laws that you should inform yourself of. The basics are: outsiders are forbidden to touch coconuts or pick fruit growing on the islands; SCUBA diving and power-driven water sports like water skiing are banned, as is public nudity; do not buy undersized fish, lobster, or octopus from local fishermen. The Kuna Congreso has also banned casual trade goods, including magazines or nail polish, innocent as they might seem. Rather than offering your new friends these intrusive items, bring a supply of quilting needles and thimbles instead. This gesture will win over local women who spend hours sewing masterful molas (exquisitely appliquéd fabric panels that are extremely popular souvenirs) without violating cultural norms.

In some places, cultural traditions have already faded: in Nargana or Wichubhuala, women wear normal western wear instead of the traditional mola, and thatched roofs are gradually giving way to corrugated iron. Other towns follow the old ways, but remember, these are not open-air museums but living communities, so consider what impact your presence will have. Some cruisers avoid traditional towns altogether for fear of intruding on local ways. While the Kuna are extremely polite and tolerant, you should reciprocate with your best behavior if you do choose to visit. Dress modestly and don't even think about snapping a photo without asking for permission (which will usually be denied). Only the younger Kuna members speak Spanish. The older generation speaks the indigenous Kuna language: start with a friendly *Na* (hello) and *Nuede* (thank you). The outer islands are not permanently inhabited, but many are dotted with small Kuna camps of one or two huts. Villagers come out in shifts of a few weeks to fish and tend the coconuts; some will also visit yachts to sell their catch or molas.

What exactly is a mola? It is an intricately sewn cloth panel that was originally de-

A mola from Kuna Yala

signed as the midriff section of a woman's blouse; hence, they are usually about fifteen by twelve inches in size. Patterns are made using deft appliqué techniques, ranging from traditional geometric designs to representations of animals or people, finished off with embroidered detail. All molas are eye-catching, but if you're in the market for a nice piece, examine each carefully. Check how straight the edges are (none are perfectly straight since they are made by hand while held on the lap) and examine the reverse side to see how tightly spaced the stitches are (small, close stitches are a sign of good workmanship). Molas cost about $10 and up; the more detail, the more expensive.

## Safety and Transportation

The Kuna are generally a gentle and kind people, and security issues are rare. However, instances of petty theft and even armed robbery have been reported off larger villages such as Nargana, where it pays to take sensible precautions. In the outer islands, we felt very safe and didn't take our usual precaution of hoisting the dinghy on deck at night. Navigational challenges of this reef-strewn archipelago are considerable: don't trust your GPS blindly and stick to principal reef approaches, which are well-described in the Bauhaus book. Reports of rough groundings are a weekly news item on the morning radio net. Occasionally, boats even sustain enough damage to be declared a total loss. Don't let this island paradise lure you into letting your guard down!

It is possible to receive visitors or pick up crew once you're in the region. The easiest way is for incoming friends to book a puddle-jump flight from Panama City to El Porvenir. However, the "airport" there is really just an air strip; don't expect any staff to sell you a ticket on the spot. It is also possible to reach the airport in Panama City via local *lancha* (a local power boat to Carti) and jeep in roughly five hours for about $50 per person. Some cruisers sail fifty miles west to Portobelo, where there are frequent, easy-to-use buses to Panama City (two to three hours). This is also a good place to make a major provisioning run: Portobelo has a well-sheltered anchorage, an ATM, a few small food stores, and buses that will bring you directly to the large El Rey supermarket in Sabanitas in one hour (departing roughly every half hour; $1.30 one way). If you need tips on how to arrange such things, just ask on the cruiser's net and you will get excellent, specific advice (long-term cruisers seem to keep giant rolodexes of helpful local contacts).

Sabanitas is also the closest place to buy a Panamanian SIM card for your phone, though top-up cards (for credit on your phone) may be found in the small Kuna Yala shops. Some San Blas islands even have public phones, which are listed in the cruising guide. The nearest marina to the San Blas area is Green Turtle Cay, thirty-five miles east of El Porvenir, with water and power but poor road connections. For an extended cruise in the San Blas islands, it goes without saying that your boat must be entirely self-sufficient in terms of power and water.

No matter where you point your bow, it's important to plan ahead and be prepared. This is especially true in a remote, fragile region such as the Kuna Yala. So stock up, head out, and cruise responsibly in one of the most rewarding cruising grounds of the Caribbean.

# Chapter 21

# Portobelo, Panama

Panama's Portobelo is a gem of a place, the perfect intermediary stop between the San Blas Islands and gritty Colón, the Caribbean gateway to the Panama Canal. Originally, this quiet port – a deep indentation open only to the southwest – wasn't even on our cruising radar. But after an enjoyable week's stay there, it was hard to understand why this fascinating port and safe harbor hasn't achieved a higher profile among Caribbean cruisers.

Christopher Columbus was the first European to note the inviting, spacious bay, which he named "Puerto Bello." It quickly became a key New World port, not only for the Spaniards bringing South American silver across the isthmus by mule train, but also for the English privateers stalking them. In its heyday, Portobelo's Customs House saw one-third of the world's silver passing through its doors. The 1638 structure is one of several colonial buildings still standing in town, a UNESCO World Heritage site. Today's visitors can climb creaky wooden steps to the second-story porch for an overview of the bay and the town. From there, it's easy for the imagination to populate the cobblestoned streets with Spanish soldiers – some optimistically counting their pieces of eight, others only counting down the sweltering days of their posting in one of the many fortifications ringing the harbor.

Just outside the bay lies a striking, rocky islet named Isla Drake after the famous privateer; his compatriot, Captain Henry Morgan, besieged this stronghold in the seventeenth century. Their relentless attacks eventually convinced Spain to abandon the dangerous overland route for a safer alternative: sailing around Cape Horn!

Nowadays, Portobelo is a quiet place left to locals and sailors. Cruisers starved for cash and supplies after an extended San Blas sojourn can re-enter civilization here (with all its pluses and minuses), replenishing cash from the ATM and buying basic supplies in

Exploring Portobelo's past

several Chinese-run "mini supers." Our favorite stops were the local bakery for delicious bread, sweet rolls, and fresh fruit smoothies; the Argentinean restaurant with its second-floor balcony seating; and Captain Jack's, a friendly cruiser hang-out that offers drinks, meals, and Internet access – in addition to hosting one heck of a Christmas party. Visitors can explore many historic sites around town, from the bayside Fort San Jeronimo to the church of San Felipe and the graceful, oft-overlooked Merced Bridge, dating back to 1597. History buffs will appreciate the informative panels erected around town, though like the crumbling buildings, these, too, have seen better days.

It's true that some visitors come away jaded, seeing only the litter and decay that tarnishes Portobelo's surface. However, those who scratch deeper will find an intriguing port steeped in history together with a commodious, well-protected bay. In the wider scope of things, Portobelo makes the perfect counterpoint to the palm-fringed San Blas Islands and the engineering superlatives of the Panama Canal, another must-see among Panama's diverse attractions.

# Chapter 22

# Canal Ho! The Approach to the Panama Canal

*Thirty-one, thirty-two, thirty-three.* My finger tapped the horizon. *Thirty-four, thirty-five, thirty-six.* What had started as a few hulking forms on the horizon became a dozen, and the dozen multiplied until we counted thirty-seven freighters. Thirty-seven looming obstacles to dodge in our approach to the Panama Canal. And that number only included freighters waiting outside the entrance. How many more were about to emerge from behind the breakwater?

Terrifying? Exhilarating? I'm still not sure which. There were ships weighing anchor, ships dropping anchor, and ships holding position for imminent action, smoke drifting from their exhaust stacks. I couldn't help but imagining a video game in which tiny sailboats attempt to dodge oncoming ships. Except in real life, you don't get three lives.

For us, the Canal wasn't just a gateway to a wide new ocean, but an adventure in itself. And though at times we felt like hapless fans plonked straight into the melee of an NBA court (time out – please?), we also reveled in the knowledge that a long-held dream was coming true. We would not only witness the awesome spectacle of the Canal, but actually become part of it, too.

Happily, all went well when our compact sloop transited the isthmus alongside the titans of the shipping world. And once the locks opened on the Pacific side, well, our next adventure could begin.

Approaching the Panama Canal

# Chapter 23

# Transiting the Panama Canal

Procedures for transiting the Panama Canal have been covered extensively in the sailing press, though constant changes mean that the prudent cruiser should check the coconut grapevine for updates. This is particularly true as the new super-locks come into operation; the increase in canal traffic may well affect the procedures for private vessels.

The good news is, the price of hiring an agent to organize transit paperwork has dropped over the years, from a reported $700 to $350 at the time of our transit in 2012. That means that the price difference between doing the paperwork yourself and hiring an agent has narrowed to the point that many cruisers can now consider the luxury of hiring an agent, whose fee covers everything from the legwork between offices down to lines and tires (to serve as oversized fenders). Organizing the transit yourself involves roughly $150 to $200 in bank fees, taxis, and line/tire rental. In brief, the steps involved are: calling for a measurement appointment, bringing the $609 transit fee and $891 security bond to the bank in cash, and calling again for a transit date (all in the official canal language of English). Whether you use an agent or do the paperwork yourself, the transit fee remains the same: $609 for any vessel up to fifty feet.

One of the principal advantages of hiring a bonded agent is that you don't have to post the $891 bond; you pay for only the transit fee and the agent. This eliminates multiple trips to ATMs, as well as the potential risk of carrying wads of cash around crime-ridden Colon (not to mention waiting for your bond to be refunded and yet another bank fee). We were delighted with the promptness and efficiency of our agent, Erick Galvez of Centenario Consultant Agency.[1] The only thing an agent cannot do is speed up the process should there be any delays in high season. Normally, transits can be organized

---

[1]Email: info@centenarioconsulting.com

in two or three days, but waits of up to a week can develop, and there have even been odd instances of month-long delays (and worse) for small boats in high season (starting late February on the Caribbean side).

Vessels can be measured either at anchor in The Flats or at their berths in Shelter Bay Marina, the only marina on the Caribbean side and the place from where most cruisers organize their transit. The advantage of having the boat measured in a berth can be significant: by doing so, Nadine was able to stay on the boat, completing projects in Shelter Bay while awaiting the measuring officer. Meanwhile, Markus could leave to help another boat transit the canal and thus gain a preview of what was in store for us. Otherwise, he would have had to pass on that opportunity.

One cannot stress enough the value of previewing the canal. While awaiting our own date, we each volunteered as line handlers for different sailboats. In this way, we were able to familiarize ourselves with canal procedures and consequently felt much less anxious about our own transit. I highly recommend that sailing couples try to go through individually, helping different boats on different dates. This exposes you to a greater number of variables: one trip may see a boat going through the locks rafted up with others, while another may go through center lock (alone in the middle of the lock), or tied up to a larger vessel which is made fast to the side wall. This doubles your chances of experiencing the type of transit that your own boat will ultimately have. Canal authorities are extremely organized, but they don't announce the lock configuration in advance. Unless you're rushing through the canal in minimum time, it is usually easy to find boats in Shelter Bay looking for line handlers, and many crews swap duties to obtain the requisite four line handlers.

Meeting fellow sailors as line handlers was one of the unexpected highlights of the canal experience for us. We each met wonderful crews when we helped other boats through, and chance brought us a delightfully international and interesting crew for our own transit. The first helper we secured was our neighbor in the marina, Sylvia. Together with her husband, Ken, this Japanese grandmother had crossed the Pacific nonstop from Japan to Vancouver in fifty-three days! We also took on Victor, a retired Czech dam engineer with another incredible sailing story. While cruising in Haiti, his small boat went aground. Before he could float it, the boat was boarded and looted by locals. Threatened by knives and machetes, Victor jumped overboard and swam to safety, but he lost everything and was looking for crew positions on other boats. Rounding out the guest list on *Namani* was Hobin, a Canadian ecology student from McGill University who was doing field studies in Panama. Each of our line handlers brought us more than just a pair of helpful hands: with fascinating stories, insights, and discrete areas of expertise, they helped make our transit smooth and thoroughly enjoyable.

And the transit itself? We are happy to report that it was mostly uneventful. *Na-*

150

*mani* went up the three Gatun locks tied to a seventy-five foot sport fishing boat from Louisiana: after they motored into each lock and made fast to the rough side wall, we would approach and raft up along their port side. This proved to be the easiest of all configurations, since our cleats did not have to take the upward strain of long lines made fast to the canal walls. Our advisor cleverly made up for the difference in our respective hull shapes by doubling the bumper tires, one on top of another, for a wider buffer. At first, we had some doubts about the neighboring crew, who seemed more intent on the football game running on their large screen TV and the kebabs grilling on the aft deck! However, they proved to be competent, and their vessel absorbed most of the strain caused by the rapidly rising water level. The 585-foot cargo ship positioned ahead of us in the same lock posed no danger. After anchoring for the night and then crossing Lake Gatun the next morning, we descended the Pedro Miguel and two Miraflores locks in the same easy manner, this time tied to a large tour boat – not a grill or TV screen in sight!

Transiting the Panama Canal has always been a highlight of any sailor's resume, but thanks to recent developments, the process has become even easier. From watching rushing water make boats "dance" in the locks, to crossing the Continental Divide through the amazing Culebra Cut, and sharing the transit with new friends, the experience will remain a singular one among many cruising memories.

In the Culebra Cut

## Post Script: Panama City Fact File

In Panama City, you're likely to find just about any part or tool you need. The problem is finding the right place and negotiating traffic to get there. We found most of what we needed (eventually) at one of these four stores:

Head to Dimar for anything related to the engine, hydraulics, pumps, bearings, or seals.[2] They also carry Jabsco parts (Dimar SA, Centro de Balineras, Vista Hermosa, Edificio La Balinera. Tel. 229-1444, email dimarventas@dimarsa.com).

For general boating supplies, try Centro Marino.[3] Although their emphasis is on motor yachts and fishing, they also carry hoses, sealants, teak sealer, and the like (Avenida Nacional, Tel. 225-6654, info@centromarino.com).

Just a few blocks and around the corner from Centro Marino is Protecsa, where we found the best prices on shackles, cables, etc. (Protecsa, Via Bolivar y Camino Corozal, Tel. 227-3533, www.protecsa.com.pa, email info@protecsa.com.pa).

Marine Warehouse is a chandler located out at Las Brisas on the Amador Causeway.[4] Whatever they don't have in stock, they can order from their North American store with relatively quick turnover times (tel. 507-6702-9256).

Otherwise, turn to Gente de Mar, a boater's agency that can import just about anything you need from a US chandler at reasonable prices. They also fill propane tanks, deliver fuel, and run an informative radio net with weather, position reports, and general announcements (VHF channel 74 at 08:00). They're within walking distance of Balboa Yacht Club at Avenida Amador Edificio 900 (email: gentedemarinternational@gmail.com or tel. 6700-9133).

Before heading out into the Pacific, most cruisers stock up on as many staple foods as possible (six-plus months of stocking up) at the three big supermarkets: El Rey, Super 99, or Riba Smith. Of these, Riba Smith seems to have slightly higher prices but a greater selection of North American products or their equivalents if you are looking for something specific. These are the last big supermarkets for several thousand miles, and you won't see prices this low anywhere in the Pacific (including Tahiti, New Zealand and Australia).

While you'll find basics such as rice, flour, and milk powder everywhere, some speciality items are particularly expensive or hard to find in the Pacific. Items that get expensive after Panama include cheese, canned butter, olives, pickles, dried fruit, nuts,

---

[2]http://www.dimarsa.com

[3]http://www.centromarino.com

[4]http://www.marinewarehouse.net

and sunflower seeds, so stock up before departing the Americas. Wine is incredibly expensive in French Polynesia, so carry as much as you can for personal consumption or to trade for fruit, carvings, etc. Bakers should stock up on specialty items like whole wheat flour, oat bran, flax, spray-on cooking oil, bake mixes and chocolate chips.

Panama was the only place I found canned red peppers which gave meals some variety. If you like quality oil, vinegar, mustard, canned ham, quinoa, sprouting seeds, or a particular brand of cereal, stock up in Panama. Likewise, get a good supply of baby wipes and household cleansing wipes before you depart. And that's just as far as the household goods are concerned! Spare parts for all boat systems and a huge supply of sealant go without saying.

It pays to carry a selection of gift items for the islanders you'll meet along the way. In our experience, few islanders were interested in fish hooks. Lengths of fishing line and rope, on the other hand, make great gifts or trade items just about everywhere, as do cosmetics. We brought magic markers to give to island kids, though many expressed a wish for a pair of Crocs or similar sandals. If you have the space to carry a few pairs, they'd make good gifts for special occasions.

# Chapter 24

# At Work and Play in Panama's Islas Perlas

Something had gone terribly wrong in our Panama cruise: the work / play ratio was badly out of proportion. We had planned to enjoy a few weeks in Las Perlas – an unspoiled, quiet archipelago at the doorstep of Panama City – before heading out across the Pacific. But no sooner were we through the canal than a cloud of reality settled over us in the form of a leaky hatch, blocked plumbing, and broken anchor windlass. Instead of kicking back in secluded anchorages, we were sweating over repairs and scavenging the capital city for replacement parts. Our Las Perlas cruise was tantalizingly near, but oh, so far.

Then, I had it: why put off the trip when we could cruise and repair at the same time? Las Perlas are within a day's sail of Panama City, making it possible to tackle jobs in a beautiful, quiet setting and still return for a final provisioning run before departing for the Galapagos Islands. We quickly stowed newly acquired tools and parts and set off, if not for a relaxed splash-and-drinks cruise, then at least a working visit.

Sailing south in a fresh breeze, we left city tension behind and were pleasantly reminded that many things on the boat still did, in fact, function properly. The hull was keeping the water out and the sails were pulling *Namani* along nicely on a broad reach. Playful dolphins further lightened our mood, seabirds swooped overhead, and a whale breeched straight out of the water in the distance. We felt magically transported back into the joys of the cruising life instead of the gritty negatives. Forty miles later, we anchored off Isla Contadora: a short distance, but a big mental step away from the point of low morale we had just escaped.

Of course, the magic of the sea doesn't solve everything, and the job list would not work itself away on its own. And so it was that Contadora, island of blooming frangipani and shy roe deer, became Contadora, island of frangipani and the clogged toilet pump. Hoses were disconnected, parts cursed over – but night fell in sweet silence, with sparkling bioluminescence imitating the stars above, all the clearer without a city's dimming effects. The outgoing morning tide exposed a wide beach with enticing caves at the foot of steep bluffs, just the place for our young son to dig for buried treasure. The archipelago had served as a pirate's den since the sixteenth century – but I was beginning to suspect that buccaneers spent more time here tarring the rigging and repairing torn sails rather than counting their treasure.

A short sail south brought us to the lee of uninhabited Viveros, island of diving pelicans and anchor windlass repair. There we had a huge bay and endless sand beach all to ourselves, at least during short breaks in our dawn-to-dusk efforts on board. Work even took on an aspect of pleasure as I dove into the clear water to replace the corroded propeller anode. Ah, the satisfaction of a quiet anchorage and another item ticked off the job list!

While the southern portion of Las Perlas consists of large chunks of land dotted with a few small villages, the northern half is an explosion of mini islets. We headed back to that enticing maze of land and water to anchor off a pristine, gold-hued beach backed by tangled green vegetation. Isla Chapera is well known as a film site of the "Survivor" television series, but for us, it provided the perfect, quiet location to scrub *Namani's* hull. Unfortunately, the plan backfired when a raging current blasted clouds of plankton past – with dozens of jellyfish in silent, tentacled pursuit. Later, we savored the glowing sunset – not over cocktails in the cockpit, but over a tube of sealant on the coach roof, rebedding a leaky hatch. Still, our mission was accomplished: we were enjoying the wonders of Las Perlas and getting critical work done.

Too many cruisers endure the exposed anchorages of Panama City for too long, coming away feeling jaded as a result. We learned that it is best to load up on what parts are readily available and get away, improvising the rest in more pleasant – even rejuvenating – surroundings. Our getaway even helped us economize, considering the mysterious way that cash slips away in a city setting – a taxi ride here, a fortifying ice cream there. Ultimately, we also made efficient use of our time, logging solid days of satisfying work with concrete results. Best of all, we did it in a beautiful, solitary location. Lesson learned: sometimes, you really can have it all!

Enjoying a pristine beach in Las Perlas

# Part VI

# The Eastern Pacific

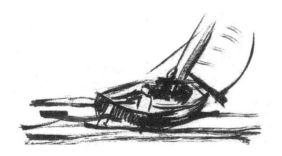

# The Eastern Pacific

We use the term "East Pacific" loosely as a catch-all phrase for what may be the most exciting part of your voyage. You've left the Americas at last, and a whole new ocean stretches ahead. As you sail west into the setting sun, you can look forward to a long list of highlights that stretch from the storied islands of the Galapagos to French Polynesia, plus the 3,000 mile "hop" in between – the single longest passage in the Coconut Milk Run. And although no two sailors experience the same conditions on any ocean passage, most cruisers who take on this part of the Pacific in the early months of post-cyclone season report easy downwind passages.

This section is rich in both facts and flavors: there's a practical guide to navigating the highly restricted waters of Darwin's islands, an introduction to the "Dangerous Archipelago" of the Tuamotus, as well as overviews of the best anchorages, hikes, and sights of two of the most spectacular island groups in the world. Those would be the Marquesas (with magical Fatu Hiva and stunning Nuku Hiva) and the Society Islands (think Moorea, Bora Bora, and their jaw-dropping cousin, Maupiti). We also cover lessons learned on passages in between. But there are plenty of flavors, too: a witch's broth, we'll call it, of anecdotes covering Tahiti's spectacular Heiva festival and the unusual comings and goings on a lonely Tuamotan atoll. Chances are, most of the postcard images you associate with the South Pacific come from here. Now picture your own boat in the foreground of that scene, and you've got it: paradise found.

# Chapter 25

# Panama to the Galapagos Islands

Having crossed the Atlantic via the Milk Run some years earlier, we felt we were ready for the Coconut Milk Run in the Pacific. Our son Nicky had crossed his first ocean at age four; now he was a "grown up" eight year old, the master of more useful knots and connoisseur of more constellations than the average suburban adult – or even the average weekend sailor. So he was ready, too, with a Lego collection that rivaled the depth and breadth of our tool box and spare part reserves.

In some ways, a passage from Panama to the Galapagos resembles the typical opening leg for an Atlantic crossing from Gibraltar to the Canary Islands. After all, both trips cover 750 to 900 miles – about a week, give or take – and both are the prelude to a much larger venture on the order of 3,000 miles. But the similarities end there, a point we were acutely aware of on the eve of our departure from Panama.

That's because the Canary Islands are a populated, well-connected outpost of Europe; the Galapagos, in contrast, are "only" an off-lying territory of Ecuador. For sailors on their way across the Atlantic, the run to the Canaries is often a shakedown cruise: just a week at sea, followed by the chance to re-assess, re-provision, and repair. The Canaries offer plenty of chandleries, boat yards, hardware stores, and supermarkets. Crew or special equipment can easily be flown in. Problems that arise do not have to develop into full-fledged dramas, and anyone with cold feet can always sail back the way they came.

Not so the Galapagos Islands. Jumping off from Panama to the Galapagos is the mental and physical equivalent of jumping off a much higher diving board into a much larger swimming pool. Galapagos-bound sailors cannot afford to learn things the hard way, because there's no way out from there (short of extreme measures). Even when you arrive in the Galapagos, you've still only reached a tiny island outpost and a national park, at that, not a cruiser-friendly playground. There's a lot of blue water west of the Galapagos, and whichever route you choose to follow onward (be it a 3,000 mile run to the Marquesas or 2,000 miles to Easter Island) will only bring you to a different, tiny island outpost, all the way to Tahiti (3,650 NM as the booby flies). And even there it's a long, long way to the next well-stocked port in New Zealand. And that is, after all, part of the appeal of crossing the Pacific.

Different ball park, different ball game.

## Into the Wild Blue Yonder

So there we stood, on the diving board of the Pacific, taking a very deep breath. *Namani* was laden down not only with food and water for this leg, but as much as she could possibly carry for the months to follow. She didn't so much sail away from Panama as waddle like an over-fed guest from a Thanksgiving feast. To make things more interesting still, we had our friend Bill on board, who would give us not only good company but also the luxury of a three-person watch rotation for our maiden Pacific voyage. However, Bill absolutely positively had to be in Santa Cruz for the start of a non-refundable Galapagos tour, giving us a two-week window to make the 900 mile passage. Easy, right? We didn't dare hope, knowing that any ocean-going venture is unpredictable.

Every passage has its defining challenge, be it weather, broken gear, or even crew harmony. We had read many reports of uncomfortable windward beats into contrary currents on this piece of ocean; other reports, meanwhile, were more focused on the problem of chafe over this sometimes windless, trans-equatorial passage. As we watched the skyscrapers of Panama City fade beyond the horizon, we wondered which challenge our voyage would bring.

Spillover from Caribbean trade winds in late February gave us a rip-roaring start, with the added thrill of a rollercoaster ride over the edge of the continental shelf. Here, 200 foot depths fall off into a 2,000 foot undersea precipice, a geography that manifests itself in lumpy surface waters. We were all glad when the bumps evened out twenty-four hours later, but not so glad to watch the winds flatten with them. By the end of day three, we had broken into the threes: three degrees north latitude, and a meager three knots of speed made good in light air. By 6 p.m., we were chowing down on pasta and drifting along at a mere two knots – in the right direction, we thankfully noted. By midnight, *Namani* was going nowhere but rolling everywhere. More correctly, we were tracing circles: the quarter moon shone a teasing spotlight on our pathetic silhouette from all angles: first from starboard, then around the bow, and whoops, there it was to port. I was rapidly running out of synonyms for "lurch" as we rolled, floundered, and tottered along in the vicinity of 03°45 N, 081°17W.

And it was only downhill from there, at least in terms of speed. Our twenty-four hour run over day three was a passable 108 miles; day two, a determined ninety-four; and day five, a scanty sixty-eight miles made good. It was high time to test whether our new Parasailor was worth the investment. This sail is a spinnaker-like, symmetric expanse of light fabric that works best slightly off the wind. Thanks to its cut-out "wing," the Parasailor is much easier to set and maintain in light winds than a traditional spinnaker. Essentially, it's a kite that flies itself, towing our docile sloop behind. All hands agreed that the wonder sail also provided immediate relief for our rolling motion, thanks to the lifting force of the wing. Always in pursuit of the perfect noon sight, Markus took advantage of the stable platform to put our Astra sextant to use. The results, in fact, were satisfyingly close to our GPS position.

Delighted with our colorful new look and "speed" (it's all relative when forward motion "jumps" from two to three knots), we set about on another home improvement program: namely, a good scrub up for each of the crew. Having time a-plenty and a relatively stable platform under us, we filled Nicky's inflatable kiddie pool with salt water and each enjoyed a thorough soap-down in the cockpit, followed by a fresh water rinse. Luxury!

## Taking It Easy

The defining challenge for this passage had become apparent: speed, or lack thereof. Therefore, it was to be a test of patience more than endurance or fortitude. It seemed that we were destined to approach the Galapagos Islands at a ponderous, turtle-like pace. (Appropriate, no?) But what's an unbearable curse to some is a blessing to others. Our passage became a leisurely, serene affair, exactly the antithesis to our anxious preparation period back in Panama. In fact, it turned out to be one of the most enjoyable passages we ever had. Even the rolling seas gradually eased to very long, gentle swell. Mixing up a batch of muffins in the galley (an unthinkable proposition during our windward passage from the US East Coast to the Bahamas), I had the fleeting sensation *Namani* was tethered in a marina somewhere, so mild was her motion.

Other than the occasional hour or two under engine for the thrill of a few miles made good, we slugged it out under sail. Why? One factor was budgetary: diesel isn't cheap and would be even more expensive to replace in the Galapagos. Another was the lack of a better place to motor to: we found no point in reaching another blank place on the chart that was equally devoid of wind. Meanwhile, *Namani* was still on track to make

Bill's deadline, even at her sluggish two to three knot pace – thanks to our quick shot out of the starting blocks and the occasional, ambitious puff of wind that treated us to a brief but exhilarating four knot gallop. One reason we had left home and jobs behind to go cruising was to escape the harrying clock that had so defined every aspect of our former lives. Instead of scrutinizing the time, we clung to reports on the behavior of the Intertropical Convergence Zone, the force with its finger on the wind controls. Since the ITCZ was weakly defined at that point in time, more of the same light conditions were expected.

Things were going swimmingly just as they were. So much so that we made a swim call, taking turns to go for an exhilarating dip in 9,000 foot depths. After Nicky suffered the only injury of the trip in the form of a jellyfish sting, we launched our inflatable kayak (on a small boat, all our toys have to be inflatable) for a quick paddle around *Namani* on the boundless, silvery blue sea. It was an eerie feeling to be even a few yards away from the mother ship, although seas were calm and visibility perfect. I wondered if the crews of early exploratory missions felt the same pang when setting out into oceans that must have seemed even more vast than they do today. Like them, we scanned our watery world from the mast top and found nothing. Or rather, we found a fascinating, fluid landscape painting in which the hills shifted, rose, and approached before shuffling toward the opposite horizon.

By day six, we could begin to hazard a guess as to our arrival date: three more days. Slow, but still on target. By that point, we had thoroughly given ourselves over to the "Qué será, será" approach to ocean sailing. Conditions were ideal for cetacean-spotting, and we glimpsed a lone orca followed by two pods of striped dolphins. They seemed a little disappointed in our pedestrian speed, however, and raced off to find less geriatric playmates. Then it was time to make a dent in Nicky's home schooling and stitch together a flag of Ecuador. The moon was nearly full now, stealing the celestial stage from the stars but bringing us a welcome visitor every night. I was gradually wading through a 700 page book on the building of the Panama Canal, a process that mirrored our journey: though the pages seemed to turn slowly, my bookmark made steady progress toward the end. As if on cue, birds began to appear around us. Land couldn't be too far now.

## Across the Equator

*Namani* was rapidly approaching the equator, and we had a party to plan for day nine. Having never crossed that milestone by sea before, we were all pollywogs, as per naval tradition. Therefore, we assigned the role of Neptune to Nicky's stuffed animal, a monkey named Frodo who was "born" in Indonesia and had therefore presumably crossed

166

the equator at some point. Frodo made a solemn Neptune who presided over the polly-wog trials, accusing each of us of dastardly crimes. Those were formulated in secrecy the previous night, each crew member writing one accusation for each of his crewmates: heinous misdeeds along the lines of leaving Lego for the barefoot night watchman to find the hard way. During the trials and subsequent punishment, Nicky got a little carried away in smearing the guilty parties (including himself) with shaving cream, and all of us sported silly headgear. Finally, each crew member dutifully sacrificed a piece of his or her celebratory brownie to Neptune. From then on, we could call ourselves shellbacks and note our latitude in degrees south, a rewarding feeling to say the least.

Neptune watching the GPS as Namani crosses the Equator

Dawn on day ten brought the sight of Cristóbal's sloping, crater-poked form: our first Pacific landfall. The only hiccup of a passage full of impressions (if not dramatic events) came when we turned the key to the ignition and listened to the engine sputter, then die. Having patiently waited all these days, we were suddenly itching to get in to port – preferably before the rapidly approaching Friday 5 p.m. mark in order to clear in. The clock, a lesser member of our passage-making cast until now, immediately took center stage with its loud ticking.

Just as Markus cleared up the problem (a clogged fuel line), the wind came back in a rush, ushering *Namani* briskly into Wreck Bay. On the way in, we were treated to a final ocean spectacle: a patch of boiling water stirred up by an agitated school of fish, preyed upon by leaping dolphins and swooping frigate birds who delicately plucked snacks out of the sea. We had "made it" on all counts: not just in to port, but with enough time to clear customs and a full two days to spare before Bill's tour began.

This passage showed us the ocean at its most serene: the Pacific, it seems, could really live up to its name. We grew to appreciate the value of a slow, even, and easy passage (950 miles in ten days): our pick every time over a fast, uncomfortable one, especially as a cruising family out to savor our time together in special places. And savor it we did, for the duration of the passage and over the next three weeks in the magical Galapagos Islands. Then it would be time to take the next deep breath and set sail for the big one: 3,000 miles to the Marquesas.

# Chapter 26

# Navigating the Restrictions of the Enchanted Archipelago

Six hundred miles west of Ecuador, the Galapagos Islands are a perfect stepping-stone for sailors heading across the Pacific from Central and South America. It's a Doctor Doolittle world where eons of evolution can be observed at a glance, whether you focus on Darwin's finches, lumbering land tortoises, or the surreal underwater landscape where hammerhead sharks glide alongside sea turtles. In short, it's a place that ranks on many a bucket list. So what's to stop the Archipélago de Colón, as it's officially called, from being a rewarding cruising destination? Tight restrictions, for one thing. Ever-changing regulations and rumors make cruisers wonder: what's the best way to see the islands on your own boat?

## Permits & Fees

Other than making a quick, in-transit stopover ($25 for under forty-eight hours), sailors currently have two options for visiting the Galapagos. The first is a one-port stop of up to twenty-one days. In the past, sailors could eke out a few extra days or visit additional ports thanks to a broad interpretation of what constituted an "emergency," but nowadays officials are inflexible and keep a close eye on the movement of private vessels. The one-port option may seem a bit of a dud, considering that the Galapagos are famous for the variation of species from island to island. However, only the vessel is confined by the one-port rule. Crews can travel freely between the four inhabited islands by taking ferries ($25, about two hours each way).

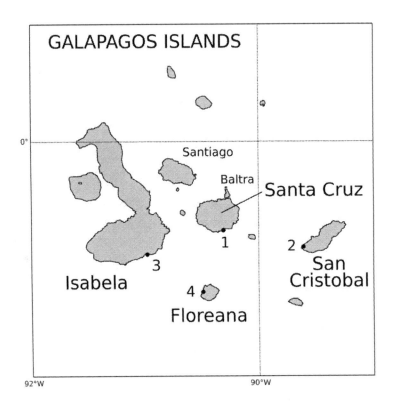

GALAPAGOS ISLANDS

Santiago

Baltra

Santa Cruz

1

2

San Cristobal

3

Isabela

4

Floreana

92°W

90°W

0°

The three-week, one-port stop option requires no advance paper work. Just turn up in one of two ports of entry (on the islands of Cristóbal and Santa Cruz), and agents will appear to help you (and take your US dollars, the official currency of Ecuador). All told, a two-person crew aboard a six-ton vessel will pay approximately $500 (cash only) in immigration, customs, and national park fees, plus an extra $100 for the required agent. A fumigation certificate is also required: a meaningless $50 document that can be obtained upon arrival from an agent, but may be cheaper to get ahead of time (in Panama, for example, canal agents sell the certificates for $35 to $40).

The second option for private vessels is to obtain a cruising permit, or *Autografó*. An Autografó grants your vessel ninety days to move between four inhabited ports on four islands: Cristóbal, Santa Cruz, Floreana, and Isabela. An Autografó can only be obtained through an agent (typically charging $300 to $500) and takes three weeks to process, so begin the process long before your departure date from the Americas. Other entry fees still apply, so even small boats will spend close to $1,000 to enter the Galapagos with an Autografó. (Technically, there is a third option, in which you pay thousands of dollars to declare your boat a tour vessel and hire a private guide.)

Of course, every rule has an exception, especially when South American bureaucracies are concerned. There are indeed reports of sailors obtaining an Autografó for "only" $300 upon arrival. Still other cruisers report that ill-tempered port captains have randomly curtailed the normal twenty day permit to only fifteen. All of this falls outside official guidelines and is difficult to verify. The vast majority of cruisers, however, report that officials hold a firm line with either of the two official entry options regardless of pleas, repeated attempts, or bribes.

So what's best: paying for an Autografó or doing day trips from a home base at one port? Frugal sailors who view the Galapagos as a stopover are usually satisfied with the one-port option. Those who see their visit as a once-in-a-lifetime opportunity might be better off paying for an Autografó and gaining an overview of several different islands. The key point to keep in mind is that both these options only grant permission for inhabited islands. No matter where you anchor (and anchoring is the only option), you will be at arm's length from the prime sights on smaller, wilder islands. But don't lose heart: it is possible to see a great deal by combining travel on your boat with independent excursions and organized tours. Last minute deals on live-aboard tours abound in Puerto Ayora. For example, four-day tours on a sixteen-person tourist class boat go for $525 to $600 (down from a regular price of $1,500) in the week prior to departure. The main hurdle to joining a tour is leaving your own boat unattended, which some crews solve by leaving one person on board or trading boat-sitting duties with other crews. The bottom line is, a visit to the Galapagos is entirely worth the expense and effort.

A marine iguana in the Galapagos Islands

## Port Comparison

Given the limitations, which is the best port to head for? Each has its pluses and minuses, and all are connected by two hour ferry services via the central "hub" of Santa Cruz. Credit cards are rarely accepted, so most transactions on the islands are made in cash (including large outlays such as tours). The only ATMs are on Santa Cruz and San Cristóbal, where you will also find painfully slow Internet access.

Puerto Ayora (#1 on accompanying map) on Santa Cruz is the most centrally located of the four principal ports. As the biggest town, Puerto Ayora offers the widest choice of tours and general services in the Galapagos. Unfortunately, the anchorage is exposed and usually very rolly. There are ATMs and Internet cafes, and supermarkets stocking a slightly wider range of goods than those on other islands (though none offer much more than basics). There is a bank, hardware store, plus the usual traveler services: laundry, restaurants, post office, and even recycling points for glass, paper, and plastic. The vast majority of Galapagos-bound flights land at Baltra airport, making Santa Cruz the best place to meet friends or exchange crew.

Santa Cruz is surrounded by a cluster of small islands, each with its own endemic species. This makes Puerto Ayora the best place to stay in terms of covering the most ground by taking multiple day trips. Daily tours depart for places like Seymour Island, Bartolomé, Floreana, and even Isabela. Local sights on Santa Cruz that can be reached without a tour include the Darwin Research Station, spectacular Tortuga Bay (a beach and neighboring lagoon where you can snorkel with sharks), the canyon-like cleft of

Las Grietas, and sights in the highlands ecosystem (giant turtles, sink holes, and lava tubes).

Puerto Baquerizo Moreno (map, #2; also known as Wreck Bay), on the island of San Cristóbal, is (usually) a more sheltered anchorage with space for dozens of boats. The approach is straightforward, with a marked reef off one side of the entrance. More sailors choose to base themselves out of this southeast corner of the archipelago than anywhere else. The town offers a number of eateries, basic grocery stores, Internet cafes, a post office, ATMs, and a bank. There is also a daily farmer's market, a hardware store, and the occasional recycling point. A number of tour companies offer local and inter-island trips – but often require a six or ten person minimum to operate. Several interesting Cristóbal sights can be reached without a tour, including a turtle reserve, a highlands lagoon, and several nearby walks. A handful of dive shops offer day trips to the offshore cliff of Kicker Rock, where hammerhead sharks and sea turtles are a common sight. Water taxis operate in both Puerto Ayora and Wreck Bay, and most sailors prefer paying $1 per person per ride than leaving a dinghy unattended, since dinghies are used as convenient resting spots and public toilets by local sea lions.

Crews with an Autógrafo may also visit the islands of Isabela and Floreana (though not as a first or last port of call unless making a special arrangement through an agent). Villamil (map, #3) on Isla Isabela is a well-sheltered spot with a more complicated, reef-lined approach and enough space for up to a dozen boats. This anchorage has a quiet, local feel. Sailors based here have the run of the largest island in the archipelago – albeit most sights can only be visited with a certified guide as part of a tour (these can be booked locally at short notice). There is a weekly farmer's market and several minimarts that sell basic goods, but no bank or ATMs. On Isabela, penguins, marine iguanas, and flamingos are a common sight, and excursions to view the volcanoes, endemic turtles, and flightless cormorants are possible.

Puerto Velasco Ibarra (map, #4) on Floreana (an island also known as Santa María) is the least visited port, an open roadstead with few amenities. Local sights include a black sand beach, turtles, and outstanding bird life, plus historic Post Office Bay.

Ultimately, each crew must make decisions on where and how to go based on practical considerations and budget. And while we have focused on the monetary facts of visiting the Galapagos, don't lose sight of the rewards. Think of the value you place on swimming with penguins at the equator, following the tracks of marine iguanas, or observing blue-footed boobies perform their mating dance just a wingspan away from your camera lens. No matter how you choose to explore the islands, the superlatives of the Galapagos will stay with you a lifetime.

# Post Script: Agents

An informal poll helped me produce this list of four agents who have received positive reviews (be forewarned, however, that each has also received at least one negative review). In addition to facilitating entry into Ecuador and processing your Autografó, they can arrange for fuel and water to be delivered to your boat at competitive rates. Of the four, only Ricardo Arenas answers emails written in English promptly.

Ricardo Arenas of Servigalapagos (www.sailingalapagos.com.ec): info@arenas.bz, cell 09 9480859, based on Santa Cruz but has representatives on other islands, speaks English.

Bolivar Pesantes of Naugala: naugala@hotmail.com, cell 09 4205158, speaks limited English, based on Cristóbal but has contacts on other islands.

Pablo Quiroga of Yachtgala: pabloquiroga@1969.com, cell 08 0040979, can organize local day trips. Speaks limited English, based on Cristóbal.

Carmela Romero of Nautigal: yachtgala@hotmail.com, cell 09 9330494, speaks limited English. Based on Cristóbal and can arrange day trips and accommodations on other islands.

Tour Agencies: Moonrise Travel on Avenida Darwin in Puerto Ayora (across from Banco del Pacifico) is one extremely professional and knowledgeable tour agency that sells last-minute, multi-day tours of the islands. Contact English-speaking Ivonne or Jenny at moonrise@easynet.net.ec or call 593-5-2526402.

# Chapter 27

# Galapagos Islands to the Marquesas: Life is but a Dream

On the eve of our departure from the Galapagos Islands to the Marquesas, each member of our crew was preoccupied with his or her own thoughts. We had already crossed the Atlantic, completed a round trip from the Caribbean up the US East Coast, and sailed 900 miles beyond Panama into the Pacific. But the remoteness of this next stretch of ocean – all 3,000 miles of it – was something entirely different. I was thrilled to be standing on the starting line of a lifelong dream, but slightly overwhelmed by the scale of it all. Then there was nagging concern about provisioning: had I stocked enough food, water, and (most importantly) chocolate cookies to last the distance?

Markus devoted most of his attention to tracking the immediate weather conditions around the Galapagos, an area of strong currents and fluky equatorial winds. Nicky, on the other hand, was too busy with ambitious Lego projects to think of pesky details like preparations aboard *Namani*. Bidding a fond *adiós* to the cavorting sea lions, blue-footed boobies, and marine iguanas of Darwin's archipelago, we were off and away on April 2, 2012.

As things turned out, the passage could be divided into three distinct parts: an awful beginning; a long, glorious middle; and the home stretch. We couldn't be choosy about a weather window once our twenty-one day Galapagos permit expired (and – shhh! – after overstaying that by two days). The first three days underway were squally with wind from the southwest. On the port tack, *Namani* could only manage a heading slightly north of west. On the starboard tack, she tracked an even less inspiring eastward course due to the strong current. Where was the favorable west-setting current we had read about? In one miserable twenty-four hour period, we tacked over one hundred miles to make ten good. It was a squally trial of patience and faith in many ways.

## Into the Trade Winds

Luckily, our misery was short-lived. The wind abated over days four and five, when we motored south-southwest. On day six, we found steady fifteen knot southeasterly trade winds at last, and the tune of our days made a drastic change for the better, something along the lines of "Merrily, merrily, merrily, life is but a dream." The sky was a swath of blue dotted with a few fair weather cumulus clouds. What a pleasure to lean back, let the Hydrovane do the steering, and watch the log tick off the miles as *Namani* sailed in pursuit of the setting sun.

Back in the Galapagos, we had made many new acquaintances and set up two SSB radio nets: one English and another German-speaking (in fact, these were just two of many, including the well-established Pacific Seafarer's Net and a French-speaking net). These provided twice-a-day social contact and just enough structure to pleasantly punctuate days on the open sea. As it turned out, the nets were populated by an entertaining cast of characters: listening was a little like tuning in to radio entertainment in the era before television. That's one reason why *Namani* followed the ticks of two different clocks: UTC, for our constant appointment with the radio net crews spread over many degrees of longitude, and our ship's clock, which we adjusted periodically as our sloop sailed west.

Otherwise, we were on our own. In fact, we had more contact with animals than humans, given occasional dolphin, whale, and seabird visits. Only once did we spot a fishing fleet, not far west from the Galapagos. Interestingly, other crews reported regular sightings of fishing boats throughout their passages, so perhaps this was just luck. It certainly wasn't for lack of a good lookout, since Markus and I spent our watches in the cockpit, ducking below only briefly to write in the log or dig out a snack. Standing watches can be a trial, as they were during those wet early days hard on the wind, or they can be glorious, as in the middle section of the trip.

## Of Sails and Stars

After a shaky start, we were treated to the loveliest passage imaginable. Fair weather and steady progress were the order of the day, every day. Weather systems that normally keep sailors on their toes seemed to be slumbering somewhere far away. In our little bubble around latitude 08°S, every day was pleasant, and we slept soundly in the knowledge that tomorrow would bring more of the same. In fact, we hardly had to trim the sails. *Namani's* slight rolling motion lulled us into a state of supreme contentment, like daydreaming babes in the cradle of the ocean. Where else but a boat can you be perfectly content to literally watch a day go by? A week? We could relate to the French sailor Bernard Moitessier, who got so into the groove that he didn't stop upon completing one circumnavigation. He simply sailed on into the setting sun for another half circle of the globe – all in one nonstop journey poetically chronicled in his book, *The Long Way*.

By day, we flew the Parasailor, our light-wind miracle machine. What had originally been a long-winded operation to set the sail quickly became a smooth, fifteen-minute process, with Markus hoisting the sock on the bow and me tending sheets in the cockpit. Once up, the Parasailor required next to no tending, and the Hydrovane kept things steady with small rudder movements. We were free to sit back and enjoy the eco-friendly ride.

At night, we would swap back to the genoa. For this trip, we replaced one of our old foresails with a special twin sail (two flaps sewn on one luff tape) that flies like a twizzle rig minus the extra set up. Downwind, the flaps open up like a small spinnaker – one that can be furled to any size with an easy adjustment from the cockpit, even while one flap remains poled out. As a cautious crew who values undisturbed sleep for the off-watch person, we prefer trading comfort for speed and therefore douse the Parasailor even on apparently quiet nights. It's a strategy that pays off: another crew reported midnight shenanigans when trying to douse their spinnaker in one of the few squalls to cross our general cruising track.

Keeping a steady schedule of four-hour watches, day and night, was another aspect of the pleasant rhythm that we fell in to. Markus took the early watch, from 06:00 to 10:00, serving as one of two controllers for the English-speaking radio net during this time. I took over from 10:00 to 14:00, a time partly devoted to home schooling, plus baking bread (and other goodies) every third day. Night watches had a quality of their own, with both the Big Dipper and the Southern Cross in view. Standing port and starboard, they were like buoys leading us along a marked channel to land, far to the west. Clear nights also meant that Markus could aim our sextant at the sky just about any time he wanted for a star sight – quite the luxury! Other than scanning the horizon, reading, and counting the minutes to snack time, I passed thirty minutes of my 02:00 to 06:00 watch with an easy session of step aerobics. After all, thirty-five feet of fiberglass doesn't provide much room for blood-pumping exercise.

And what exactly does an eight-year-old do for twenty-eight days at sea? Doesn't he feel bored? Cooped up? Lonely? None of the above! With a greater part of the morning devoted to school (plus a shorter afternoon session in his second language,

German), Nicky happily kept himself occupied in his remaining free time. To begin with, there were Lego boats to build: massive marvels of engineering complete with working winches, cloth sails, and swing keels. Then there were the adventures of Percy Jackson (the schoolboy demigod son of Poseidon) to read, and decks to patrol for flying fish. Nicky also spent part of the early night watch in the cockpit, clipped in beside me, watching the stars. How many eight-year-olds are treated to down time like this, contemplating the grandeur of the universe with their parents? How many parents can claim the same?

Our weeks at sea were punctuated by special occasions, too. After a flurry of cake-baking and craft-making, Nicky and I helped Markus celebrate his forty-sixth birthday at 08°S 110°W. We hadn't brought gifts from "civilization" for this special day; instead, we applied our hands, hearts, and a little creativity to the materials available on board. The results (commemorative artwork, a bar of soap carved into the shape of a turtle, and personalized new lyrics for a favorite song) made it a birthday to remember in both location and spirit.

*Namani* photographed from *E Capoe*

Most exciting of all was our mid-ocean rendezvous with a French sailboat called *E Capoe* – the name translates to something like "What the heck!" Position reports on the radio net showed that we were very close to this family of five. We had chatted on SSB, but never crossed paths – until now! *E Capoe's* crew is made up of a French father, Austrian mother, and three trilingual kids (both their parents' native tongues plus the Spanish they picked up while living in the Galapagos Islands, where their parents worked as researchers). So it was with great anticipation that we compared positions and scanned the horizon for a sail. Our first sighting came in the pre-dawn hours, just a dot of light ahead. Eventually, we raised a white sail and the mirage-like shape of a boat appeared on the horizon.

Like naval encounters of centuries past, the excitement stretched over half a day as the boats steadily drew closer. When *Namani* finally pulled alongside at noon, we all broke into silly grins and waved for all our arms were worth, compressing all our social energy into that one brief encounter. Then the mid-ocean photo shoot of a lifetime commenced, producing countless images of each boat from all possible angles and various sail configurations. When we finally did get to spend time together in the Marquesas, we felt like old friends. The kids got along beautifully, and we were delighted to be able to cross paths on many later occasions – all the way from 118°W to 163°W longitude!

## And What About the Boat?

Not every minute of an ocean passage is fun, but this particular passage had an embarrassingly high percentage of good and great moments. Smooth sailing and steady winds helped in that respect: there was little chafe or undue stress on the rigging, as regular checks reassured us. One day, my big job was to replace a slider on the largely unused mainsail. On day twenty-six, Markus got a new perspective on our little universe when he climbed the mast to fix a weak connection in the tricolor light. Otherwise, the only "work" on the boat was topping up our water tank from a separate cache of reserves and refilling the diesel burned early in the trip with fuel from jerry cans.

All the boats we were in contact with complained of shaggy forests of gooseneck barnacles sprouting from their hulls. The radio net buzzed with solutions that ranged from the inventive to the insane. Someone suggested running a line under the hull to rub the barnacles off, a recipe that brought mixed results. From the "don't try this at home" school of thought came the plan to go overboard for hand-to-hand combat. Bruce from *Adventure Bound* not only cleared the growth in this way, but even speared two fish while he was at it! This was not, however, an approach anyone else chose to try. We went with the "ignore" option and attacked the inch-long pests at anchor at the end of our journey.

## The Home Stretch

The radio nets also hosted discussions on the feasibility of making an illicit stopover in Fatu Hiva before officially clearing into French Polynesia on Hiva Oa, forty-five miles farther downwind. It was a tempting prospect, indeed, to avoid a long windward run. The gorgeous Bay of Virgins on Fatu Hiva ranks as one of most beautiful anchorages of the South Pacific, and nobody wanted to pass it by. Radioing ahead to crews who had already made landfall brought a halt to all this speculation, however, once a report came through of regular patrols threatening hefty fines for illegal stopovers (whether or not these fines were ever collected was an unresolved question). In a way, this is a good thing, as the windward passage weeds out much of the fleet and leaves Fatu Hiva in relative peace, a true reward for those willing to tough it out for a day.

Land ho! The Marquesas

The wind only faltered on the last four days of our passage, a mere Force 3 that wafted us gently forward. The Parasailor helped eke out the last few miles, but boats behind us fell into a windless void. Some inched in to port after a total of thirty-five days underway. A few even came non-stop from Panama, a trip of over fifty days! When the lush, craggy cliffs of Hiva Oa came into view, we were thrilled, but also sad to end this lovely passage. One of the most peaceful, magical times our family has ever enjoyed was coming to a close. It was entirely unlike our Atlantic crossing a few years before, which had been an erratic, trying passage with conditions ranging from dead calms to ugly squalls. Now we arrived fresh and eager for more sailing. And a good thing, too, since inter-island passages within the Marquesas have more in common with open ocean sailing than coastal cruising.

By lunchtime on April 30, *Namani* was anchored in the tight quarters of Traitor's Bay, with one anchor ahead and another astern to keep her oriented into the light swell along with twenty-odd other boats. One of our radio net buddies kindly dinghied up with a welcome basket for us: huge, succulent pamplemousse (grapefruit the size of bowling balls), crisp green lettuce, and, of course, a fresh baguette. With misty mountains all around, we immediately fell in love with the Marquesas. *Namani* had covered 3,300 miles in twenty-eight days. The big one – the longest single passage of our three-year cruise – was behind us, and will forever remain a sailing highlight.

# Chapter 28

# Highlights of the Magnificent Marquesas

Isolated, wild, brooding; bold mountain landscapes jutting up above a vast, rippling sea. The magnificent Marquesas have attracted many an escapee from western "civilization" over the centuries – including us modern-day sailors, willing to cross a seemingly infinite ocean on small, frail boats with small, all-too-human crews. Many of us are pulled as much as pushed, lured by a siren song composed by those who came before us. But it's hard to know what's legend and what's reality among these storied islands. So where to begin?

As Thor Heyerdahl wrote, "A painter is better armed to convey the majesty of the Marquesas than a writer." The islands are long-extinct volcanoes that rise high above the ocean floor, their slopes deeply chiseled by the elements. It's a wild and enticing landscape like nowhere else in French Polynesia. The islands fall into two clusters: a southeastern (windward) group consisting of Hiva Oa, Fatu Hiva, and Tahuata, and, seventy miles to the northwest, a leeward cluster made up of Ua Pou, Nuku Hiva, and Ua Huka. Given the absence of fringing reefs, this is by no means a sheltered archipelago; passages between islands are exposed. Each island is truly unique and offers its own special highlights to the cruiser. Marquesan people are open and friendly – strike up a conversation and you will immediately be plied with more juicy pamplemousse than you can possibly carry.

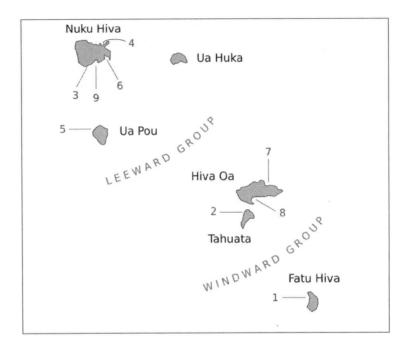

## Great Anchorages

Fatu Hiva's Bay of Virgins (see map, #1) is one of the most visually dramatic anchorages in the world, where sheer cliffs and eerie rock formations plunge from thousand-foot heights into the sea. The last hours of daylight make for a mesmerizing light show every evening, when the rugged features molt to ever deeper shades of gold. The bay is not much more than a narrow cleft in the coastline and relatively deep at thirty feet or more. Being on the lee shore, it's usually quite calm – except for gusts funneling off the slopes. There's a free, fresh water tap right on the shore, where you can fill up with deliciously refreshing and safe drinking water. The tiny settlement of Hanavave is a very welcoming place where locals offer home-cooked dinners and wooden carvings. Beware that Fatu Hiva is not a formal port of entry. Technically, cruisers who make a stop here without clearing in at nearby Hiva Oa can be subject to hefty fines (whether those fines are only threatened or actually collected is unclear).

Tahuata's Hanamoenoa Bay (map, #2) is another favorite, located just around the corner from Hiva Oa's tightly packed Tahauku Bay. Here, a perfect sandy crescent fronts a quiet anchorage with depths of ten to twenty feet. It's a rarity in this archipelago, otherwise typified by rugged, boulder-strewn coastlines. Wild horses graze on the green slopes in this uninhabited corner of the island, and the resident manta rays are another prime attraction (see below).

*Namani* in Fatu Hiva's Bay of Virgins

While there's no such thing as an ugly bay in the Marquesas, Taioa Bay (map, #3, also known as Daniel's Bay) on the southwest corner of Nuku Hiva is the only anchorage that can really hold a candle to Fatu Hiva's Bay of Virgins. There, mountain slopes descend to the sea in echoing folds, each catching and scattering light at different angles. This is also one of the better protected anchorages in the archipelago; when you approach from the sea, it's almost hard to believe there's more water beyond the jutting headland. There is a potable fresh water tap at the head of the bay, where a number of gardens but no permanent population is located. Anchor in twenty to twenty-five feet.

Anaho Bay (map, #4) on the northeast coast of Nuku Hiva is unique as the only reef-lined anchorage in the Marquesas. It's just far enough off the usual track that few boats make the trip out here, but hugely rewarding for the isolated beauty of the place. This might just be your best chance to escape the cruising crowds while anchoring in a secure place with a scenic sandy beach (anchoring depths twenty-five to thirty feet).

## Great Hikes

After twenty-eight days at sea, we worried that our legs might not be up to exploring the Marquesas afoot. As Jack London wrote, "Two months at sea, bare-footed all the time, without space in which to exercise one's limbs, is not the best preliminary to leather shoes and walking." We made do with light sandals and found that the stunning scenery always kept us inspired.

185

A perfect introductory hike is the short (thirty to forty minutes one way) hike to the waterfall behind Hanavave on Fatu Hiva (map, #1). It's a gorgeous, sunny spot where you can swim beneath the refreshingly cool waterfall. One of the sensory highlights in the Marquesas is resting on the rocks of the creek, shifting with the shade throughout the day and catching a different watery tune each time: the constant hum of the cascade, the high babble of closely-spaced rocks, or the low-pitched gurgle of broader gaps between large boulders.

Once you've warmed up with that, how about an epic, ten mile hike from Hanavave to Omoa? The rough jeep track offers incredible views of the island interior and the sea. As Thor Heyerdahl put it, "Nature on the seventh day." In Omoa, visit the petroglyphs, buy a cold drink, or send a "Greetings from paradise" postcard from the small post office. To make this a one-way trip, ask Marc or another boat owner in Hanavave the going rate for the fifteen minute motorboat "shuttle" back.

Ua Pou (map, #5) has several hiking trails, long and short, leading to close-up views of the stunning pinnacles in the island's central massif. A great one-hour walk that offers a little of everything runs from the rolly anchorage in Hakahetau, past the interesting Tetahuna archaeological site (village ruins explained through interpretive panels), and on to a stunning – if chilly – waterfall tucked into the mountain slopes. The wet, shady spot is also a favorite of mosquitoes, but you can hide from them behind the curtain of the waterfall. There, the roar and sting of the water is another delight for the senses.

Nuku Hiva offers two not-to-be-missed hikes. One traces Herman Melville's beautiful "Typee" valley. Anchor in Comptrolleur Bay (map, #6) at the southeast end of the island and ask directions in Taipivai village to the Paeke cult site. It's a pleasant walking trail that leads to interesting shrines with smiling tikis (thirty minutes each way). The queen of the cascades in the Marquesas is Vaipo, a sheer 800 meter drop reached by a two hour hike from Taioa (Daniel's) Bay, on the southwest end of Nuku Hiva. The first section of the walk winds through a lush, golden valley that can only be described as a Garden of Eden.

## Great Sights

Many cultural traditions ground to a halt in the dark years following contact with the first Europeans, whose diseases decimated the local population. The population of Hiva Oa alone fell from an estimated tens of thousands to a mere 2,000 today. Therefore, cult sites like the Iipona archaeological site (near the village of Puamau on Hiva Oa, map, #7) remain cloaked in mystery, even to locals. But there is no mistaking the spiritual

A smiling welcome in Fatu Hiva

aura of this vine-clad site, where huge statues perch proudly on massive stone pedestals. If there's one archaeological site to visit in the Marquesas, this is it. You can brave the rolly north coast anchorage or hire a driver in Atuona for an all-day island tour. One well-known local tour driver is Marie-Jo. Bouncing along the hairpin curves of the coastal road in the back of her pick-up with a hibiscus flower tucked behind one ear is a minor adventure in itself!

Paul Gaugin ran restlessly around the globe until he found this verdant speck of land far, far from his native France. A small museum at the site of his atelier in Atuona on Hiva Oa (map, #8) is well worth a visit. You won't find originals here, only copies, but you will see the works within the context that inspired the artist to create some of his best-known paintings. Gauguin's grave in the hillside cemetery above town is also something of a minor pilgrimage site.

Ua Pou's skyline is unique even among islands known for their dramatic profiles, with vertical rock pinnacles that puncture the clouds. Even half-shrouded, the sight is breathtaking. Although many cruisers seem to bypass this island, it pays to make at least a one or two day stop in either Hakanai or the less-frequented Hakahetau Bay (map, #5). The latter may be your best chance for an anchorage of your own.

## Great Experiences

One of the most memorable experiences to seek in the Marquesas is a visit to the manta rays of Hanamoenoa Bay on northwest Tahuata (map, #2). Packs of three or more of these graceful, black-coated behemoths sweep through the bay, vacuuming up plankton with their huge mouths. To snorkel alongside these beauties is simply an awe-inspiring experience. Although we were careful not to crowd the mantas, they showed no such inhibitions, swimming right past and even brushing against us. It's an incredible experience if you're lucky enough to catch the mantas on one of their irregular sweeps through the bay; they seem to come and go on a two to three day schedule.

Throughout the Marquesas, cruisers are frequently offered meals by local families at a price of $15 to $30 per person. Much more than a delicious meal, it's also an opportunity to "taste" local life and culture up close and personal. You'll be swept into the house, into the family, and into conversation on everything from politics, education, and island economics to local gossip. Of course, it helps to speak a little French, but sign language works, too. It's amazing to witness the preparation that goes into the meal: instead of running to one of the tiny local shops, the family hunts and gathers in the immediate vicinity of their garden. Fruit grows in abundance, chickens are cornered in the yard, fish hauled from the sea, and a hunting expedition heads to the hills for fresh goat meat. It's a multi-course meal to remember!

## Great Reads

Three thousand miles of open ocean makes for a lot of reading hours. Each of these books describes the Marquesas from the point of view of sailors of past generations. Topping off the list is Thor Heyerdahl's *Fatu Hiva*, in which the Norwegian explorer struggles to find equilibrium living with nature and natives in the 1940s. His poetic descriptions of the island as he found it seventy years ago show today's sailors what has changed and what hasn't.

Herman Melville's *Typee* is a semi-autobiographical account of his time spent among cannibals on the eastern end of Nuku Hiva. It's an entertaining read as much for his detailed descriptions of the Marquesan way of life as for its quaint reports of local scenes ("The varied dances of the Marquesan girls are beautiful in the extreme, but there is an abandoned voluptuousness in their character which I dare not describe"). Following in Melville's wake was Jack London, who brilliantly captured his voyage from Hawaii to Nuku Hiva (and beyond) in the entertaining *Cruise of the Snark*. Hilarious passages discussing the mysteries of celestial navigation lead in to beautiful descriptions of Nuku Hiva.

## Practicalities

French and Marquesan are the two languages of the Marquesas: start things off with a friendly *kaoha* (hello). The two ports of entry are Atuona on Hiva Oa and Taiohae on Nuku Hiva. Atuona (map, #8) is the less practical of the two, with a long walk to town from Tahauku Bay and no potable water. On the other hand, the surroundings are beautiful and it's a practical gateway to the windward end of the archipelago. The pros of Atuona are its medium-sized grocery stores, bakery, and Internet connection right in the harbor. The cons are having to anchor fore and aft in very tight quarters in Tahauku Bay (also known as Traitor's Bay). Woe is the hapless soul who anchors beyond the boundary formed by two yellow crosses on either side of the bay! Some sailors find out the hard way with the 04:00 arrival of the supply ship, the *Aranui III*, which will summarily evict anyone blocking the dock.

Nuku Hiva's Taiohae (map, #9), on the other hand, is a spacious bay with plenty of room for everyone. The only crowded area is near the dock where the Internet signal is strongest. Taiohae stores are the best-stocked in the archipelago, but inexplicably,

189

the twice-weekly produce market is often a dud. The village also has a small hardware store, a few mechanics, and the opportunity to fill propane bottles (with butane, that is). While Hiva Oa was rationing fuel, there was plenty to be found in Taiohae. While in town, don't miss the delicious sashimi at the open-air Viaki restaurant at the dock, where the fish is fresh and the portions are large enough to satisfy even the hungriest sailor's appetite.

Certain luxury goods make good gifts to exchange with friendly locals who offer bushels of fresh fruit from their trees. Wine is much appreciated, as are cosmetics and nail polish. Children admired our Crocs and wished for some for themselves. Basics like fish hooks are not in demand, but a good length of rope is worth its weight in gold – or juicy pamplemousse.

## Getting off the beaten path?

The only disappointment (if that's the word) of our Marquesas cruise were the crowds we found at each of the main anchorages. In the peak months of April, May, and June, hundreds of boats pass through the archipelago. Our record lows were in Ua Pou (two boats) and Comptrolleur Bay (four), whereas Atuona was packed with thirty boats and Fatu Hiva's Bay of Virgins hosted a full complement of seventeen. Of course, you can anchor in any number of less-frequented bays, but many are avoided for good reason: they can be uncomfortable or downright perilous, such as either of the two slender bays in seldom-visited Ua Huka. "We wanted to get off the beaten track," lamented one sailor who ventured her own way. "Now we know why there is a beaten track!"

The Marquesas were our first taste of Polynesia, and what an introduction it was. Again and again we found ourselves in awe of our surroundings. We were infinitesimally dwarfed yet entirely at peace with our small existence within this magnificent world. The wild, welcoming islands gave us a deep appreciation of how good life can be when days unfold slowly, our family taking its pick from the many possibilities that each island offered. It was only the promise of more Polynesian islands beyond the horizon that drew us – ever so reluctantly – away.

## Post Script: the Dreaded Bond

Non-E.U. nationals are required to post a bond upon arrival in French Polynesia, a sum equivalent to the price of an airline ticket to your home country. There are a number of agents in the Marquesas and Tahiti who can facilitate the process and even obtain a bond exemption. The bond is one consideration that makes the (free) Pacific Puddle

Jump rally attractive, since the organization partners with reputable agents to smooth the entry process.[1] Sailors with E.U. passports, on the other hand, can clear in to French Polynesia for three months without any fuss.

---

[1] http://www.pacificpuddlejump.com

# Chapter 29

# Marquesas to the Society Islands

Having sailed all the way from the Galapagos Islands to the Marquesas – 3,000 miles of very open ocean – it's easy to think of the next 770 miles to Tahiti as a mere hop. Especially when the hop is broken in two: 550-plus miles to the Tuamotus, and a mere 250 miles to Tahiti. A couple of days! Nothing to it! Right?

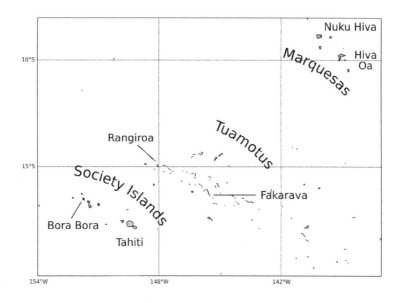

Be warned: these passages may be relatively short, but they are not to be underesti-mated. Conditions west of the Marquesas are such that the weather may be consider-ably less predictable than that of the previous leg. Which isn't to say that every day will be a challenge; this is, after all, the Coconut Milk Run. However, complacent sailors can easily be caught unaware and consequently report rougher passages than expected.

A case in point: we lucked into a brisk and mostly pleasant trip, whereas boats just a few days behind endured rough, squally conditions. One crew we later met in New Zealand called their Marquesas-to-Tuamotus run the worst of their entire Pacific season, with heavy seas and howling winds. Given a choice, who wouldn't choose a pleasant journey over a trial?

## Choosing a Weather Window

So what exactly should you watch for when planning this passage? Track the broader Pacific weather picture carefully, paying special attention to two main factors: first, low pressure systems and associated fronts moving east from New Zealand, and second, the South Pacific Convergence Zone (SPCZ). Think of the SPCZ as the neighborhood troublemaker – you'll want to keep an eye on its intensity and position at all times. If the SPCZ shifts south of its usual haunt at around 10°S and combines with a front extending from one of those New Zealand lows, you can expect a disturbance of the trade winds and squally conditions.

Keep in mind that global forecast models (such as NOAA's GFS GRIB forecasts) are not very good at predicting the behavior of tropical phenomena such as the SPCZ. In fact, GRIB files might show light winds when squalls of thirty to forty knots may be on the prowl. Therefore, sailors should cull multiple weather sources, including synoptic charts and satellite imagery. (See weather resources detailed in *Atoll Cruising 101: The Tuamotus* on page 199 and *Weather Notes* on page 79 of this book.) If you choose your weather window carefully, this passage will likely turn out to be the pleasant hop you'd like it to be.

## Planning Ahead

Every beginning starts with an end: a farewell to the land behind. For us, four weeks of blissful Marquesas cruising inevitably gave way to three days of provisioning, rig checks, and fuel runs to get *Namani* ready to roll. This, too, can be more of a project than it initially seems. The passage itself should only take about a week, but crews planning to spend time in the Tuamotus will easily be stocking up for a month or more. Don't count on finding many (or any) food, fuel, and water options in the Tuamotus.

The good news is, the best shopping of the central Pacific awaits in Tahiti, with chandlers, grocery megastores, and hardware stores.

Another plus is that all of French Polynesia is one administrative area. Once cleared into the Marquesas, you are clear for the Tuamotus and Society Islands as well. Sailors are technically required to check in with the local gendarmerie (police station) in large towns, but not in the Tuamotus. Therefore, once you notify the gendarme in Nuku Hiva of your departure, you're clear until Papeete.

In addition to gathering supplies and weather data, another important consideration for this "easy" passage is arming yourself with information on the atoll passes. What are the general pass conditions for the atolls you hope to visit? Are your tide tables accurate? When will slack water be? Even the widest, deepest, "easiest" passes in the Tuamotus can make for roller coaster rides (and worse) when attempted in the wrong conditions. One excellent – and free – resource is the wonderful *Cruising Compendium for the Tuamotus* compiled by the crew of s/v Soggy Paws.[1]

Thinking about visiting multiple atolls? Make sure you have a realistic view of what that involves. Neighboring atolls may appear to be an easy day sail apart, but even a short hop can turn into an overnighter once you factor everything in: departing Atoll A at slack water and with the sun sufficiently high for good visibility, traveling twenty to forty miles, then running the pass into Atoll B when slack water again coincides with good visibility. Squeezing all that into one day takes planning and a little luck. For a more thorough look at what the Tuamotus have in store, see the next chapter: *Atoll Cruising 101: The Tuamotus* (page 199).

## Underway At Last

As we set sail on a course of 215°, dolphins escorted *Namani* away from the Marquesas, and we caught our last sunset views of the islands' spectacular silhouettes. Steady Force 4 winds made for a pleasant broad reach and a solid 120 miles in our first twenty-four hours. We immediately slipped back into passage-making mode: reading, watching the horizon, and checking our lures for dinner. Had we not been downloading weather forecasts constantly, we might have been lulled into expecting more of the same over the entire 540 miles to Fakarava. After all, most of our month-long passage from the Galapagos to the Marquesas had been carefree, easy sailing; why expect anything different?

But the wind dropped, and a series of mild squalls set in. We reefed the sails in an-

[1] http://www.svsoggypaws.com

Dinner en route to the Tuamotus

ticipation of each dark cloud line, only to wallow in the vacuum left when each burst passed by. An inconvenience, nothing more. As it turned out, *Namani* was just ahead of an unsettled patch of atmospheric conditions that made life very unpleasant, indeed, for boats just one hundred miles behind. For those crews, watching the horizon was a much more urgent pastime, with endless waves of powerful squalls keeping them on their toes throughout the passage.

For us, the next days were variable in every sense: skies clearing from full cloud cover to a more pleasant 2/8th cover, then back again; sails in and out; motor on and off. The moon was nearly full now, lending the night watch good company. When the moon did set in the early morning hours, the effect was like turning a dimmer switch up on the rest of the stars, so brightly did they shine. The sky closed up again over day three, and much of day four was spent in a drizzle, like sailing within a wandering cloud.

Our fishing lures attracted little interest over the first part of the passage, then suddenly drew too much interest from seabirds. Having no desire to add that type of meat to *Namani's* menu, we reluctantly drew in the lines. As it turned out, those birds may well have spared us complications, as we were to find out a few minutes later.

The next patch of ocean was in a wild, frothy commotion. A full feeding frenzy was on, with a tasty school of fish under attack from all directions. Birds dive-bombed into the fray from above, while large fish flashed and attacked from below. In the midst of it all, we spotted three tall, curved dorsal fins, sleek black bodies with a flash of white. A trio of huge orcas was muscling in on the feast. The fins grew closer and closer to *Namani*

196

with each successive breath at the surface, until one of the orcas appeared not four yards off the stern. After an alarming Moby Dick moment in which the orca had a good, close look at us and "killer whale" attack stories rushed through my mind, the giant dove and disappeared. Whew! My heart rate was slow to recover but the spectacular memory of that close encounter will last forever. When things calmed down again, we trawled the lines and came up with *Namani's* all-time record catch: three tunas struck four hooks almost simultaneously, and we landed two for a delicious sashimi dinner.

## The Transit of Venus

A more sedate, slow-motion highlight of the passage was the transit of Venus. We had our protective eclipse glasses ready in anticipation of the event, but would the clouds cooperate? As we anxiously scanned the sky, counting down the moments to the big event, we felt a close affinity to Captain Cook. Unlike him, we were not sent into the Pacific specifically to observe the transit of Venus, but like him, we were under considerable time pressure. After all, the next time Venus travels across the face of the sun will not be until the year 2117!

At the same time, the tower marking the northeast corner of Fakarava was just pulling into view. As usual, everything was happening at once. Luckily, the clouds parted enough for us to get a good look at a dark speck crawling slowly across the face of the sun. This also provided good visibility for navigating the pass of our very first atoll. By the time we ran the north pass and entered the lagoon, Venus was halfway through its transit and the sun high overhead. A few hours later, with *Namani's* anchor down off a palm-lined tropical paradise, Venus slipped off the opposite edge of the sun and continued its journey through space. We had been just in time to catch the event, just as our passage was completed in time for a nasty series of squalls to descend over the area.

## Onward, Ever Onward

We opted to visit the central section of the Tuamotus, with Fakarava as a practical starting point, but many sailors stop over in Rangiroa, at the northwestern extremity of the archipelago. Others head off the beaten track to lonely atolls like Raroia or Kauehi. But sooner or later, all roads lead to Tahiti, a distance of approximately 250 miles. And this really is a hop, just two nights of downwind sailing.

This passage, too, is not without its minor challenges, but the short distance makes it feel like a walk (or a dash) through the park. Though *Namani* was bumped and thumped by irregular beam-to seas, she made good speed as yet another series of mild squalls passed overhead. Our principal preoccupation was the condition of the port aft shroud after two weary strands parted, succumbing to the strain of 20,000-plus miles of use. Spectra line worked well as a quick reinforcement, and we added one more expensive item to our "Papeete parts" list.

As the lights of Tahiti appeared on the horizon, so, too, did masthead tricolors appear all around us. The sailing fleet was reconverging after their respective exploits in the Tuamotus. When the sun rose, another sail joined the westbound gang, then another and another as we rounded the northwest corner of Tahiti. Excitement grew as we spotted Point Venus, where Captain Cook made his observations, and finally, the capital city of Papeete.

## All Clear?

New arrivals have several choices of where to stay in and around the Papeete area. There are several marinas, including the public docks in downtown Papeete and well-run Marina Taina a few kilometers south. The only catch may be to find a free berth in the peak months of June and July. A reef outlines the entire coast, but the main passes are well marked and easy to traverse. Not so the many secondary passes, which should be treated with caution. Inside the reef is a calm, seemingly endless lagoon in which to anchor, though crowds are thick all the way past the Taina area. A limited number of rental moorings are available as well. Boats heading south from Papeete to Taina will pass the international airport, and a call on channel 12 is required to make sure you don't tangle with low-flying aircraft (English is fine; French appreciated but not a must).

No matter where you tie up, you should report to the port captain in Papeete (the office is located in the large ferry building) within a couple of days of arrival. While you're at it, hoof it out to the industrial port to obtain the document needed for purchasing duty-free diesel on your way out the other end of the Society Islands. Be forewarned: this document cannot be obtained in Bora Bora.

But after that, business matters can be pushed to the back burner. You're in the Society Islands at last, a place where the creature comforts of home are wrapped in stunning South Seas packaging. Tahiti is just the gateway to far greater treats, such as craggy Moorea, lovely Huahine, and incomparable Bora Bora. If only the ticking clock could somehow be put on hold!

# Chapter 30 *Be Sure to Read + Re-Read*

# Atoll Cruising 101: The Tuamotus

By now, every cruiser has certainly heard of the Tuamotus, a string of low-lying Pacific atolls straddling the central section of French Polynesia. Although the wonders of GPS have "downgraded" the Tuamotus from their earlier status as "the Dangerous Archipelago," enough obstacles remain to give many cruisers misgivings – and rightly so. For many, the Tuamotus represent a first encounter with narrow passes and coral-strewn lagoons where landmarks are practically nonexistent and eyeball navigation is the name of the game.

So just how easy – or how dangerous – are the Tuamotus? You won't know until you get there. That's why we recommend that newcomers master the basics of atoll navigation at the most accessible, "tamer" Tuamotus first, and then graduate to more challenging atolls once gaining first-hand experience. It's a matter of piecing together an irregular puzzle of reefs, passes, anchoring techniques, and weather patterns. Ultimately, a brief sampler of the Tuamotus proves to be enough for some cruisers. Others move on to the greater challenges – and rewards – of atolls off the beaten path.

The sprawling archipelago's seventy-seven atolls are made up of large fringing reefs marked by a few tiny islets (motus) that barely rise above sea level. Within each atoll is a relatively calm lagoon littered with unmarked coral heads. The only things abundantly available in these watery oases are coconuts, fish, and pearls. Fresh water, provisions, and fuel, on the other hand, are all hard to come by, so cruisers must be as self-sufficient as they would be for a long offshore passage.

Enjoying a quiet anchorage in Fakarava

## Gateways to the Tuamotus

The two most-traveled gateways to the Tuamotus are Rangiroa, at the northwestern edge of the group, and Fakarava, at roughly the central point of the chain. Each of these atolls feature wide, well-marked passes that even cruise ships can enter, with easy-to-follow channels inside. Naturally, these user-friendly passes mean that Rangiroa and Fakarava are the atolls most impacted by outside influences in terms of both culture and environment. On the other hand, both offer relative safety and peace of mind, making a balanced trade-off.

Rangiroa lies on a direct line from the Marquesas to Tahiti and therefore makes a natural stopping point for many west-bound sailors, especially those on a tight schedule. This atoll is so vast (the second-largest in the world) that you can build an entire cruising itinerary within its sea-like lagoon. For this reason, some make Rangiroa their one and only stop in the archipelago before continuing on to Tahiti. Others add in neighboring Ahe, which likewise promises a straightforward pass and easily accessible lagoon anchorage. Fakarava, a centrally located atoll within the archipelago, calls for only a minor deviation from the direct line from the Marquesas to Tahiti, and is also a logical stopping point for sailors arriving via the less-traveled Gambier Islands. Next door to Fakarava is lovely Toau, population two; this atoll is the perfect second step along a natural progression through the archipelago.

# Running the Passes

In pre-GPS days, sailors avoided the Tuamotus for fear that the slightest navigational error might put them high and dry on a reef. Nowadays, navigation to and among the atolls is generally straightforward. The first real challenge cruisers face is entering an atoll. Happily, the main passes into both Rangiroa and Fakarava are not only clearly marked, but extremely deep and wide as well. However, timing is everything! Throughout the atolls, you must plan your entry (and exit) carefully and use the prevailing southeasterly winds to your advantage. Avoid strong contrary tides (peaking at five knots or more in some passes) as well as strong wind-against-tide situations. The best time to enter a pass is at slack tide, even if that means waiting. After all, sailing is a game of patience.

Of course, there are a few exceptions to this rule of thumb. For example, passes located on the leeward side of an atoll may be cautiously attempted at the tail end of an outgoing tide (in other words, against the wind and a weak tide). Conversely, windward passes may be transited with a weak incoming tide. Unfortunately, the tide tables incorporated into some chart plotting programs are inaccurate for this region, giving many sailors a nasty surprise. We used the French SHOM tide tables instead and found these to be very reliable (see *Weather and Tide Resources for the Tuamotus* on page 204).

Another factor to take into account when entering a pass is the sea state. Because the southern and western sides of the atolls are usually very low, seas will break over the reefs after a period of strong, sustained winds from a southerly or westerly direction, or if a southerly swell of more than six feet has been running for some days. All the water pushed into the lagoon this way will flood out through the atoll's passes, causing an enhanced outgoing and a weakened incoming tidal stream. This effect will also delay (or even eliminate) the low water slack tide while advancing the high water slack tide by an hour or two. Ultimately, you should calculate the window of opportunity as best you can, then carefully observe pass conditions upon approaching. If in doubt, use VHF channel 16 to contact boats anchored inside the lagoon or to reach a local dive operator for local advice. Don't be put off by a bit of uncertainty – the atolls will repay your patience many times over.

At oft-traveled passes like those in Rangiroa and Fakarava, there is absolutely no need to send someone aloft to eyeball the route ahead. We saw one sloop crashing its way into Fakarava's north pass in a wind-against-tide situation with one crew member perched up in the spreaders for "safety." How the poor man kept from being launched overboard as the sloop pitched and slammed wildly was a mystery. It's far better to wait for a favorable tide and save the second-story acrobatics for unmarked passes in other atolls – at slack tide, mind you!

Once through Tiputu Pass in Rangiroa, it's a simple matter of slinging directly to the nearest village anchorage. In Fakarava, running the north pass and navigating the main channel is straightforward, thanks to excellent markers. Assuming the sun is high in the sky, isolated coral heads are easily distinguishable as shallow green or brown patches against the darker blues of deep water. In fact, newcomers will quickly realize that markers are largely superfluous in fair weather. Conversely, cloudy skies or low sunlight will make coral heads much harder to spot. At the same time, crew members must keep an eye out for the small buoys that mark pearl farms inside the lagoons. These are lessons that one can quickly learn in the tamer Tuamotus before going on to navigating unmarked sections of the main lagoons or in atolls off the main byways.

## Anchoring in the Atolls

Once safely in an atoll, sailors can head for a tantalizing, isolated motu of their very own, even in relatively populous Rangiroa and Fakarava. But there's one last hurdle: anchoring, which presents two sub-challenges. First, finding a well-protected spot behind the low-lying, tiny islets of the atolls can be like trying to hide an elephant behind a telephone pole. As soon as the wind shifts, you're likely to have to move – a major effort in large atolls, where traversing from one side to the other can be an all-day effort, and where fetch can create considerable seas. When looking for a good spot, keep in mind that though the wind can blow from any direction, you should be especially wary of the powerful southerly winds, called *mara'amu*.

The second challenge of atoll anchoring is keeping your ground tackle from wrapping around coral heads (bommies), since it is rare to find a broad enough sandy patch to accommodate your entire scope. The solution is to "float" your chain with fenders set at intervals of roughly 1-1.5 times the depth. When the chain is not under load, the fenders will suspend it above bommies as the boat drifts from side to side. Anchoring in twenty feet of water, for example, set your first fender at about thirty feet, the second at sixty feet, and a third at ninety feet. Just keep in mind that a perfect set will take some adjusting after you snorkel to observe how the chain behaves. The greatest threat comes from bommies close to the boat, which can catch the chain and shorten the scope – just what you don't need when a squall suddenly kicks up.

## Weather

Conditions in the Tuamotus can change rapidly, so it is critical to track weather developments using all the resources at your disposal. Weather systems moving east from New

Zealand and tracking south of French Polynesia may work in concert with the South Pacific Convergence Zone (SPCZ) to disturb the trade winds and cause squally conditions and wind shifts. Therefore, the prudent cruiser should monitor weather forecasts that provide some measure of atmospheric instability as well as describing general trends. In our experience, NOAA's GRIB files sometimes indicated very light winds when in fact gusts of up to thirty knots occurred. We therefore augmented use of the GRIBs with a number of additional sources, such as Meteo France text forecasts, NOAA weather charts (particularly Lifted Index found in their Spot forecasts), and NADI Fleet Codes (see details in *Post Script: Weather and Tide Resources for the Tuamotus* on page 204). As at sea, our SSB and Pactor modem proved to be indispensable tools for receiving meteorological information.

## Enjoying the Atolls

As far as we're concerned, the atolls are a place to enjoy solitude rather than sample village culture. However, the main settlements in Fakarava (population 1,000) and Rangiroa (population 3,000) do offer the advantages of Internet, small shops, and dive outfitters who can shuttle SCUBA enthusiasts to some of the most spectacular dive locations in the world. One notable site is Fakarava's legendary South Pass, where dozens – even hundreds – of sharks feast on the multi-course meal the currents sweep past, a particularly action-packed scene during full moon phases. Not every venture into the water has to be an exhilarating thrill, however; there is also the pure serenity of snorkeling off your boat in idyllic green-blue shallows.

Many sailors find that their thirst for atoll living is quenched after one or two stops in the Tuamotus. Some find the experience nerve-wracking, especially when unsettled weather demonstrates just how exposed the anchorages really are. Other sailors can't get enough of this paradise and linger in the archipelago for an entire season. They revel in largely untouched atolls such as Makemo, Kauehi, and Raroia. Ultimately, the length of time sailors devote to cruising the Tuamotus depends as much on their ability to tolerate the challenges as on their luck with weather. Outside time pressures also conspire to interrupt the reveries of some cruisers, who find themselves hurrying to Tahiti to meet scheduled guests. Air Tahiti Nui offers regular flights between Tahiti and many of the atolls, so you might ask visitors to book last-minute connecting flights to the Tuamotus rather than rushing away from this unique location.

Are the Tuamotus truly dangerous? Given a fair degree of prudence, no. On our 1981 Dufour 35 with a six-foot draft, we used GPS as well as both paper and computer charts, but we didn't have a chart plotter at the time, and we never needed the radar. We did use our SSB radio and Pactor Modem to download weather information daily.

Consequently, we were able to keep a step ahead of unpleasant conditions and truly enjoy the magic of the Tuamotus. What's to keep you from doing the same?

# Post Script: Weather and Tide Resources for the Tuamotus

The Tuamotus lie within the French Polynesian time zone: UTC-10.

Accurate tide tables can be downloaded from the French Hydrographic Office (SHOM).[1]

There are several weather forecasts available for the archipelago:

Meteo France issues both marine and land forecasts. The forecasts are available from *www.meteo.pf* or on request from Saildocs (send an email to query@saildocs.com with no header and the message `send fr.poly`. Of course, these forecasts are in French, but the basic vocabulary is easy to decipher.

NOAA Spot Forecasts detail a number of useful weather parameters. Request by sending an email to query@saildocs.com with an arbitrary subject line and the following message body:

```
send Spot:16.1S,145.7W|7,3|PRMSL,WIND,WAVES,RAIN,LFTX
```

This example requests a 7 day forecast at 3 hour intervals (|7,3|) for the location 16°06'S 145°42'W (16.1S,145.7W), including sea level pressure (PRMSL), average wind speed and direction (WIND), significant wave height, swell direction and period (WAVES), precipitation (RAIN), and Lifted Index (LFTX, a measure of instability in the atmosphere). You can alter each data point as needed, keeping in mind that positions must be specified in decimal degrees (rather than minutes) to one decimal point.

NADI Fleet Codes are synoptic charts issued by Fiji's meteorological service that cover the southwest Pacific. Send a message to query@saildocs.com with the message body saying `send fleet.nadi` or `subscribe fleet.nadi` for a fourteen-day subscription with daily delivery. To display these fleet codes as synoptic charts, you will need a free, small software application called PhysPlot which can be downloaded at the Pangolin website.[2]

---

[1] http://www.shom.fr/en/services/tidal-predictions/predictions-en-ligne/
[2] http://www.pangolin.co.nz/physplot

# Chapter 31

# Spotlight on Fakarava and Toau

Fakarava is a perfect location to learn the lessons of "Atoll Cruising 101" because one long, thin motu shelters the entire east coast, with a marked channel leading several miles away from the small-scale "development" of Rotoava village. Atoll novices will be relieved to discover there is nothing life-threatening about leaving the channel and finding a place to anchor. With the sun high overhead, it's easy to pick your way through coral heads to sandy patches fifteen to thirty feet deep. Even though Fakarava draws a fair number of sailors, it is possible to find your own anchorage. That is, if the copycats don't find you. Often, we were happily enjoying our solitude until the magnet effect drew in a handful of other boats. Perhaps they reasoned that we had found "the" anchorage when in reality, they could have strung themselves out almost anywhere along the long shoreline.

From Fakarava, it's a pleasant day sail to Toau. On the northwest side of this atoll, two distinctive white range markers lead the way into Anse Aymot. This is a false pass that breaches through the fringing reef of the atoll without breaking all the way through to the inner lagoon. The result is a mini lagoon with excellent 350° protection – a rarity in the Tuamotus. In Toau, one friendly couple live off the bounty of the land and sea, occasionally offering evening meals at an open-air "restaurant" by the shore. However, Valentine and Gaston are extremely busy with multiple atoll pursuits and may not be able to offer regular meals. Consider it a treat, not a given. They have even set up several moorings (a herculean effort involving repeated free dives to depths of fifty feet and more) to eliminate the hassle of anchoring over coral heads (not to mention the damage this inflicts). Some cruisers linger for weeks in this unhurried place, snorkeling the reefs and wandering the wild, tangled edges of the motus.

Entering an anchorage in Fakarava

# Chapter 32

# The Spice of Life:
# Roll Up Your Sleeves

You'd think that a solitary South Seas anchorage filling up with sixty sailors aboard six charter catamarans would spell bad news for the handful of full-time cruisers already moored there. Instead, the impending arrival of the fleet heralded one of the highlights of our Pacific crossing. We were drawn to the atoll of Toau by reports of outstanding diving and the hospitality of the two sole inhabitants. So we were surprised to find Valentine and Gaston in a somewhat agitated state as they prepared to host their biggest-ever dinner two days hence. "I am praying," Valentine confided, wary of the task ahead.

Word spread quickly among the four cruising boats tucked into the cozy bay. Without hesitation, all rolled up their proverbial sleeves and turned the ramshackle waterfront homestead into a beehive of activity and bon esprit. The men worked nonstop for the better part of an afternoon to filet a massive heap of fish brought in from a funnel-shaped trap on the reef. Black-tipped sharks darted along the nearby shoreline, poaching for offal, as island dogs perched atop shallow coral heads and barked furiously at the intruders. Meanwhile, we women kneaded dough, minced garlic, and plaited palm fronds into decorations. A more gender-neutral task was wringing milk from handfuls of sweet white coconut flesh, an ingredient that found its way into every dish on the menu, from bread to poisson cru. A pig was butchered; lobsters were collected from a pen in the atoll's protected waters; the sun dropped ever closer toward the deepening colors along the sparkling horizon, and the day drew to a weary close.

Picking up where we had left off the next morning, everyone contributed what they could. One cruiser, an electrician, wired overhead outdoor lights, while the SCUBA

Fileting fish in Toau's 'Polynesian Sweat Shop'

divers of the group installed an additional mooring to accommodate the incoming fleet in the bommie-strewn bay. This came as a great relief to Gaston, who would otherwise have to free-dive repeatedly to fifty feet. Valentine sent us off to pluck flowers for the table and leaves to wrap barbecue-bound treats in. Sixty new plates and cutlery sets had been brought in to the isolated atoll for the occasion, and were now carefully arranged on the long dinner table under the palms – just the job for my eager son. Napkins were folded, torches fashioned from bamboo stalks, chairs counted and re-counted.

Our excitement peaked that afternoon as one after another yellow-canvassed catamaran glided into the sanctuary of the bay. We had been led to believe that the charter group consisted of the heads of a major marine insurance company, and we prepared to share our – ahem – customer feedback when the opportunity arose. In fact, the group that came ashore was none other than *Cruising World* magazine's Adventure Charter group on their inaugural Tuamotus cruise, organized by the tireless Peter and Carol King! They were equally surprised to discover an international troop of sailors scurrying about under the direction of their Polynesian hosts.

As evening fell, the barbecue overflowed with juicy meat and the colorful dinner table beckoned. Some cruisers served the guests while others manned the kitchen, relaying loaves of sweet bread in and out of the single oven, then delivering them to the tables, steaming hot. As things settled down, we had the opportunity to chat with the newcomers. They were just like the sailors we once had been, dreaming about sailing into the sunset and wistfully eyeing the rugged yachts of full-time cruisers. I was also delighted to meet the authors of *Cruising World's* "Log of the Ithaka" column, the gracious Bernadette and Douglas Bernon. It's a small world after all, even in the remote atolls of the Tuamotus!

The next morning, the catamarans headed off to other destinations, other adventures. We cruisers with vaguer, slow-motion schedules drifted back ashore to clean up, starting with a stack of dishes that seemed to form the highest point of the low-lying motu. But many hands make light work, and things were soon back to normal along the azure waters of the bay. All agreed to hold a potluck that night to give Valentine and Gaston a night off and to socialize. The shared experience had brought us together as more than just anonymous neighbors. The high note of a magical South Seas evening was the heartfelt musical merci that our hosts sang, Valentine strumming her ukulele to Gaston's accompaniment on the spoons. One song listed the wonders of various Polynesian islands before concluding "Mais j'aime les Iles Tuamotus" in the refrain. We agreed most heartily, and dreamed of one day returning to this Garden of Eden, as Valentine fondly called her home.

What is it that sailors seek in their travels? Unique experiences in isolated corners of the globe, insights into foreign cultures, and often, a wish to contribute to local endeavors in some way. We found all that, and more, in Toau. So thank you, *Cruising World* Adventure Charterers, for facilitating new friendships and bringing us a rich experience we would never have otherwise enjoyed. Fellow cruisers, take note: next time you get word of a charter fleet heading your way, don't flee. Head to shore instead, and roll up your sleeves!

Rainbow over the atoll

# Chapter 33

# Highlights of the Society Islands

You know you've been spoiled by the South Pacific when Bora Bora just isn't good enough. Or when you have to drag your protesting child to snorkel with "just another" manta ray. Your floating home rests in one beautiful, placid lagoon after another, with the sound of distant waves on the reef like a lullaby each night. If this isn't the good life, what is?

So where exactly does one find this paradise? Before visiting, I have to admit to having rather vague notions of what constituted the Society Islands. Tahiti and Bora Bora were on my radar, but the true gems, places like Maupiti, I had never even heard of. The following is a cruiser's primer to the destination of many sailors' dreams, named by Captain Cook in honor of the Royal Society, a scientific body spearheading the Age of Enlightenment in eighteenth-century England.

Tahiti is just one island, the administrative capital and gateway to the Society Islands. The archipelago is made up of two loose clusters: Tahiti and Moorea lie at the eastern, or windward edge of the group, two towering beauties separated by a mere twenty miles. From there, it's a good ninety miles to the nearest island of the leeward group, made up of Huahine, Raiatea / Tahaa (two islands that share one lagoon), and Bora Bora. At the far westernmost end of the chain are quietly overlooked Maupiti and Maupelia. All are lush, green islands with stunning volcanic silhouettes, except the black sheep of the family, Maupelia, a low-lying atoll in this otherwise lofty group.

Alas, the pleasures of this island group are fleeting for anyone crossing the Pacific in a single season. Compounding the sheer distances is the fact that North Americans are entitled to a mere three months in all of French Polynesia – from the wild Marquesas to the atolls of the Tuamotus and the jaw-dropping landscapes of the Society Islands. That leaves the average cruiser with about a month to whirl through the Societies. Given

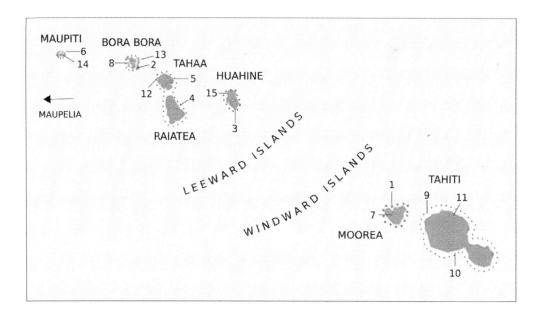

a finite amount of time, how do you whittle down the possibilities to the very best of the best? If we had to name our top picks in the Society Islands, the Oscars would go to...

## Great Anchorages

For panoramic photos of your boat in the foreground of a stunning Society Islands landscape, nothing beats the sheer, chiseled heights of Moorea's Opunohu Bay (map, #1). You can anchor on either side of the entrance or at the head of the bay, where the holding is generally secure. A good thing, since gusts can funnel wildly down the steep valley. You can dinghy ashore for fresh baguettes or play hermit in your own little corner of paradise.

Having almost written off Bora Bora as spoiled by over-development, we had to revise our verdict after a blissful week in the southwest corner of the lagoon (map, #2). The gorgeous, sandy anchorage quickly won us over with its peaceful aura, views to Bora Bora's iconic central peak, and great snorkeling (see *Great Snorkeling* on (page 215 below). Getting there means circling Bora Bora in a clockwise direction and slaloming through a narrow, snaking pass through an inner reef in the northwest corner of the lagoon. It's a nail-biter, but the pass is marked and depths are at least nine feet.

Avea Bay on the southwest corner of Huahine (map, #3) draws cruisers more for its serenity than its dramatic beauty. There's plenty of space for boats to spread out, each

At anchor in Bora Bora

with their own swath of views to the distant reef and Raiatea on the horizon. You can snorkel, take walks ashore, or feast on a traditional earth-oven roast offered by a low-key resort. Reaching Avea Bay via the narrow, sheltered lagoon is a scenic cruise in itself, with gorgeous views opening to the island interior. The lagoon channel is buoyed all the way to Avea, with minimum depths of eight to ten feet.

You'll find gorgeously isolated anchorages at many of the motus within the shared lagoon of Raiatea and Tahaa. Tiptoe up to the inner edge of the reef and anchor on a sandy bottom; you'll feel like you're at the edge of the universe. Some spots are shallow, others deep. All resonate with the quiet roar of ocean swell pounding the outer reef. Raiatea's Motu Tipemauo (map, #4; off Iriru Pass) and Tahaa's Motu Mahaea (map, #5; off Toahotu Pass) are only two gorgeous, solitary examples among many.

The gem of them all, however, is sleepy little Maupiti (map, #6), located twenty-five miles downwind of Bora Bora. In fact, it's a miniature Bora Bora, with the same stunning aquamarine coral ring surrounding a tall central peak. Maupiti sees very little tourism; there is only one small village and no visible hotels marring the lagoon. Boats can anchor just inside the pass near a spot frequented by manta rays, or off the village for walks ashore (both detailed below). The only trick is getting in (and out), since the narrow pass can be potentially dangerous in a sizable south or southwest swell. In other conditions, range markers make running the pass a breeze.

213

# Great Hikes

Cruisers based in Moorea's Opunohu Bay can dinghy to the head of the bay and hitch-hike up to the Belvedere (view point) to reach the trail head for the Three Coconut Trees Pass (map, #7). This moderate walk leads through beautiful wooded stretches and eventually gains views high over both Opunohu and Cook Bays (one hour each way starting from the Belvedere). On the way back, reward yourself with a delicious pineapple ice cream at the Agricultural College, two-thirds of the way up the valley road.

For eagle-eye views over breathtaking aquamarine lagoons and the deep blue horizon, scale the central summits of Maupiti or Bora Bora. Maupiti's Tiriano peak (map, #6) is a 1000 foot uphill trek, manageable in under an hour. The very last section requires scaling steep rocks, but a sturdy rope installed there will help you reach the top safely. Scaling Bora Bora's Otemanu peak (map, #8), on the other hand, is a serious endeavor at twice that vertical distance. Steep sections are not for the faint of heart and the trail calls for serious footwear.

# Great Sights and Experiences

The annual Heiva festival on Tahiti is one of the true highlights of the Pacific cruising season (every July in and around Papeete; map #9). Events range from hula-style dance competitions to traditional sports such as gaily colored fruit basket races. Tickets are available at the Carrefour supermarket box office (see next chapter for details).

Paul Gauguin lived in Tahiti before moving on to greener pastures in the Marquesas; the site of his home is now an interesting museum (map, #10). It's a perfect day out by rental car that can be combined with hikes and waterfalls on the leeward shore of Tahiti. While you have a car, take a driving adventure through waterfall-lined Papenoo Valley in the island's interior (map, #11; even 2WDs suffice).

Bicycling any of the quieter islands can provide a great change of pace for any sailor. Many islands have ring roads that run along the lagoon, staying (more or less) flat. Great destinations are the southern half of Huahine, any shore of Moorea or Bora Bora, and the six manageable miles around little Maupiti. The roads are generally in good condition, "navigation" is easy, and rentals are available in most cases.

## Great Snorkeling

Tahaa's coral gardens (map, #12) truly deserve the name. Snorkel the shallow slot between two small motus on the west side of Tahaa, where fish swim through canyon-like slots between the tightly packed coral. Leave your dinghy on the east side of the motu and wear sandals for the walk to the west side, then float back through the coral gardens. Sunset views from this anchorage are nothing short of spectacular with the profile of Bora Bora punctuating the western horizon.

Sadly, much of Bora Bora's reef has fallen to storm and human damage, but a few captivating spots still remain. The southwest corner of the lagoon has some poor, but also some truly spectacular reefs with coral of all shapes and sizes, in addition to a good variety of tropical fish. If you're lucky, you might even catch a glimpse of the granddaddy of all moray eels. Anchor your dinghy carefully in a remote spot far from the beach hotel of Motu Piti Uu Tai for the best spots (map, #2).

Snorkeling or diving among resident manta ray populations is an incredible experience. One community frequents a spot near Bora Bora's Hotel Meridien, on the east side of the lagoon. Look for the patch of deep water midway between the outer motus and the "mainland" (map, #13). Another population can be found at the anchorage just inside Maupiti's pass (map, #14). Both these places are deep and neither is crystal-clear, but the excursion is well worth the effort, particularly if you find a cleaning station: a sort of manta ray wellness spa where tiny fish fuss over the mantas' sleek tuxedo coats.

## Off the Beaten Track

Maupiti is the insider's pick of the Society Islands, a gorgeous little island lost in time. Cycling around Maupiti and scaling its peak both make our short list of absolute high-lights in the entire Pacific. Good quality drinking water is available from public taps scattered along the island's ring road, and three tiny shops offer the basics. Fishermen sell the catch of the day at the roadside, your best bet for a tasty tuna dinner.

Unlike its cousins to the east, Maupelia (also spelled Mopelia) is a low-lying atoll. This is the least frequented of the Society Islands with navigable passes, since the pass is so narrow. Even some seasoned cruisers describe the narrow slot as terrifying. Good conditions are a must. Those who do visit report memorable snorkeling, diving, and island hospitality.

## Practicalities

French and Tahitian are the two languages of these islands. Though the islanders are well accustomed to tourists, they usually take the time for a friendly exchange. Try greeting people with a friendly *iorana* instead of bonjour. ATMs are few and far between, so be sure to stock up on CFPs (Cours de Franc Pacifique, a currency tied to the Euro) before heading away from Tahiti's Papeete (map, #9) or Bora Bora's Vaitape (map, #8). Your best bet for provisioning outside the massive Hypermarchés of Tahiti (chains such as Carrefour and Champion in Papeete and near Marina Taina) is the large supermarket in Huahine's main town, Fare (map, #15). There, you can anchor in deep water (twenty-five to thirty feet) and dinghy in or tie up alongside the small dock for a short stop. While one crew member tops up the water tank for a small fee, another can go shopping just a few hundred yards down the road. Even Bora Bora's shops are not as well stocked as this one. Eggs are a rarity throughout all the islands, so grab several dozen when you get the chance. The Society Islands are the last place you'll find canned butter for many miles to come, so stock up before departing.

Tahiti itself has lost a lot of the magic that once so captivated sailors, including the mutineers of the *Bounty*. On the other hand, Papeete is the best place for spares, repairs, and general supplies between Panama and New Zealand. We found that prices were comparable with those we later found in New Zealand and were glad not to have put off the new standing rigging our boat so sorely needed. Tahiti and Raiatea both offer several options for haul outs. Cruisers who must leave their boats unattended for visits home can consider Tahiti's Marina Taina (moorings or berths; reservations for peak season recommended) or the public quay in Papeete. In past years, stories of rats and theft marred the reputation of the public docks, but we heard only positive reports during our visit.

Bora Bora is the last place to purchase duty-free fuel before heading west to the Cook Islands or Samoa, but you'll only be granted this privilege if you obtained a tax-free form back in Papeete. Plan ahead or you'll pay full price!

## Onward, Ever Onward

Months of superlative scenery and impressions in French Polynesia had us spoiled rotten, so these tips are truly the best of our best. Ultimately, even Bora Bora redeemed itself, in spite of shore-stealing hotels that had initially turned us off. The kids among our cruising friends complained of months of being dragged out on one stunning, unforgettable excursion after another, but someday, we reckon, they'll appreciate what we've given them. We adults, on the other hand, don't suffer from delayed gratification: the Societies were grand in every sense of the word. But time is short, and the siren song of other South Pacific destinations eventually lured us away. We packed our boat with supplies and memories, and, like Captain Cook, directed our "Course to the West and took our final leave of these happy isles and the good People in them."

# Chapter 34

# Spotlight on Tahiti's Heiva Festival

The summer of 2012 was London's Olympic summer, but half a world away, we were enjoying spectator sports of a different type. Who needs Track and Field when you can cheer competitors in events like Fruit Basket Races, Stone Lifting, or Coconut Husking? At Tahiti's annual Heiva festival, tickets are cheap to free, audiences enthusiastic (but everyone gets front row views), and at break time, you can refresh yourself with coconut ice cream or passion fruit soda. Ah, the South Pacific!

Each July, cruisers pack the marinas, mooring fields, and anchorages in Tahiti's protected lagoon, drawn as much by the festival as the alluring landscape and excellent ship services. Over the 130-year history of the Heiva, the festival eventually expanded from its roots in song and dance to showcase traditional sports as well. And so it was that we found ourselves cheering *va'a* (outrigger canoe) races against a stunning tropical backdrop, then checking the schedule for *Grimper au Cocotier* (Coconut Tree Climbing) – between checking the rigging and repairing the anchor windlass, that is.

A Polynesian twist on a familiar event is the team javelin competition, in which participants aim for a coconut at the top of a thirty-foot pole. The team with the most hits after seven hectic minutes wins, and the best athletes are immediately whisked aside for interviews on local television. Meanwhile, the crowd shifts excitedly over to the Stone Lifting venue, settling down on the lawn to watch competitors in several weight classes heave a 160-pound boulder to their shoulders in a race against the clock.

Another highlight is team coconut husking, in which three-person teams speed-husk 150 coconuts. It's a wild scene with the crowd cheering, coconut milk splashing, empty husks flying, and chunks of white copra piling ever higher. The athletes in each of these events – men and women – are a sight themselves, dressed in colorful pareus (sarong-like wraps) and lush leafy headwear, with swirling tattoos on shoulders, legs, backs

– even faces. For us, it was also a chance to witness the normally serene, unhurried Polynesians move into high gear!

Coconut husking competition

Exciting as the sports events are, the Heiva's primary attractions are the dance and song competitions that spread over eight evenings, each featuring two dance and two musical troops. Though the events are judged and winners take home hefty prize purses, it's all about prestige. We were absolutely wowed by the spectacle of one hundred synchronized dancers wearing gorgeous flower and shell-adorned costumes that sway with swinging hips to a blood-pumping drum beat. The open-air, seaside setting in Papeete's grassy To'ata Place truly makes the evening one to remember. Sailors moored at the public docks are only a five minute walk away from the arena and have front row views for the fireworks on France's national holiday, July 14.

Best of all, the Heiva remains a largely non-commercial, local affair despite its highly professional organization. Tahitians make up the majority of the audiences; there are no souvenirs for sale and no hawkers, just a lot of color, culture, and fun. Tickets to the song and dance performances in the main arena go for between $10 and $30, while the sports events are free. All in all, the Heiva is a unique, month-long celebration of tradition, folklore, and artistry that should be on every Pacific cruiser's calendar.

# Part VII

# The Central Pacific

# The Central Pacific

Reefs, reefs, and more reefs: in this section, we cover an area we loosely term the "Central Pacific," including the Cook Islands, Niue, and Tonga. But along with the navigational challenges come an artist's palette of incredible greens and blues, genuine island folk, and unique sights both above and below the waterline.

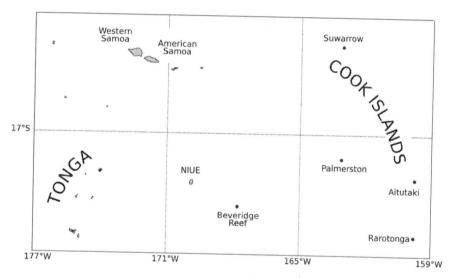

It's also an area of choices that divides the cruising fleet. While some maintain a westerly course, calling in at Suwarrow and Samoa, others dip south to visit Aitutaki, Rarotonga, Palmerston, Beveridge Reef, and/or Niue. Each of these remote specks on the charts have their pluses and minuses, many of which are detailed in the relevant chapters. Admittedly, we can't cover everything without having crossed the Pacific a few more times – but give us time for additional "research" and we'll be happy to get back to you in a future edition of this book!

It's around this point in the crossing that you'll come across a number of fresh faces to the cruising fleet, which will have coalesced into a tight-knit group. The "newcomers" are sailors sailing southwest from North America via Hawaii and Palmyra, and who knows? You might just pick up another buddy boat or two.

Ultimately, it seems that all roads in the Central Pacific lead to Rome – er, Tonga. The Vava'u group is a regular cruiser's Mecca, where you'll find cruisers' hang-outs, basic services, as well as chit-chat about the route ahead. But there's more to Tonga than just Vava'u, which you'll learn in the "flavorful" chapter "A Tongan Feast." Enjoy!

# Chapter 35

# Connecting the Dots in the South Pacific

Cruising can be a game of connect the dots, and for most of the Coconut Milk Run, a sailor's choices are fairly straightforward. The Marquesas can be cruised from windward to leeward in a more or less logical series of hops. From there, the trade winds usher you straight toward the northern end of the Tuamotus. The atolls, in turn, practically spill over into Tahiti, gateway to the Society Islands. And once you've cruised on to Bora Bora (and its little sister, Maupiti), the next logical destination is Tonga, 1,400 miles west.

But between the two lie the Cook Islands, and that's where the choices multiply – sort of. We quickly discovered that the stepping-stone route that seemed so logical on a chart – from Aitutaki to Palmerston, Beveridge Reef, and Niue – was full of disclaimers. Aitutaki's shallow pass means only boats that draw five feet or less can call there – and even some of those scrape their way in. Palmerston gets mixed reviews due to the open roadstead anchorage as well as the possessive manner in which island families claim and coddle visiting sailors. Meanwhile, Rarotonga's harbor was undergoing dredging, or so rumor said. Beveridge Reef sounds like paradise afloat, but we realized there'd be nowhere for our eight-year-old to stretch his legs. Suwarrow lies closest to the rhumb line to Samoa, but that lonely paradise was threatening to draw a crowd.

So which would it be? The cruising fleet that had formed an agreeable little community throughout French Polynesia suddenly splintered into several cliques. A few hardy crews decided to zig and zag, determined to try and see it all. Most, however, were of the pick-and-choose mindset, not quite willing to wander a hundred miles off the rhumb line or sail too hard on the wind. As for us, well, we succumbed to peer pressure

225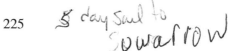

and followed the kiddie contingent to Suwarrow. Five blustery days out of the Society Islands, we eyed the horizon in anticipation. Was our decision the right one?

Let's just say that even when we finally pried ourselves away seventeen days later, it was only under the cracking whip of an all-too-short cruising season. Because time moves differently in Suwarrow – even more so than in the most bucolic of South Pacific islands. Sea and sky, day and night melt into each other so seamlessly that before we knew it, our first week had zipped by. Mornings were perfect for a dip in the crystal-clear water or snorkeling with manta rays. Afternoon was the time to relax in one of the fishnet hammocks strung up among the palms. Those who felt ambitious could join the accommodating rangers of this otherwise uninhabited National Park on an excursion to the far side of the atoll, and the sailors left behind could amble on foot over one of the most vivid reefs to be found along the Coconut Milk Run. Evenings were a time for beach potlucks or simply counting the stars. In fact, there's just enough to do on Suwarrow to make not doing *anything* an attractive choice.

Rushing ashore on Suwarrow

Every sailing cohort, it seems, sets its own trends. Crews who preceded us by three years reported that Palmerston had been all the rage at the time. In our year, Beveridge Reef seemed to be garnering the popular vote until almost everyone headed to Suwarrow instead. Did that detract from our experience? Not at all, at least for the families: fourteen kids from seven boats and seven nations at the time of our stay. Other crews, well, they might have had a different definition of paradise!

Of course, the party had to break up sometime, and when it did, the fleet headed off in various directions: some west to Samoa, others on a more southerly bearing to Niue. But in this neck of the ocean, all roads lead to Tonga's Vava'u group, where we were happily reunited for another sweet sailing sojourn. And that's the South Pacific for you – one highlight after another, no matter where you linger along the way.

# Chapter 36

# Trash or Treasure?
# The Sailor's Book Swap

I was prepared for South Pacific cruising in every way: not only was my sloop low in the water with weeks of supplies, but my electronic reader was filled to its two gigabyte brim. Yet I still found myself inexplicably drawn to book exchanges – serendipitous treasure troves of dusty reading for those long, tropical evenings under a thousand and one stars. Even Suwarrow boasted a thriving book exchange, despite being a tiny speck of land hundreds of miles from – well, the next tiny speck of land in the vast, watery Pacific. Perhaps Suwarrow boasts such a well-stocked book swap because of (and not despite) being such an isolated place.

On second thought, "well-stocked" might not be the best descriptor for a cruiser's book exchange. It's more of a mixed bag, in the words of Tom Neale, who brought Suwarrow minor fame with his memoir of solitary atoll living, *An Island to Oneself.* Neale took one glance at the castaway books he found and "decided that half of them were not worth reading at all – a decision I reversed after a year when I was only too glad to read *anything*." Indeed, some of the faded paperbacks on Suwarrow today look as if Tom Neale himself might have thumbed through them back in the 1950s.

After all, sailors do not abandon their cherished copies of Joshua Slocum to the merciless pits of book swaps; they ditch the forgettable flotsam and jetsam of the literary world. But among the outdated cruising guides and marine supply catalogs, a few masterpieces lay secreted away. Of course, there's a catch: the worthwhile reads are usually in a rather obscure foreign language, such as Ernest Hemingway's classic *Hvem ringer klokkerne for* (*For Whom the Bell Tolls* – in Danish), or Ian Fleming's Dutch bestseller, *In Dienst van Hare Majesteit* (*On Her Majesty's Secret Service*).

The jettisoned English-language titles, on the other hand, run the gamut from outrageously unbelievable spy novels ("a final showdown with an enemy more sinister and deadly than has ever been seen before"), John Grisham bestsellers ("Just released!" – in 1997), and gushing romance novels ("Now she must flee – and seek refuge in the arms of a virile and dangerous stranger"). It's like visiting a public library stocked not by a prim, conservative professional, but by a hairdresser's miniature poodle.

I found myself intently studying the jackets of trashy novels, wavering between the virile stranger and the ruggedly handsome super agent. Finally I spotted an Agatha Christie mystery in a foreign language I do read. Salvation! But two weeks in a small atoll leaves plenty of down time, and I eventually succumbed to temptation in the form of the studly super agent. Oh, the shame! The only thing saving my scarred dignity was the fact that I hadn't actually paid for these books.

The Suwarrow book exchange

So why was I reading this junk? I couldn't help myself! There's something about the element of surprise, like visiting a new restaurant with a seductive menu full of exotic flavors. No matter how many titles fill the screen of my Kindle, I still covet the moldy paperbacks of these deliciously unpredictable book swaps. And who knows? I might discover a priceless jewel, like Suwarrow itself, with its reef walks, superb diving, and groovy fish net hammocks. The irresistible pleasure of perusing book shelves is like beach combing on a tropical island: you never know just what treasures the tide will wash in.

# Chapter 37

# Niue: the Rock of Polynesia

For all his discoveries, Captain James Cook did register a few misses. The great navigator sailed right past Sydney Harbor, for one thing, and failed to notice New Zealand's gorgeous Milford Sound. In the grand scheme of his three epic voyages, these oversights can be excused, but we can't quite forgive his dismissal of little Niue, a speck in the Pacific he called Savage Island. After a brief encounter with stone-throwing natives, Cook made a quick exit and curtly noted in his log: "Seeing no good was to be got of these people or at the isle we return'd on board . . . and made sail to WSW." Admittedly, a lot has changed since 1774, but we humbly beg to differ.

Today's Niue is a delightfully welcoming place, a unique steppingstone along the South Pacific Coconut Milk Run. Nowhere else in Polynesia did we find such unbelievably clear water, a comparable landscape, or as warm an association with the letters NYC (that's Niue Yacht Club, for the record, not New York City). Locals include visitors in community events, whales let you snorkel alongside, and yes, even the poison sea snakes are friendly.

## Getting There

Sadly, many sailors bypass the little island. Those traveling via the northern Cook Islands often head to Tonga nonstop rather than facing winds and seas from forward of the beam. Happy winners of the South Pacific weather lottery, we snagged a perfect window of ESE winds for a brisk four-day, 560-mile beam reach from Suwarrow. Wind direction is less of an issue for cruisers who arrive via the southern Cook Islands, although that route often brings capricious winds (calm today, blasting tomorrow), a result of greater proximity to low pressure systems tracking to the far south.

Few Pacific landfalls are as laughably simple as arrival in Niue. Except for a few FADs (Fish Aggregating Devices marked by large orange buoys), the island is free of any off-lying dangers. It's a straightforward matter of pulling into the deep, wide bay of Alofi and picking up one of NYC's twenty hefty moorings. Curious sea snakes popped their heads up as we made fast to one of the many free moorings and took in our new surroundings. We were reassured to learn that the fangs of these venomous reptiles are located so far back in their narrow throats that it is virtually impossible to get bitten. Yes, cruising is a great learning experience, and on our way across the vast Pacific, we shed one paranoia after another: first our fear of sharks, and now, our instinctive aversion to sea snakes.

Having triumphantly announced our arrival to Radio Niue and conquered the notorious dinghy crane (more on that later), we were greeted with a friendly "Welcome to Niue!" by customs officials on the wharf. Soon, we were walking south past Alofi's "commercial center" (a sprawling, one-story building subdivided into small shops) to Niue Yacht Club, "the biggest little yacht club in the world." Run entirely as a volunteer effort by good-hearted people such as Ira Merrifield and Commodore Keith Vial, NYC offers boaters warm showers, a cozy reading corner, free Internet, power outlets, and a small bar area open six days a week. They even hosted our son's ninth birthday party in the clubhouse, going so far as to decorate a table with balloons and a colorful tablecloth for the special occasion. For an optional NZ$20, we couldn't resist the impulse to join NYC, whose membership exceeds the island's population of 1,500. Thanks to Ira at NYC and the extremely helpful tourist office just a coconut's throw away, we soon had all the information needed to explore the "Rock of Polynesia."

## Under the Sea – Diving

The uplifted coral island resembles a Pacific atoll that has been hoisted high and dry one hundred feet above sea level. One of Niue's principal drawing cards is its fascinating underwater world, where visibility seems limitless. Checking the mooring is a question of glancing from your deck through crystal-clear water, even to one hundred foot depths. Niue's pitted coral bulk extends underwater in a series of slopes and deeply etched gullies, making for snorkel and dive experiences like nowhere else. SCUBA divers can explore underwater caves where the sea glows with shafts of intense blue light or ascend an enclosed underwater "chimney" from depths of sixty to twenty feet. The friendly folks at Niue Dive run guided trips to various locations and fill bottles for cruisers with their own gear.

232

It's not just the ringed sea snakes that make Niue's sea life interesting. Whales are frequent visitors during the July to October calving season, as are dolphins. At the call of a whale sighting near the mooring field, I geared up in record time to snorkel beside an adult humpback. Observing the magnificent creature splash its black body and white fins on the surface was a humbling experience, topped only when the whale dove effortlessly out of view into its private realm far, far below. At times, it's even possible to hear humpback songs resonating through the water and into the cozy quarters of your own hull. On rare occasions, the cetaceans get closer, closer – too close! In 2012, a passing whale entangled itself in a mooring line, seriously damaging one sailboat's bow roller in its efforts to pull free. In true community fashion, locals and boaters pitched in with materials and expertise to patch the vessel so that it could safely continue to Australia. That said, this was an unprecedented and hopefully one-of-a-kind encounter – for both sailors and whales!

Diving in Niue's clear waters (photo by s/v Gudrun V)

## Shoreside

When we weren't in the water, we wandered bucolic Alofi nibbling sweet coconut bread fresh from the bakery, and found a handful of cafes, a supermarket, and two gas stations. Something struck us as unusual in the bank: the absence of bars at the cash counters. Obviously armed robbery is not an issue in this friendly island nation! Foreign tourism to Niue is low-key, with a single weekly flight from Auckland that carries a mere 160 passengers. They quickly disappear into a handful of inconspicuous hotels or into the homes of relatives. In fact, more Niueans live abroad than on the island itself. Many islanders have immigrated to New Zealand in recent decades, most recently after Cyclone Heta struck in 2004. Indeed, a drive around the island revealed many abandoned dwellings sitting cheek by jowl with their tidy neighbors. Still, the population is upbeat and the living standard quite high (thanks to support from New Zealand) despite the island's isolation and status as one of the smallest sovereign nations in the world.

Tourist infrastructure is unobtrusive but well conceived, like the many well-signed "sea tracks," coastal walks that range from five to twenty minutes. Visitors are pampered with amenities such as clean toilets and fresh water showers at nearly every trail head. Together, the sea tracks offer a feast for the senses: the rich, musky smell of old growth forest at Huvalu Forest Conservation Area; the roar and hiss of waves smashing into rock pinnacles at windward Togo Chasm; the dark, damp echoes of Avaiki Cave; and the sensation of a powerful sea surge trying to flush swimmers out of narrow Matapa Chasm and into the open sea. Topping the list of island superlatives are the magical Limu Pools, sparkling aquamarine basins where snorkelers can swim through the shade of a small sea arch. Fresh and salt water mingle here, creating blurry strands for a psychedelic underwater effect. We took in all these sights along the island's forty mile circumference by rental car, splitting the NZ$100 daily rate of an eight-seater van among three crews. To drive on the island, visitors are required to apply for a local driver's license at the police department, a ten-minute process that costs NZ$22. Like our NYC membership, we considered the colorful photo ID another trophy of our memorable stay on Niue!

## Unique Niue

Niue is a nation of early risers, so we dragged ourselves ashore at o'dark-thirty for the Tuesday produce market, optimistically anticipating fresh, vitamin-rich goodies. Sadly, this was the one disappointment Niue was to deliver. Savvy buyers snapped up the pitifully small quantities of produce before they even hit the sales tables by intercepting vendors in the parking area. Being a quick study, I copied the maneuver with the next arrival. After "window shopping" through the windshield, I helped myself to bananas right out of the hatch and proceeded to make change among three eager buyers for one quick transaction with the vendor – all before she had "finally" emerged from behind the steering wheel. Eventually, we discovered that the true key to successful produce procurement on Niue is simply smiling: several times during our stay, friendly residents gave us bananas and paw paws (papayas) growing on their properties. One woman even made a special trip to the wharf to present the yachties with bunches of deliciously sweet bananas. Welcome to Niue, indeed!

Which brings us to the town wharf with its infamous dinghy crane. Since the towering dock is exposed to the pulsing swell, small craft cannot safely remain tied up in the water. The solution is an ingenious crane that lifts everything from small dinghies to heavy fishing skiffs bodily out of the water. We quickly discovered that much like the poisonous sea snakes, the dinghy crane is all bark but no bite. You simply approach from the water, attach your dinghy's three-point harness to an oversized hook, and step ashore. Then it's a simple matter of pressing the "up" button on the electronic control box, swinging the craft ashore, and rolling it out of the way on a hand trolley (considerately provided by NYC). Using the crane is a smooth and easy operation, unless of course the swell gets up, when the lift can get "interesting," "challenging," or downright "unusable," in the words of Commodore Keith.

We ended our stay on Niue at a "village show," a monthly event hosted in turn by each of the island's communities. In addition to handicraft exhibits and dance presentations, the program included events like an uga contest, in which bowling ball-sized coconut crabs tipped the scales. In the show's finale, the few foreign visitors were called up for a special contest: speed coconut husking. We immediately observed that "speed" is a relative term when sailors take on coconuts. As we hacked, thumped, tore, and swore at our stubborn coconuts, locals erupted in laughter at our pitiful techniques: the over-the-head, slam-it-down with all your might approach; the pound-and-grind in close quarters approach; and the even less effective chip-chip-chip from the wrist technique. Unable to watch such ineptitude any longer, local women leaned in with pointers until one slightly more coordinated sailor conquered two coconuts in two minutes. Then, the locals rolled up their sleeves and demonstrated how it was done properly: in a mere twenty or thirty seconds (men's "warrior" and women's divisions, respectively). We all enjoyed the fun and laughter, feeling a touch of kinship with the islanders who had so kindly included us in their community get-together.

We had to ask ourselves: could we find one negative thing to report about Niue? By nature, the island is a destination rather than a cruising ground: you sail to the single port and then explore ashore. The main drawback for sailors is that Alofi's bay is scarcely more than a light indentation in the western coastline, so it's important to track weather developments at all times. The NYC moorings are exceptionally strong and well-maintained (not to mention reasonably priced at NZ$15 per night), but a fair amount of rocking and rolling is to be expected. Strong, sustained west winds or south swell can even drive yachts away entirely. That said, most sailors find the usual motion tolerable and depart the Rock of Polynesia with fair memories.

Pushed by approaching cyclone season and pulled by our next destination, we eventually admitted that it was time to drag ourselves away from yet another "most favorite" island. To paraphrase Captain Cook's comments, I'll state for the record: "Knowing much good was to be got of these kind people and at the lovely isle, we return'd on board ... and with heavy hearts, made sail to the west."

## Niue Fact File

Language: Niuean and English

Currency: NZ$ (available only as cash for cash exchange or Visa card cash advance at the bank).

Customs: No cruising permit or entry fees (weekend fee NZ$20); departure tax of NZ$34 per person.

Niue Yacht Club: *www.niueyachtclub.com*

# Chapter 38

# A Tongan Feast

Apparently, we had it all wrong. The best thing about Tonga is not the sailing. No! The true highlight of this island kingdom is in fact a Tongan feast. This message was continuously reinforced from the moment we cleared customs. *Must go to a feast!* admonished cruisers who had arrived a few weeks earlier. *Come to our village feast!* called the friendly voice of a local whose community made a fundraiser out of the event. Such offers were a regular feature on the morning cruisers' radio net. *Have you signed up for the weekend feast?* urged neighboring sailors.

We felt a little disoriented, because we had actually come to Tonga for the sailing, not the feasting. After thousands of miles of sailing between isolated Pacific Islands, we had finally reached a compact, sheltered cruising ground. In Tonga's northern island group, Vava'u, we looked forward to the novelty of short, frivolous day trips. Our sloop became a hyperactive beehive of activity as we tacked, winched, and trimmed away. We could bask in comfortable beam reaches, kick back during placid downwind runs, and thrill in windward beats – all in a single afternoon! On the menu were deep, wide channels, snaking slalom runs between islands, and challenging, reef-dodging routes. We were in Tonga to feast, all right – to feast on the sailing.

## Sailing the Vava'u Group

Firm in our resolve to overindulge in sailing at its best, Markus, nine-year-old-Nicky, and I made a quick, two-day turnaround after our arrival in Neiafu, the administrative capital of Vava'u. The next week went by in a flurry of maneuvers since no two anchorages in Vava'u, it seems, can be connected by a straight line. Our sloop romped

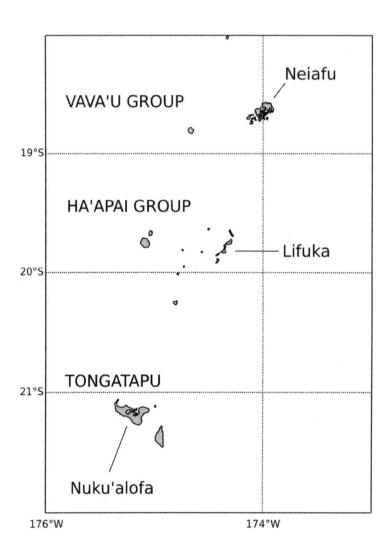

through the watery maze like a frisky pony set loose in an aquamarine pasture, throwing in twists and turns just for the sheer joy of the movement. The route we followed on the first day traced an upside down J; day two drew an uneven letter U. Day three saw us covering a mere nine miles on a route shaped like a bent fish hook, with a downwind leg, a beam reach, and finally an alpine ascent of zigzag tacks. The wind, blowing a steady Force 4 or 5, came in three flavors: northeast, east, and southeast. The sky was blue, and thanks to a long line of reefs on the windward side of Vava'u, the water was flat. We were happy, relaxed, and eager for more.

Reinforcing our emphasis on sailing was the fact that many of the established anchorages are best known by number references, due to a scheme invoked by the Moorings charter base that has (sadly) stuck, at least among the cruising community. So we zipped from anchorage number six to neighboring number seven, skipped right over to eleven, and then made our way to a true gem, number thirty. Which isn't to say that we ignored the shoreside charms of Tonga. On the contrary, we had a wonderful variety of experiences: attending a church service near Mala Island, where the congregation sang gorgeous, vowel-rich hymns at the top of their lungs; collecting our fill of ripe, juicy mangoes on a long walk from Tapana; snorkeling among plump, indigo starfish at Port Morelle; and trading colored pencils for bananas in a peaceful village on Kapa. Since education is a national priority in Tonga and English is emphasized, we were able to converse freely with locals whose lives, like ours, are defined and delineated by the water.

Our most glorious day sail in Vava'u came when we weighed anchor in Tapana and set course for Kenutu Island on the less visited eastern fringe of Vava'u: three miles as the crow flies, but fifteen over the shortest water route. With tacks, *Namani* covered twenty-three miles that day as we eyeballed our way around green islets resting like so many wallowing sea turtles, each with a golden, sandy ring encircling its shell. We even found ourselves enjoying two hours of tacking into the easterly wind. Maybe all that tropical sun was getting to us, after all.

When at last the froth of the outer reef boiled just off our bow, we seized our reward: easing the sheets to fly northward on a beam reach. Markus stood at the bow, signaling a quick jog to port, then starboard as we dodged coral heads that littered the narrow channel between two spitting reefs. What a glorious sensation to sail this serpentine route without the noise of an engine or the filtering effect of a chart plotter! We were back to the basics of sailing and loving it. When at last our anchor bit the sand in the lee of uninhabited Kenutu, we felt a warm glow of accomplishment.

Kenutu's location behind a gauntlet of reefs poses a selection process of sorts, and we were proud to have made the cut along with six interesting and highly accomplished crews. Two South Africans were on their way to a new life Down Under, and a Japanese

Snorkeling in Tonga's Vava'u Group

couple was circling the Pacific. One family was heading home to New Zealand after a nine-year cruise to Norway via Chile, while another was about to close the loop on a "normal" four-year circumnavigation. All congregated on the beach to share sundowner snacks and companionship. Though this wasn't a feast in the literal sense, we savored delicious anecdotes and chased them down with scrumptious jokes as our driftwood campfire crackled in the sand.

Sailing back into the heart of the Vava'u group, we headed for little Lape, population thirty. There, Nicky was invited to spend a day at the one-room schoolhouse. His favorite subject? Recess, naturally. As an after school treat, we snorkeled on the magnificent Coral Gardens, spotting whole colonies of clownfish among the rainbow assortment of shapes. We had ticked off all the best of Vava'u in two brisk weeks, including swimming into submerged caves and braving the narrow, rocky pass into the lagoon of doughnut-shaped Hunga Island. We were ready to move on, content to have done everything. Everything, that is, except a feast.

I had to ask myself: what was this obsession with feasting, anyway? Apparently, it all goes back to 1953, when Tonga's Queen Salote attended the coronation of a young Queen Elizabeth in London. In spite of the pouring rain, Queen Salote insisted on keeping the hood of her horse-drawn carriage down throughout the long procession as a sign of respect. Salote's symbolic gesture and winning smile earned her legions of adoring fans all over the world. When Elizabeth visited Tonga soon after, Queen Salote

A day at school on Lape Island

laid on the feast of the century: an open-air affair that stretched over a hundred meter-long table laden with tropical fruit, roast pigs, succulent seafood, and countless other leaf-wrapped goodies. Grainy black-and-white images of the feast spun to newspapers around the globe, and a legend was born.

## On to Ha'apai

All very nice, but as I said, we were in Tonga for the sailing. So we ventured back into open water, sailing sixty miles south. In the less frequented Ha'apai group, a tangle of reefs and exposed islets make navigation more exacting and good shelter difficult to find when weather conditions go from benign to bad. Consequently, only a fraction of the cruisers who crowd Vava'u venture into these azure waters. When we checked in with the port captain in Lifuka (a quick and easy formality), we learned that only sixty boats passed through in the peak months of September and October. That left the best of Ha'apai to a select – and scattered – fraternity of sailors. Here, we could each retreat to our respective anchorages, and a good thing, too, since many are small and only partially sheltered. All the more reason to rave about the rewards: uninhabited islands, superb snorkeling, and in the right season, a better opportunity to see whales without the stampede of snorkelers these behemoths attract in Vava'u.

Like Vava'u, the Ha'apai group offers a veritable smorgasbord of post-sailing activities. In Ha'ano, giant bats hung like so many oversized, upside-down fruit in the trees. That

241

is, until the sound of our voices shook them into the air like a foreboding (but ultimately harmless) scene from a Hitchcock movie. Tiny Luangahu proved to be a difficult place to find shelter, but once settled in, we could circle the entire island on foot in a few minutes, or linger over the exotic seashells underfoot. Nicky, meanwhile, was in his element digging giant sand pits and collecting driftwood for a full moon campfire on our private island.

Throughout our Ha'apai sojourn, we were keenly aware of how the sailing skills and smooth teamwork we had developed over the past months were paying off. For us, the ultimate test came at O'ua, a long, thin island encapsulated by reefs. Many charts neglect to indicate the small, winding pass on the south side of the island. In fact, we had little more to go on than outdated way points and rumors of defunct navigational aids. This was a challenge we would never had dared attempt at the start of our journey, but now we were confident enough to give it a try (albeit ready to turn tail at a moment's notice).

After tacking *Namani* boldly up to the reef's edge, we struck the sails and motored cautiously ahead with a constant lookout on the bow. The early afternoon light lit the reef brilliantly as we scanned for any sign of a break. There it was: a crooked pole marking the entrance between two frothing shallows. We were in, drawing a wide arc to reach the deep basin that harbored a handful of other boats. They, like us, were drawn to O'ua by its promise of good shelter when a forecast trough was to pass over the area the next day, bringing torrents of rain.

Every cloud has a silver lining, and in O'ua, this came in the sturdy form of a young local named Freddy. We were initially bewildered when this twenty-something-year-old swam out to our boat at the height of a squall and perched on our stern ladder. What on earth was he up to, swimming in such weather? What did he want? His broken English and our nonexistent Tongan did little to clarify the situation at first. But Markus, with his patient heart of gold, joined our visitor in the downpour, communicating through basic English and hand gestures. It was a little like navigating with paper charts: it requires some use of the brain, but ultimately gets you to your destination. Our visitor didn't appear interested in fishing gear, nor was he particularly curious about our boat. And he certainly didn't harbor any evil intentions. It seemed that all Freddy wanted was to initiate a little contact with the outside world, an impression confirmed later when we visited him on land. Living in an isolated island village with fewer than one hundred crowded inhabitants has its limits. What's a little rain when the outside world comes knocking at your door?

Little did we know that this strange encounter was to pave the way for a very unique experience. When Freddy returned the next (sunny) day with a bunch of bananas, we invited him to join us for lunch. Freddy raised his heavy eyebrows in the Tongan equivalent of a nod and savored every bite of freshly baked bread and canned ham as if they were gourmet treats. Then he promised to return the next day with a feast for us. Now it was our turn to raise our eyebrows and nod. This we had to see.

True to his word, Freddy appeared the next day on a borrowed skiff and stepped aboard *Namani* with his promised feast: Tongan takeout, as Markus later quipped. The meal had been cooking in an *umu*, or earth oven, for hours, and was now spread across our cockpit table in succulent, leaf-wrapped packages. Each dish came with a deceptively spartan title that belied the explosion of flavors it promised. "Fish" referred to three steaming, juicy reef fish marinated in coconut milk. "Chicken" was the unassuming name of a deliciously soft, steamed meat. Accompanying them were octopus, taro, and cassava, plus fresh-off-the-tree papaya for dessert. It was a feast fit for a queen and a day to remember. Freddy borrowed Markus' guitar to strum a few tunes while his son Anis joined Nicky in climbing the rigging and tinkering with Lego. Among the many facts we gleaned from Freddy that day was that secondary education is much harder to obtain in the Ha'apai group, explaining why fewer people had the same mastery of English that we observed in Vava'u. No matter: friendships can be made with or without language. With few words yet generous gestures, Freddy left a lasting impression.

Our time in Tonga was not yet over, but we knew there would be no topping this high. Weighing anchor the next day, we bid a sad goodbye to our friend, hoping he would find many new acquaintances among other cruisers who passed O'ua, few that they might be. How pleased we were to have made the journey not only to Ha'apai, but to Freddy's doorstep. Tonga had provided us with a feast for the senses, and we could indulge no more. After clearing out in the kingdom's capital, Tongatapu, sixty miles south, we headed out to sea once again, our eyes fixed on Minerva Reef and Opua, New Zealand. A season of unforgettable Pacific experiences – and unlikely friendships – was drawing to a close.

*Note*: See the *Picking a Weather Window for a Tonga-to-New Zealand Passage* chapter (page 251) in the New Zealand section for notes on Tongatapu in the southernmost section of this island kingdom.

# Chapter 39

# The Spice of Life:
# The Boater's Barter Economy

Out on northern Tonga's remote Kenutu Island, we had it all: a lush, uninhabited paradise, turquoise anchorage, vibrant coral reefs.

We even had good company, a merry little group of accomplished sailors. The Kiwis had just been to Norway and back – via Cape Horn. The Japanese had navigated the treacherous waters of their country's medieval sailing bureaucracy. The South Africans were emigrating to Australia, the slow way. We had a lot in common, including empty pantries. The Americans were out of coffee; we were low on flour. The South Africans needed outboard fuel. But the shortage most keenly felt was by the Japanese: no beer! What to do?

We could, of course, head back to the nearest shop, two day hops away. But the whole point of being out *here* was not to go back *there*. Plus, getting to Kenutu wasn't exactly a breeze. Breezy, maybe, but not easy: a narrow, reef-strewn gauntlet; the kind you squeeze through, then look back on with a heavy gulp.

But wait! The Japanese couple did have flour. The South Africans had coffee, the Americans had fuel, and we were willing to part with a few bottles of beer.

Ah, the feeling of kicking back in a remote anchorage with everything you need!

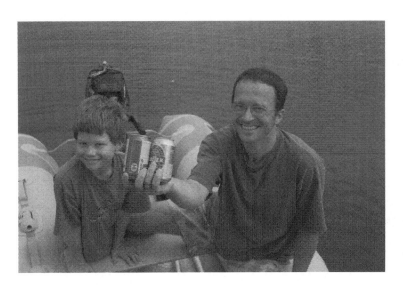

A boater's barter economy in Tonga

# Part VIII

# New Zealand

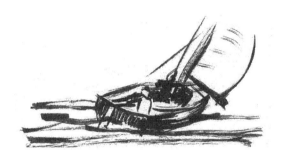

# New Zealand

Once cyclone season looms over the tropics, cruisers must decide where to pass those risky months. While some choose to hole up in the handful of proven cyclone shelters in French Polynesia, Fiji, or New Caledonia, most take themselves out of the line of fire by sailing out of the cyclone belt. The vast majority who do so head for New Zealand. After all, it's hard to resist the siren call of beautiful scenery, a familiar language and culture, and top-notch boat services.

We spent six relaxed months in New Zealand, and time flew. Even in a suitcase crammed with exotic Pacific memories, New Zealand stands out for us as a special place and time. There's something for everyone, from quiet hidy-hole anchorages to the city vibes of Auckland and the magnificent alpine scenery of the South Island. In fact, many cruisers find themselves boomeranging between New Zealand and the tropics for years on end. (It's a rough life, but somebody's got to do it.)

In this section, we discuss the tricky passages between New Zealand and the tropics – the biggest challenges of our Pacific crossing. We also detail cruising options on and off the beaten path, as well as list options for boat work and land travel. Ultimately, New Zealand will not disappoint, no matter how you choose to spend your time.

# Chapter 40

# Picking a Weather Window for a Passage to New Zealand

Exactly a year after leaving Beaufort, North Carolina for the Caribbean, we faced a similarly tricky passage on the other side of the world. Now in Tonga with an idyllic season of Pacific cruising behind us, we were watching for a weather window to make the 1,100 mile trip to New Zealand. The symmetry was striking. A year earlier, our challenge was to find a gap between successive lows coming off North America in November, preferably with cooperative northerlies to ease our way across the Gulf Stream. And no late season tropical storms, please! In Tonga, we warily eyed lows spinning eastward off Australia – southern hemisphere lows spinning clockwise, that is. Again, timing was everything. Too early in the season meant that potential gales south of 30°S would be at their peak; too late, and we could be chased by an early cyclone above that imaginary line.

Naturally, we weren't the only sailors eager to get our timing right. A seasoned fleet of international cruisers had gathered in Tonga, all fixated on the figurative beacon of New Zealand shining ahead. After months of relatively carefree tropical sailing, signs of obsessive-compulsive behavior were cropping up in every tanned, weather-beaten face. On beaches, in cafes, on the radio: we scrutinized weather reports and compared notes. For most of us, it promised to be an eight to ten day passage, plus or minus a possible stopover in North Minerva Reef, nearly 300 miles out of Tonga. Many crews had signed up for the All Points Rally, an informal event that offered the benefit of pre- and post-passage information sessions as well as social gatherings and general weather advice – all for a price irresistible to any cruiser (namely, free). A number of crews were also plugged into professional weather services based in New Zealand and beyond, faithfully waiting their sage advice. The question in everyone's mind was, which window was the window?

So when the pros gave the green light for a Thursday through Saturday departure in the first week of November – exactly coinciding with the general time frame of the rally – many cruisers jump-started over the starting line. Some of us, however, waited to see how a mischievous-looking depression forecast to spin off the South Pacific Convergence Zone northwest of Fiji would develop. As the fleet disappeared over the horizon, I couldn't help but feeling slightly... wimpy. Were my misgivings a simple case of pre-passage nerves? On the other hand, as a family with a young child, we like to play it safe, especially with any hint of trouble brewing on the horizon. And didn't John Martin, organizer of the All Points Rally and veteran of thirty-seven Tonga-New Zealand passages, specifically note in an early bulletin: "Keep a good lookout for anything with a closed isobar in the tropic region to your west. If you see one, don't leave until it passes or disappears"?

Two days later, our fears were realized as the depression off Fiji materialized and developed into an unmistakably onerous system with the potential to become the first named tropical storm of the season. It was expected to track southeast toward Tonga and the very ocean sector that the fleet was sailing directly through. Later, it became clear that the depression would inch toward a high pressure system located over New Zealand, creating an intensified squash zone. In some ways, the general scenario paralleled that of the infamous 1994 Queen's Birthday Storm, which claimed seven vessels and three lives (weather services underestimating a depression forming off Fiji; a high pressure system over New Zealand creating a squash zone; a cruising rally giving a subconscious feeling of a deadline).

Soon, it was clear to everyone that the storm spelled trouble. However, theories on how to handle it varied widely. Part of the fleet resolved to stay put in Tonga. Other vessels, already well underway, calculated that they could hasten south, out of the predicted storm track. Still others agonized over backtracking to Tonga. But sailors hate backtracking – especially when the finish line to a long cruising season beckons so seductively. Several outward bound yachts wavered, turning back for Tonga, then pointed their bows back toward New Zealand after all. A few even made a third course change, about-facing one more time for shelter in Tonga – a wise decision, as events were to prove.

The trouble with racing to beat a storm's predicted path is that atmospheric forces hold very little regard for human weather forecasts. The low's expected intensity and track changed from forecast to forecast, playing with the hopes and fears of those underway. What eventually materialized was more serious than the initial warnings had suggested: a more intense low moving farther south than expected and closing in on those underway. The idea of speeding south to keep ahead of the storm was complicated by light air conditions during the first days of the passage. That meant immediately relying on engine power – all well and good for large sailboats with huge fuel reserves, but smaller vessels with limited capacity had a lot of optimistic calculating to do. Many were forced to burn most of their fossil fuels early on, leaving no Plan B for the latter part of the trip – a point when sailboats often motor to reach New Zealand ahead of the next low pressure system coming across the Tasman Sea. No matter how you packaged it, the scenario was littered with ugly possibilities.

## Forecasted vs. Actual Track and Intensity of Tropical Depression between 7th and 10th of November

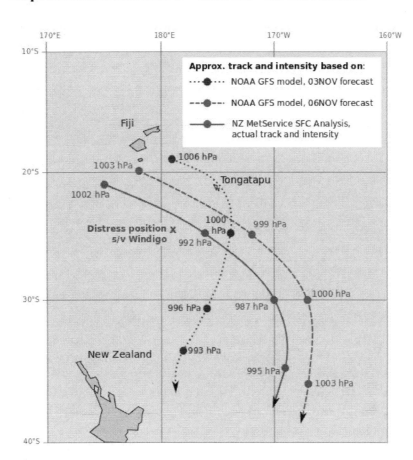

# Meanwhile, back at the ranch...

Those of us who had hung back in Tonga faced a different dilemma: where to seek shelter. Sailors in the Vava'u group had the straightforward choice between several secure anchorages, including Neiafu and Tapana. Down south in Tongatapu, our options were less clear cut. We were among a dozen boats anchored off Pangaimotu, a small island across the wide lagoon from Nuku'alofa, Tonga's capital "city." The holding in sand felt secure, but we were uneasy at the prospect of the open seven-mile fetch to the west – exactly the direction from which twelve hours of high winds were expected at the height of the storm.

The alternative was to move across the bay into the Nuku'alofa harbor, but that required an extensive set-up of two anchors plus lines ashore rigged with rat preventers. Rats – ugh! In the evenings preceding the storm, we all huddled at Big Mama's open-air restaurant on Pangaimotu to weigh our options. Several crews felt harbor-shy after a recent domino-effect dragging incident back in the central Ha'apai group of Tonga. Better to stay in the open anchorage and allow space to react, they reasoned, than be squeezed into a corner. Others favored the harbor's superior shelter and proximity to town. Meanwhile, our children played on the beach, blissfully unencumbered by the anxiety-producing distractions their parents were suffering. The fact that our numbers were swelled by several boats who had turned back from their passages did, however, reassure us that we had made the right decision to stay in Tonga.

With two days remaining before the storm, we opted to move to the inner harbor, going stern-to the breakwater with seven other yachts (and space for several more). The muddy bottom provided excellent holding, and the breadth of the harbor allowed us to get a good 150 feet of chain out on our primary bow anchor. We also set a secondary anchor to the west on another one hundred feet of rode. Once settling into a spider web of criss-crossing lines (all sporting discs to discourage stowaway rats), we sat back, watched the barometer drop, and crossed our fingers for those at sea.

It's hard to put a price on safety and comfort, but consider this: one couple who sat out the storm in Tonga forfeited very expensive flights they had already booked from New Zealand. Still, they were relieved to be safe aboard their floating home in relatively sheltered waters. Meanwhile, many yachts who did brave the storm sustained damage and consequently paid for repairs by the oh-so-obliging New Zealand yacht industry. It's a trade-off that's difficult to quantify, but certainly bears keeping in mind.

At the height of the storm on Wednesday, the maximum wind speed measured within the harbor was forty-nine knots, while a boat off Pangaimotu reported a peak of seventy-four knots. In the harbor, our hulls lay in quiet water, while boats in the anchorage were buffeted by an uncomfortable but harmless two-foot chop. A sharp wind shift had all of us in the harbor leaning hard a-lee, while boats anchored out in the bay were momentarily knocked down, but none the worse for wear (other than cabins in complete disarray). Ultimately, all the vessels in Tongatapu weathered the storm well, whether secured behind the breakwater or anchored out at Pangaimotu.

## Drama at Sea

The same could not be said of boats at sea. Unfortunately, the storm tracked farther west and built larger waves than expected. Consequently, many sailors who thought they would be in safe territory were now directly in the path of the storm or in the squash zone. Most of the fleet on passage reported the likes of fifteen foot waves and sustained forty knot winds: taxing, but not life-threatening. However, the worst of the storm brought thirty foot waves and fifty knot winds. One yacht, *Windigo*, a thirty-eight foot Beneteau, issued a mayday, reporting injuries and water ingress after being rolled. The nearest vessel, the sturdy thirty-seven foot Tayana, *Adventure Bound*, endured a punishing overnight beat to windward to offer support until a diverted freighter could reach the scene and take the crew of *Windigo* aboard. In the meantime, an unregistered EPIRB went off roughly one hundred miles south of Tonga, setting off more alarms. Later, this was discovered to originate from a fishing boat that had lost power but was able to ride out the storm safely on a drogue.

Thankfully, other yachts at sea did not suffer such dramas despite miserable conditions and a number of breakages, from torn sails to broken autopilots and dislodged dinghies, not to mention frayed nerves and general exhaustion. But they were not yet home free. A calm set in after the storm, preceding yet another low sweeping toward New Zealand from Australia. Crews who had already played their fuel joker were forced to sail through the calm at turtle pace, eventually making landfall under another assault of wind, rain, and heaving seas. However, most crews were able to view the experience in a positive light, gaining confidence in their vessels and in their own abilities.

## A Better Window

As the storm passed, we in Tonga were relieved that our friends were safe. Now our thoughts could return to our own upcoming passages. As it turned out, we had a much easier ride south. Just as the storm had exhausted many sailors, so too did it suck the energy out of the atmosphere, leaving a harmless series of disorganized high pressure systems and weak lows floundering in its wake. We were therefore among a second batch of southbound sailors who set off on November 11 with a forecast that promised a slow but hopefully uneventful passage. For us, it was exactly a year to the day that we had left the East Coast for the Caribbean.

This time, the forecast was spot on, and our passage to New Zealand proved to be a calm, even zen-like experience. We enjoyed a few fast days, but also set new low-mileage records of ninety-eight, fifty-four, and a wallowing forty-seven miles in successive twenty-four hour periods. On the other hand, with nothing threatening on the wider horizon, we were content to save diesel, drifting quietly along and counting our blessings. Unlike the boats one system ahead of us, we could put into North Minerva Reef for a one-of-a-kind, mid-ocean anchoring experience, and then resume our passage at an unhurried pace. Eventually, the wind did pick up again, propelling us toward New Zealand's North Island on a comfortable beam reach.

A relaxed passage to New Zealand

When we arrived to a sunny week in the Bay of Islands, one of the social organizers of the All Points Rally lamented that we had arrived too late; too late, she meant, for the post-rally events that had been held in Opua. *Actually*, I thought, *we arrived at exactly the right time*. Sailing is about bending to the will of the elements, rather than attempting to bend a forecast to one's will. In fact, many of us are out cruising to escape a world of artificial, pressing engagements and an ever-ticking clock. But habits are hard to break, as the story of the first departing fleet demonstrates.

## Looking Back

In retrospect, we couldn't help but examine how so many crews found themselves in such a precarious situation at sea. There were a number of contributing factors. First, the difficulty in picking a weather window is that choices can't be compared ahead of time; you can only weigh the latest forecast against very vague notions of what the future might bring. Consequently, "good enough" is often taken as a reassuring sign. Complicating this was the fact that respected weather routers gave the waiting fleet a thumbs-up to depart. But even experts make mistakes, particularly with a "science" at the mercy of the elements. They and many crews were aware that a depression would form, but gambled with the high odds that the tropical depression would not amount to much (indeed, many forecast lows turn out to be false alarms).

In this case, playing it safe paid off. We benefited from the advice of a locally based amateur weatherman, the veteran of multiple passages between Tonga, Fiji, and New Zealand. He was correct in taking a conservative approach, reminding us that the track and intensity of a tropical system is nearly impossible to pinpoint in advance. In other words, trusting computer software that suggests a vessel can stay ahead of a tropical depression's theoretical track five days hence is a dicey proposition at best, especially in the southwest Pacific. Instead, he heeded his own experience and intuition, and ultimately proved to be spot on.

Furthermore, it seems that many crews heeded a natural urge to get moving "on schedule." The fact that this coincided with the general timing of the rally served to reinforce a dash to the exit door, compounded by subliminal peer pressure. After all, it can be awfully hard to sit still while an anchorage empties out around you. Impatience was another factor, as some crews admitted they were just plum tired of waiting. Picking a weather window really did prove to be an exercise in disciplining oneself to scrutinize the fine print – in both weather forecasts and in expert advice, such as that appearing in John Martin's early bulletin.

Of course, hindsight is a 20/20 phenomenon. Our observations seek to learn from a trying experience so that we can be all the wiser the next time around. That's the theory, at least. Since one of the morals of this story is that theory and practice often differ vastly, well… let's just say we'll plan for the worst and hope for the best!

# Chapter 41

# A Season in New Zealand:
# A Practical Guide

For many trans-Pacific sailors, New Zealand is the promised land: a safe, English-speaking place south of the cyclone belt, a place to slow down, relax, and catch up with boat projects. After all, most will have come all the way from the Americas in one long, 6,000 mile season and are more than ready for a break. But six months can feel like a long time to spend in one place, especially for the cruiser accustomed to a harried pace. Where to go? How to divide your time? This chapter outlines the options for a season in New Zealand, the better to plan your stay.

Most inbound yachts choose Opua in the Bay of Islands as their port of entry; others head straight for Auckland or Marsden Cove (Whangarei). New Zealand requires an advance notice of arrival for private yachts, but this is a simple matter of downloading and submitting an online form.[1] The form must be filed at least forty-eight hours before arrival, but you can send it in weeks earlier and update your arrival date by email. Upon clearing in, most passport holders are granted a free three-month visa, which can be extended for up to nine months by mail (NZ$165 per family). Once such business is taken care of, the travel-weary fleet slowly dissipates to sample their pick of the myriad choices on water or land.

---

[1] http://www.customs.govt.nz

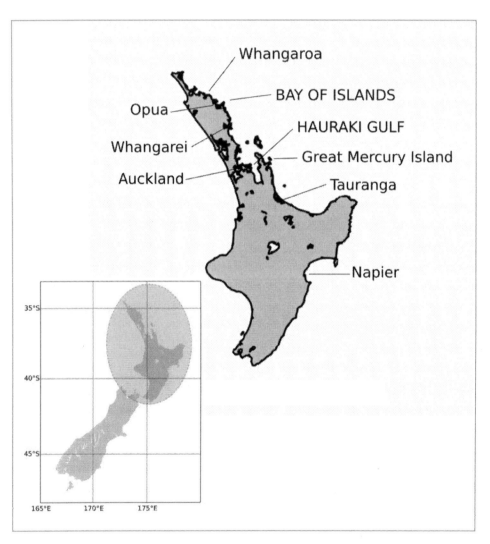

New Zealand's North Island

# Cruising Grounds: the Bay of Islands

After months devoted to long blue water passages, sailors delight in New Zealand's rich cruising grounds, starting with the Bay of Islands. There, a smattering of uninhabited islands offer anchorages for every wind direction – not to mention pristine beaches, hiking trails, and a hurricane hole or two. You'll awake each day to emerald views and exotic bird calls, like the wavering, gong-like call of the tui. Most – but not all – dangers to navigation in the Bay of Islands are marked and the tidal range is a mere five feet. For us, the area summons memories of swimming, hiking, and dolphin spotting.

Each island is unique, yet part of the singular tapestry of the bay, and all offer excellent walking tracks. One of our favorite spots is undulating Urupukapuka with its numerous trails, duck blind, and Maori *Pa* (fortified hilltop village). Motorua offers a different perspective from a World War II lookout bunker on its heights. The sandy beach at Oke Bay is a real treat, as are any of the trails that crisscross the peninsula there. Mainland Russell is one of the oldest settlements in New Zealand, and worth the discomfort of anchoring in the busy harbor. Across the bay, historic Waitangi is another must-see, though access is difficult from the water. To reach sights like Waitangi or to go shopping in Paihia, we'd usually anchor off the beach in Paihia (if conditions were settled) or anchored more securely in Opua, then hitched a ride into town.

Whenever a northerly gale piped up, we'd drop anchor in muddy Orokawa Bay. And when the weather settled again, we could set a course for Roberton Island, a thin strip of land nearly trisected by tidal lagoons. If conditions are very settled, Waewaetorea is another nice option, thanks to its pleasant beach and the hilltop views.

Still, the Bay of Islands is much smaller than its reputation suggests. Although there are dozens of lovely anchorages, the prime destinations boil down to a handful of islands and mainland bays, none of which are more than fifteen miles from each other. Two weeks is plenty of time for a laid-back circuit of the bay. More is better, but many sailors get itchy feet once they exceed the six-week mark.

That's when it's time to check the continuous VHF weather forecast and head farther afield. We quickly learned to take forecasts with an extra grain of salt: with no land mass to buffer the island nation from the Antarctic, weather is notoriously unpredictable. On the other hand, we found David Thatcher's cruising guides (including a section on weather) spot-on throughout our stay in New Zealand.

A frequent sight in the Bay of Islands

## Beyond the Bay of Islands

Two enticing destinations beckon just a day sail north of the Bay of Islands: the Cavalli Islands and Whangaroa, a perfectly sheltered, fjord-like bay. We spent a happy two weeks there, sometimes as the sole boat in one of the many anchorages. The sail north can be exhilarating, with the feel of the open ocean even on this short coastal hop. Still, it's all line-of-sight navigation – a real treat after months of blearily eyeing the compass. Great Cavalli Island is essentially a taller, larger cousin of the places we'd become familiar with in the Bay of Islands, with wooded trails and views of a fractured seascape. Apparently, a day off the beaten track is a day too many for most: here, you can safely divide the number of visitors by ten and multiply the length of the beaches by two.

Almost every visiting sailor heads south to Auckland and the Hauraki Gulf at some point. Doing so requires a mental shift from "paradise at anchor" to full sailing mode for the trip along the raw, exposed coastline. On a bad day, this coast can conjure up images of the wild Southern Ocean. At its best, conditions will be just right for an enjoyable two to three day trip to the Hauraki Gulf. We quickly learned to follow local cruisers well offshore to avoid confused inshore wave action and unmarked hazards like appropriately-named Wide Berth Islands and Danger Rock.

The most interesting stop along the way is Whangamumu, just around the corner from Cape Brett and the Bay of Islands. It's a large, circular bay open to the east, uninhabited but for the ruins of an interesting whaling station. A number of hiking paths branch out from here. Other anchorages along the way include Tutukaka and the outer reaches of Whangarei. While several islands cluster along this stretch of coast, most are nature reserves where you can't step ashore; you'll also be hard pressed to find a safe anchorage among them.

# The Hauraki Gulf

Right at the doorstep of Auckland, the Hauraki Gulf is the undisputed queen of New Zealand's cruising grounds. Take your pick: sample city life or escape to wooded reserves like Tiritiri Matangi Island. Thanks to steady ocean breezes and relatively calm waters, the sailing is outstanding. We took to heading wherever the wind blew us, setting our Parasailor for the sheer joy of a brisk downwind run or working upwind among a fleet of pleasure craft.

Every island is unique and distances are generally short. You might hike the ashy slopes to the volcanic peak of Rangitoto one morning, then sail away on a fifteen knot southeasterly to end the day off one of Waiheke Island's posh neighborhoods. Tiritiri Matangi is the place for bird-watching: we paddled ashore and immediately spotted native species with melodic names like takehe and pukeko. The nocturnal and notoriously shy kiwi, however, is much harder to find. Peaceful Kawau Island draws many sailors (and city day-trippers) thanks to the manicured grounds of Governor Grey's Mansion. Other great destinations include Rangiahua for its secret nook of an anchorage, Motuihe for its wartime history and city views, and Rakino for its rocky outcrops. Of course, you'll be sharing this playground with a "city of sails," but most of the anchorages are spacious and the scenery is beautiful wherever you go.

One of the best places to get away from it all within a day of Auckland is peaceful Te Kouma Bay on the rugged Coromandel Peninsula. Literally capping the gulf is Great Barrier Island, where you can hike among native kauri trees to a historic dam, summit Mount Hobson (621 meters), or visit Smokehouse Bay, where a do-it-yourself woodfire hot tub awaits. Given all there is to see and do afoot and afloat in the greater Auckland area, even the most burned-out Pacific cruiser can spend months here.

## South to Tauranga

Cape Colville, the northeasternmost point of the Hauraki Gulf, marks the outer limit of many sailors' self-imposed cruising grounds; all the more room for the rest of us. Great Mercury Island, just one day farther southeast, is an absolute stunner with its long, sandy beach and beautiful scenery. Depending on the weather, there are several anchorages where you can break up a trip south, including Mercury Bay, Mayor Island, and Slipper Island.

Tauranga and its sister city, Mount Maunganui, are pleasant places that attracted us for several reasons. From there, we could rent a car to reach the best-known inland attractions of the North Island: Rotorua, for its culture and thermal activity; Lake Taupo, for beautiful scenery; and Tongariro National Park, for its lunar landscape. With some of lowest marina and yard fees on the North Island, Tauranga is also a good place for boat work (see *Haul-Outs and Yard Time* below).

Truly hardy sailors press on to South Island's spectacular Fiordland, but the more extreme weather of the south confines most sailors to the north/central part of the North Island, particularly since land travel to the South Island is so easy (see *Land-Based Travel* on on the next page ). Of course, that only multiplies the rewards for those who do sail south.

## Haul-Outs and Yard Time

After thousands of miles of ocean wear, most boats will be begging for maintenance, repairs, or improvements. A good time to schedule work might be during the school holidays from late December to early February, when it seems that three out of four million Kiwis hit the water. It's a nation of boaters, and it shows.

Whangarei offers the widest choice of services and boat yards on the North Island. It's also a good place to store a boat safely in the owner's absence. The disadvantage of basing boat work out of Whangarei is that there are no attractive options for local sailing; you'll truly be upriver. Still, Whangarei earned top marks from every sailor we know who visited, both for price and quality of services. The excellent *Whangarei Marine Promotions* guide is available online and in yachtie hangouts as far back as Tahiti and Tonga. Check out Town Dock, or Marsden Cove Marinas, and Docklands 5, Riverside Drive, or Norsand yards.

Opua is another good base for boat work, with a couple of good chandlers and yards. Prices are typically a hair above Whangarei's (try Opua / Northland Marina and Ashby

Boatyard). The advantage of working out of Opua is the proximity to beautiful cruising. We spent the final month of our stay whittling down our job list there. After applying a fresh coat of antifouling, we picked up parts and groceries and headed out to the islands to do our work in idyllic surroundings. With only a one to two hour commute back to town for more supplies, this is also conducive to saving money, as you can't spend a cent once you're out in the bay.

Greater Auckland is yet another possibility for boat work or an extended stay, though prices are a tick higher than elsewhere. The advantage of working out of Auckland are the stimulating city and fine Hauraki Gulf cruising grounds (popular choices are Westhaven and Bayswater Marinas, or Gulf Harbour Marina farther afield).

We were drawn to Tauranga by low marina rates and settled in for a month of intense boat work in a place brimming with chandlers, hardware stores, and electrical supply shops (see Tauranga Bridge Marina or Tauranga Marina). There's not much local cruising there, but we broke work up with hikes up Mount Maunganui and an inland trip.

Budget roughly NZ$25 per night in a marina for a thirty-five foot boat in any of these locations; rates drop for week/month-long stays. Word is that rates are even cheaper down in Napier, but the trip around several wind-swept capes keeps many away.

## Land-Based Travel

With so much to see in "Middle Earth", it's no wonder that many sailors opt for a period of extended land travel. Used car deals abound in Opua, Whangarei, and Auckland, including convenient buy back packages. These deals usually entail a NZ$2,000 difference between the buying and selling price, with everything from compact cars to camper vans available. The early bird gets the best pickings; if you're serious about buying a car, shop as soon as you arrive in New Zealand.

We opted to cruise for most of our stay with short periods of land travel. Jucy Car Rental's "El Cheapo" was our vehicle of choice and despite the name, it never, ever let us down. Jucy also has some of the best deals in campers, as well as last minute delivery deals. For a shorter trip to the South Island, consider flying with Jet Star. We paid NZ$150 per round trip ticket from Auckland to Queenstown and spent a grand total of NZ$2,100 for three people in ten days (including flights, car, self-catering stays in backpacker lodgings, and modest sightseeing). The local tourism industry specializes in the bold and exhilarating: bungee jumping! White water rafting! Lord of the Rings trail rides! The catch? These activities cost upwards of NZ$150 per person. We stuck to hiking, splurging only for a Milford Sound cruise and a day's mountain bike rental.

We were pleased as punch with our mini trip, just as friends were delighted with the months they spent traveling overland. The moral of the story is, there's something for every budget in this beautiful island nation.

## Other Practicalities

The first thing we did upon arriving in Opua was to open a free checking account with the local branch of Kiwi Bank in Paihia. Although we paid a fee for transferring money from our home account, we ultimately saved by having a local credit / debit card. Another early order of business was communications. Vodafone is the biggest 3G cellular provider, and their dongle can be reused in Fiji with a local SIM card. Internet coverage is good if not speedy; we hiked many a hill in the Bay of Islands to pick up a signal when coverage down in the anchorage was poor.

New Zealand will truly seem like the promised land in terms of chandlers, supermarkets, and hardware stores. Two of our favorite boat products were Uroxsys Aliphatic varnish (very tough stuff) and Soudal FixAll, a polymer adhesive sealant that's a more economical alternative to Sikaflex. We're glad we stocked up on these – as well as all our favorite foods – before leaving New Zealand for Fiji and Vanuatu.

After the relaxed standards of Polynesia, Kiwi officials can seem positively draconian in some of their regulations. Only locally certified gas cylinders will be filled with propane, for example, and only locally certified power cords can be used for shore power. And although New Zealand is an extremely friendly host nation in all respects, crews who overstay their visas are subject to heavy fines. This became an issue when ugly fall weather delayed many a boat's departure for the tropics, exactly as crews butted up against their visa expiration dates. Officials run regular patrols of island anchorages, so don't even think about laying low anywhere but the crowded anchorage of Opua. That said, customs officials in Opua didn't pressure anyone to leave in the face of bad weather; present your case in person to explore options for a short-term extension.

New Zealand might not have it all, but it comes pretty darn close. Sailing for every ambition level and a variety of attractions on and off the water made our six months whiz by. At the end of a full season in New Zealand, most cruisers have regenerated enough to look forward to new destinations in "the Islands" – the generic Kiwi term for Tonga, Fiji, Vanuatu, and New Caledonia. Some like this part of the world so much that they ricochet between New Zealand and the tropics for season after season, cultivating friendships in both places. Alas, we don't all get to sail on that kind of schedule – but even one season is enough to create a treasure trove of memories.

# Chapter 42

# The Spice of Life:
# A Day at the Museum

The helmsman barks orders; grinders sweat at their winches; the tactician eyes the field. Another day at the races? No – a rainy day at the museum! Centrally located on the Auckland waterfront, Voyager: New Zealand Maritime Museum lets visitors feel like they're on the water even when they're indoors. Traditional exhibits display Polynesian seagoing canoes and trace the history of tall ships. What really captivated our attention, however, was the recently opened permanent exhibit: *Blue Water, Black Magic: A Tribute to Sir Peter Blake.*

Besides a section devoted to the national hero of this boating nation, the new wing displays boats, everything from modest dinghies to the 1995 America's Cup winner, *Black Magic.* Of the many interactive stations, our favorite was a computer-simulated race platform where a six person team can put a racing yacht through her paces. We put Nicky into the helmsman's role and did our best to keep up with his wild but enthusiastic maneuvers: Hard aport! Gybe ho! Later, he and a seven-year-old buddy took turns at keel design on another computer, while we parents sat gaping at southern ocean footage from the Jules Verne Trophy.

To top off an entertaining afternoon, visitors can board one of the historic ships in the museum's fleet for a harbor cruise. On the scow *Ted Ashby*, we lent a hand to raise sails and listened raptly as the ship's volunteer crew shared anecdotes. Markus inquired about volunteering and whether a minimum age limit applied. "More like a maximum!" joked the seventy-year-old deckhand, one of the crew's younger members. The relaxed, friendly atmosphere they created made the experience all the more memorable, as if Auckland harbor views weren't enough to cement the experience into our minds.

267

Last, but not least, the fun and fascination of Voyager can be enjoyed at a bargain price: we were admitted for free during school holidays, and the regular family admission is a fair NZ$32 (roughly US$16). A family pays only NZ$20 (US$10) more for the harbor cruise. Even with all the outdoor pursuits available in and around Auckland, visitors to New Zealand should not miss Voyager. Plan your visit at *www.maritimemuseum.co.nz.*

Exploring Auckland's Maritime Museum

# Chapter 43

# New Zealand to Fiji:
# The Long Way Around

There's the rhumb line, the great circle route, and there's the long way around. The latter wasn't exactly our intention when departing New Zealand for Fiji one late May day, but that's what sailing is about: life at the mercy of the elements, sometimes for better, sometimes for worse.

It had been a wonderfully unambitious season in the land of the kiwi for us. Now that cyclone season was past and winter coming on, however, we were eager to explore "the Islands," as Tonga, Fiji, Vanuatu, and New Caledonia are fondly referred to. Apart from shaky sea legs, we wondered, how complicated could this be? The passage is simply the southern hemisphere version of the US East Coast to Caribbean run, without the complication of the Gulf Stream. No problem, right?

Our suspicions, however, were aroused by a contradiction: while respected sources such as Jimmy Cornell and the Island Cruising Association Rally give late April / early May as a good departure time, most veterans wait for more stable weather patterns in June – that's winter, meaning an increased frequency of Tasman Sea lows. So which would it be: an early start, toeing the line with the end of the cyclone season, or a later passage, with a trade-off between more reliable weather and colder temperatures?

## Waiting for a Weather Window

We spent nearly all of May in the Bay of Islands, finding no sign of what we would call a weather window. Boats that did depart early ran very narrow gauntlets between high latitude storms and tropical depressions that seemed determined to keep all intruders out of their territory above 25° south. Some crews got lucky in their gamble; others, not so lucky. We listened in to the radio nets and felt justified for hanging back while others reported thirty, forty, even fifty knot sustained winds with seas to match. One friend reported: "Arrived in Fiji a little blown away, but all in one piece." The boat, however, was "in a few more pieces," including a broken pushpit, a parted genoa sheet, and torn lazy bag. Meanwhile, we were happy and well occupied in New Zealand's beautiful Bay of Islands. Why rush off?

For a good passage north, we wanted the back side of a low pressure system moving east across the Tasman Sea; the leading edge of the following high would provide favorable winds up to the trade winds. In the long-term forecasts, the systems all looked promising while they built over Australia. But as time passed and the systems inched closer, they either morphed just enough to postpone our departure, or the South Pacific Convergence Zone would spawn another late season tropical depression. Time and time again, we thought we had our window and prepared for departure. The boat was ready, the crew was ready, even the vegetables were ready! But what were optimistic weather windows to begin with inevitably took a turn for the worse: the high a little too weak, a little too short; or an unstable tropical depression would pop into the scene like a loose cannon. All in all, the science of forecasting seemed more like a dark art of consulting oracles and reading entrails!

And so we waited, and waited, and waited. Lovely as New Zealand is, the island nation was taking on a Hotel California feel: you can check out any time you want, but you can never leave. Thirty-five-plus knots on the beam with six-meter seas, anyone? What about four days of strong northerlies, followed by a week of motoring? There were, in fact, a few takers for each of these "windows," many of them crews with looming visa expiration dates. We bit the bullet and applied for a visa extension instead. What's NZ$165 versus an unnecessary thrashing (and possible gear damage) at sea? As a consolation, all those perfect New Zealand anchorages were now empty of other cruisers, so we were content to wait.

It was late May and a full month after our intended departure time before the weather systems stabilized enough to put any faith in the forecasts. Finally, we had it: a low followed by a nice, strong high that would bring us into the trade winds with reliable southeasterlies. Yes, there was one tropical depression out there, but every available forecast model consistently had it tracking well ahead and out of our path before it caused any trouble. A period of northerly winds carried in by a cold front could be dealt with by stopping over at Minerva Reef. It all looked very manageable. (Famous last words?)

# In Good Company

During our weeks of waiting, we had the feeling that we were stragglers, the softies left behind while all the other kids had gone out to play. But it turned out we were in good company, as evidenced by the sight of thirty crews queued up outside the Opua Customs office on the morning of Wednesday, May 29. The atmosphere was one of an excited high school graduation: all hugs, sentimental retrospection, and eager looks forward into a warm, tropical future. Soon, the Bay of Islands was sprouting with more sails than we had seen in a month, an entire armada heading for various points north.

It all looked so good on that gloriously sunny afternoon. Initially, everything unfolded as expected, with a nice southwesterly breeze to carry us away from land. As night fell, so did the wind, just as forecast. We piled on layers of warm clothing and cranked up the motor. Never had leaving land for the open ocean felt so easy!

Escaping the southern winter in New Zealand

Until it got complicated, that is. That lurking tropical depression surprised everyone by taking its own good time to materialize. Instead of being swept away in front of an east-bound high, the cheeky thing slipped in behind the high and suddenly stood directly over our route. While some crews plowed straight on (eventually reporting sustained fifty knot winds and heavy seas), most detoured west to skirt the edge of this low. A stopover in Minerva Reef was no longer an option, so we steered *Namani* on a new heading of 330° to avoid the worst. Even with a detour that took us as far west as 173°02 E, we hit forty knot winds and rough seas. Happily, both came from behind and the boat rode it out well, even if our stomachs didn't. For forty-eight hours, we subsisted entirely on pretzels and granola bars and simply hung on. *Namani* made a solid five and six knots, even when we struck the main and genoa to sail under our "baby" staysail – a pitifully small scrap of canvas we were sure we would never, ever have to use. We were repeatedly soaked by slapping waves, and many crews bailed swamped cockpits after being pooped by following seas.

All the while, sea birds soared overhead, then swooped through deepest troughs of short-period waves, just a walk in the park as far as they were concerned. For us, it was an unpleasant two days that ultimately gave us more confidence in our vessel and ourselves, if not in interpreting apparently "stable" weather systems – especially those fickle tropical depressions! As the wind gradually abated, we headed back to the east. Nature gave us a day off, with wind dropping to below five knots and seas rapidly easing.

## The Tsar's Thumb

Our 300 mile detour reminded us of the story of the Tsar's thumb: once upon a time, Russian Tsar Nicholas I ordered his engineers to build a railroad from St. Petersburg to Moscow. He took a ruler and drew a straight line connecting the two points on a map – straight except for where his thumb jutted over the ruler, creating a slight bump. Not willing to question the Tsar, the engineers designed exactly the railroad he drew, including a mindless detour to nowhere. *Namani* had traced her very own Tsar's thumb, but at least it allowed us to avoid the worst conditions.

We used the twenty-four hour calm after the storm to dry out, rest up, and chow down before the next challenge arrived. That was an approaching cold front that would sweep in a period of twenty knot northerlies expected to gust thirty-five to forty knots – an "XL" version of the contrary winds we had originally hoped to sit out at Minerva Reef. The good news was, it was an opportunity to make back our easting by taking the wind on the beam, this time under triple reefed main and the baby staysail. The cold front hit in one nasty squall line. One casualty of the fray included the winch handle we kept at the mast; it was flipped overboard by a flapping sheet. (Call it a token sacrifice to Poseidon.) Another boat reported a shredded genoa and torn mainsail; they eventually limped in to port a day behind most others.

So what does a nine-year-old do while all this is going on? Nicky was largely unperturbed, putting supreme confidence in his parents and the boat. (Yikes!) He nonchalantly continued to read or ponder the computer programs of his dreams in his snug den of a quarterberth, making only brief appearances in the soggy cockpit. He did, however,

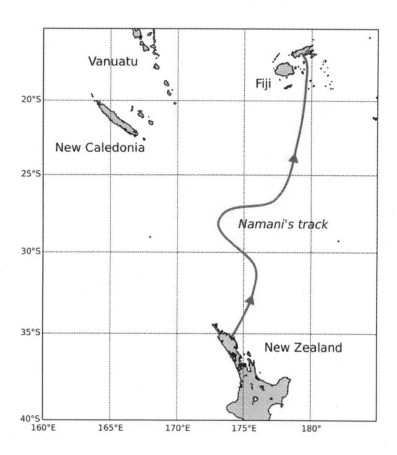

confess to feeling a little bored. The highlight, as far as Nicky was concerned, was our high speed, topping out at nine-plus knots "downhill."

Our second bout with the elements lasted twenty-four hours before the wind dropped and backed from north to northwest, west, and eventually, the southwest. Dawn brought the happy prospect not only of abating winds and seas, but sunshine, too. Given warmer temperatures and calmer seas, we finally had the pleasure of sailing with the companionway open. As the wind went to WSW and fizzled to ten knots a few hours later, we pulled out yet another sail from our arsenal of six: the Parasailor, our excellent light wind sail that significantly reduces the boat's rolling motion – a major plus in the confused slop left in the wake of the preceding systems. The galley filled with the aroma of fresh bread and muffins, and the general scent aboard was further improved after salt water baths for each of us in our inflatable kiddie pool, followed by a fresh water rinse. Markus used a stranded flying fish as fresh bait and promptly snagged a big mahi mahi, giving us a real dinner treat. Yes, passage-making certainly has its pluses and minuses.

Just a day later, *Namani* reached the trade winds for good, sailing along with fifteen knot winds from the southeast. The radio net sang with a chorus of relieved voices from crews finally making good progress in the right direction. We benefited greatly from two friends outside our little flotilla: one was a ham radio enthusiast and sailor in New Zealand who used his home Internet connection to fill us in on satellite images of the various weather systems. Another was a sailor already at our destination (Savusavu in Fiji), who added each of us to the waiting list for moorings in tightly packed, deep water Nakama Creek. Thanks to him, all the boats in our little pack of six could be accommodated upon arrival. Fifteen months earlier, we had started our Pacific crossing feeling very much alone; now, we were part of a tight network of sailors who truly looked out for one another.

As it turned out, none of us was in a particular rush to arrive, since Fiji customs officers charge high rates for weekend overtime. Several early arrivals hove-to for forty-eight hours rather than paying the additional fee. *Namani* was well on track for a Monday morning arrival, so we could fully enjoy the last section of what would be a twelve-day passage. With no excuses left, home schooling was back on the agenda, along with reading and guitar playing. The moon had gradually faded from its third quarter to a thin crescent during our trip, leaving a sky full of brilliant stars. Prominent among them was Scorpio, clawing its way up into the night sky, and later nose-diving into the western horizon.

# Land Ho!

The main challenge left was navigation as we approached the islands of southern Fiji. Sunday was a day of ticking off progress past large islands as we made our way north. In this area, the islands are widely spaced and mercifully free of isolated dangers, making the approach to Savusavu straightforward. It was only with a few miles to go that we put on our polarized sunglasses to run the reef-lined entrance into Savusavu Bay. No sooner had we made the turn into Nakama Creek than a launch from Waitui Marina came out to guide us to our mooring with a friendly hello – in Fiji, that's a hearty "Bula!"

The longest passage of our second Pacific cruising season was now behind us; we were back in the tropics at last, and could look forward to shorter hops all the way to Australia. Including our detour around the Tsar's thumb, *Namani* sailed 1,485 miles instead of a straight-line 1,140 miles. We spotted everything from small petrels to broad-winged albatross on the way from 35°S to 17°S, and flew four different sails over the course of this varied passage, from our biggest sail (the Parasailor) to the smallest (the baby staysail). We were especially glad that we had taken the time to do a test hoist of this sail back in New Zealand and that we'd stowed it within easy reach.

Having waited a long time for a good weather window, we admit to feeling a bit chagrined to find that our chosen slot was not significantly better than many earlier departure times we had rejected. In fact, we broke our own rule: never to assume that anything about a developing tropical depression is predictable. On the other hand, we console ourselves with the fact that we had been tracking the two weather systems that disturbed our passage all along; when their paths did deviate from the forecast, we could quickly go to Plan B. Of course, we could have waited another few weeks in New Zealand, but sooner or later, every cruiser has to hit the road. And ultimately, that is what separates the boats at the dock from the ones sending tropical greetings home.

# Part IX

# The Western Pacific

# The Western Pacific

For all that we had dreamed, researched, and prepared for our voyage, the western end of the Pacific remained a mystery to us until we cleared out of New Zealand and headed north. Of course, we'd heard of Fiji, but had only the vaguest notion of where to head once we got there. Vanuatu and New Caledonia are places the average landlubber hasn't even heard of, let alone found on a map. We felt very much as if we were heading into the great unknown.

So what did we find? Warm, generous people. Incredible natural scenery, above and beneath the water. Vibrant Melanesian cultures that embrace tradition while welcoming outsiders like us. Last but not least, we found challenging cruising in reef-laced waters. Now we understand why some lucky sailors linger in this magical part of the Pacific for years on end.

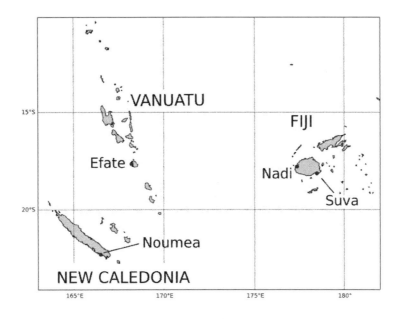

By now, just enough sailors have explored these islands to trim the danger off the edges of a cruise there. On the other hand, slowly divergent cruising tracks contribute to keeping the pleasure fleet spread out, thus preserving the area's exotic appeal. Some crews angle north with an eye on a Pacific loop, while others take a middle line for an eventual passage to Indonesia, and still others hug the southern edge of each island group on their way to Australia.

With hundreds of small islands within each of these island groups begging to be explored, sailors are spoiled for choice – a common conundrum in the Pacific. In fact, that's a topic this section closes with, when we examine the options for an onward voyage to Australia by comparing two crews' different routes west: one to Queensland via Huon and Chesterfield reefs, and another over New Caledonia to New South Wales. As difficult as some of these choices are, the good news is you can't lose no matter which you opt for.

# Chapter 44

# Fiji: Flirting with the Date Line

On paper, crossing the Pacific in one season seemed like a perfectly good plan. But once there, we were like kids in a candy store: everything looked so good. We wanted it all! So when the chance came to decelerate our cruise from a two-year run into a three-year jog, we grabbed at it like the greedy sailors we are. There is just too much to see, too quickly. So many fascinating islands and cultures. Fiji, Vanuatu, and New Caledonia were all at the far end of our itinerary. Surely they all deserved more than a quick fly-by?

Or so we supposed, because we actually had very little information on cruising in those areas. Right up to the time when we left New Zealand at the start of our second Pacific season, we had little notion of what a cruise in Fiji might look like. In part, that's because Fiji is one of the few Pacific island groups that can't be tackled in one logical, leeward-to-windward direction. There are choices to be made, zigs to be zagged, and more than what any sane sailor can cover in a single season. For the spoiled cruisers we had become, a real conundrum.

So where to begin?

## Clearing In

Most sailors coming from Tonga or New Zealand aim for one of three ports of entry on the east side of Fiji. The southernmost port of entry is Suva, a busy industrial port. The main attraction of this unattractive port is that it cuts a day off a New Zealand to Fiji passage, no small consideration for sailors ready to cry Land Ho! As capital of

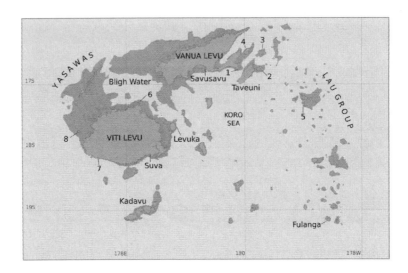

the island nation, Suva hosts a number of embassies, a practical consideration for those wishing to apply for visas for Indonesia or Papua New Guinea.

Levuka, on the other hand, is reputed to be one of the most interesting colonial towns in the South Pacific and offers all the basics, too: supermarkets, gas stations, and restaurants. However, the anchorage is too exposed to be comfortable in southeasterlies above ten to fifteen knots.

Savusavu, the northernmost of the three, has become many a cruiser's favorite, thanks to its good shelter and services. It is a medium-sized town with a big heart and everything the post-passage cruiser needs, from fuel stations to large supermarkets and a good selection of shops and restaurants. Savusavu's friendly inhabitants – both native Fijians and Indo-Fijians – provided a lovely welcome in our first Melanesian destination. However, one limitation of Savusavu is space in the narrow confines of the deep water creek, where moorings are a must. Ideally, you'd email ahead to reserve a mooring in Waitui Marina, Copra Shed Marina (which also offers docking space), or Savusavu Yacht Club. Savusavu is the home base of Curly Carswell, who runs a morning radio net and offers weekly seminars on cruising in Fiji – a great value, as are his cruising notes and way point packages.

Take note that the charge for clearing into Fiji on a weekend is far above and beyond the F$170 charged during weekdays. Wherever you clear in, stock up fully before heading out to quieter corners of Fiji. Vodafone and Digicel are two excellent phone / Internet providers; we were able to connect to the Internet in nearly every corner of Fiji (one notable exception being the southern Lau group).

## Cruising in Fiji

Fiji is not a destination for the faint of heart due to the maze of reefs that surround each island. For the first time in three years of cruising, we took to cautiously relying on a chart plotter. Still, electronic charts, GPS, and hand-me-down cruising tracks are no guarantee of safety, so the prudent sailor will always keep a careful lookout for unmarked dangers and set sail only in good visibility. At least, that's the theory.

In practice, we found it nearly impossible to sail only in good visibility, especially on the overcast, eastern side of Fiji. Even if we managed to leave one anchorage under clear skies, clouds would inevitably move in, forcing us to make more "blind" harbor entries (relying entirely on electronics) than we'd like to admit to. Distances are such that overnight trips are unavoidable when heading for off-lying island groups such as the Lau group or Yasawas.

For all the challenges, cruising in Fiji promises rich rewards. Beautiful tropical landscapes are only one plus; interactions with locals are another. It all starts with the sevusevu ceremony, a must in any traditional village (see *Fact File: Dispelling the Myth of Sevusevu* on page 289). Beyond that formality, a friendly wave and call of "Bula!" (hello) earned us many invitations to tea or lunch. Islanders in remote places are always happy for practical gifts such as tea, rice, batteries, sugar, flour, fishing gear, and the like, since supply ships often skip stops. English is one of the official languages of Fiji, and all but a few village elders and very small youngsters seemed completely fluent.

It's hard to do justice to a cruising ground as rich or complex as Fiji; this is just an overview. For detailed cruising notes, start with the excellent s/v Soggy Paws website, with its free compendium and links to other guides (all free).[1]

## Which Way Around?

Fiji is comprised of two large islands, Viti Levu ("Big Fiji") and Vanua Levu ("Big Island"). The best cruising is to be found among the smaller, off-lying islands. Once you've explored the east side of Fiji, you'll have to decide how to reach the west side. Will you sail over the top of Viti Levu or around the bottom? Going over the north allows for day hopping, but given the extensive reef system there, it's more of a connect-the-dots GPS exercise than kick-back-and-relax sailing. We found the reef reasonably well marked and Curly's way points absolutely spot on.

---

[1] http://www.svsoggypaws.com

Sailors who head west along the south coast of Viti Levu usually do so in a couple of overnights, starting with one to Kadavu (see *Under the Bottom: Kadavu and the South Coast* on page 286). Both the north and south coasts of Viti Levu are places to transit more than to linger in; you'll find yourself drawn ahead to the more appealing cruising grounds on Fiji's west coast.

Fiji straddles the International Date Line, although the entire country shares one time zone and date. It's great fun to watch logbook entries jump from longitude east to west and back again, sometimes several times a day. Either way, it's a long, long way from Greenwich, England.

## The Northeast: Vanua Levu and Nearby Islands

If you've cleared in at Savusavu, the logical place to start cruising is the northeast end of Fiji where highlights are many and varied. Viani Bay is fifty miles from Savusavu, a popular spot thanks to pleasant surroundings and world-class diving on Rainbow Reef (map, #1). Dive operators make pick-ups directly from boats in Viani and even offer a yachtie's discount (we paid US$100 for an unforgettable two-tank dive with Taveuni Ocean Sports). Thanks to a good Vodafone signal in Viani, you can easily surf the Internet and call dive operators.

The lush mountain scenery of Taveuni, the "Garden Isle" of Fiji, is not to be missed. Hire a local cab for a day trip to the windward side to hike beautiful trails and multiple waterfalls. The same cab can take you to the natural water slide near Somosomo (rated the top site in Fiji by our nine-year-old). Since its anchorages are quite exposed, Taveuni is best visited in settled weather.

Other prime destinations on the northeast side of Fiji include the lovely islands of Qamea and Matangi (map, #2), as well as scarcely-visited Budd Reef (another stop for settled weather; map, #3). The islands of Rabi and Kioa are notable as Polynesian enclaves within Melanesian Fiji (map, #4). Friends reported idyllic, virtually empty anchorages there once a weather window sparked a mass exodus of the cruising fleet to the Lau group. Even fewer cruisers venture over the reef-strewn north side of Vanua Levu, a place to truly get away from it all.

## To Windward: the Lau Group

The Lau group is something of an awakening beauty, since these islands have only opened to cruisers in recent years. Most sailors wait for a brief disturbance to the trade winds to head there, grabbing a short period of northerlies or calm days. Make sure you head out at the first opportunity, since the next chance may be two to six weeks away. Timing your arrival is important, too, since most atolls have narrow passes that can usually only be run at slack water and in good visibility.

Be warned: the secret is out. Once-isolated atolls now see more and more yachts – even dozens at peak times. The two most-visited Lau islands are Vanua Mbalavu (map, #5) at the northern end of the chain and Fulanga at the southern end. Other atolls of the Lau group have trickier passes and therefore fewer visitors.

Local chiefs levy modest visitor's fees, but who can begrudge them a chance to finance school fees and community improvements? These remote villages generally operate outside the cash economy, so the fees are well appreciated and apparently well spent, with chiefs and elders allocating funds. Other than this fee, we went a month without spending a cent in the Lau, trading small goods for fresh fruit.

Many cruisers rate Fulanga's incredible lagoon as Fiji's top spot, and we're inclined to agree. A huge, sandy expanse dotted with tiny mushroom-shaped islets, it's a paradise for swimming and kayaking. Some cruisers spend weeks diving, snorkeling, and generally reveling in the scenery here. We were given a warm reception at the main village and later anchored in fifteen feet of sand in a seemingly endless pool of turquoise water. The visitor's fee here is F$50 per yacht.

Off the grid in Fulanga

Vanua Mbalavu ("Long Land") has several attractions. One is the main island, where you can visit different villages and take scenic walks. The biggest draw of the atoll is the

Bay of Islands, a compact but captivating spot where boats anchor among cliffy green islets. Snorkeling is good if not spectacular, and a number of caves dot the pocked shore. The village of Daliconi controls fishing rights to the Bay of Islands; do your sevusevu and pay a visitor's fee of F$30 per person there.

## Over the Top

Cruisers with time to linger can pick their way across the top of Viti Levu, staying within the fringing reef and calling at a number of pleasant anchorages. This calls for a keen eye on the chart plotter and, potentially, a fair amount of motoring.

Two places along the north coast merit special mention (map, #6). First, the diving off Nananu-i-cake Island and Volivoli Point is highly rated (book dives through nearby resorts). The nearby town of Rakiraki is a good place to re-provision. To get there, anchor off Ellington Wharf or Volivoli and grab a taxi to town (F$50 round trip), where there are large supermarkets, gas stations, banks, and an open-air farmer's market. On the minus side, there is no reliable source of drinking water in this area and the anchorages are deep (forty to sixty feet).

This northern route is especially attractive as a jumping off point for the Yasawas. We weighed anchor in Volivoli in the afternoon, put the brakes on for most of the fifty-five mile crossing of Bligh Water (yes, that Bligh, who passed through during his open boat odyssey after the mutiny of the *Bounty*), aiming for a dawn arrival off Round Island Passage at the northern end of the Yasawas.

## Under the Bottom: Kadavu and the South Coast

Alternatively, you can sail around the south side of Viti Levu and call in at Kadavu for its world-renowned diving. While the island is peppered with a few low-key resorts and villages, be prepared to be entirely self-sufficient in terms of provisions. Sailors without their own dive gear can book a trip with one of the resorts.

The only other notable point of interest along the south coast of Fiji is Likuri, where the Robinson Crusoe Island Resort hosts torchlit dance performances (map, #7). And from there? You're ready to slingshot around to the west side of Viti Levu and take your pick of several marinas (including Vuda Point and Denerau) or beautiful island cruising grounds.

# The West Side: the Mamanucas and Yasawas

Conventional wisdom seems to depict these island groups as spoiled and "not the real Fiji." A pity, because the development is hardly as intrusive as some insist. Having been warned of party-all-night resorts and corrupt villagers, we were delighted to find peaceful anchorages and friendly people. Even at the Blue Lagoon, the busiest spot in the Yasawas, we found "only" a dozen spread-out boats and a very low-key resort. Small cruise ships will drop anchor and claim sections of beach for their guests, but they move on quickly. Even at peak times, island trails are virtually unvisited, a walker's paradise for the taking.

The west side of the Yasawas is one big blank spot on the chart, except for bold letters: UNSURVEYED. A constant lookout for isolated dangers is a must, even if you stick to GPS tracks handed down by other sailors. The good news is that this side of Fiji is much drier and sunnier than the east, meaning good visibility.

The south end of Waya Island has some of the most stunning scenery in the Yasawas, while Drawaqa draws visitors with its promise of snorkeling with manta rays (often too many visitors, including resort guests). The Blue Lagoon is neither as spoiled nor as overcrowded as some claim, and we found it to be a lovely place to catch up on business, using the strong Internet signal. A local farmer also makes the rounds of the anchorage by skiff, making it possible to stock up on produce. Besides these well-known spots, there are a dozen other anchorages where you can hole up for a day or a week, claiming the views to yourself.

The Mamanucas are another minefield of reefs, though slightly better charted (map, #8). High, craggy islands draw intrepid sailors to the likes of Monuriki, where Tom Hanks' *Castaway* was filmed. Sooner or later, all roads lead to Musket Cove Marina, which offers moorings, dock space, and full access to resort facilities. Musket Cove is an aggregation point for cruisers, a great place to catch up with friends – starting with the pool and barbecue area!

# Looking Back

All good things must come to an end, and for most sailors, this means clearing out in Lautoka or nearby Vuda Point Marina (a new service that will hopefully be continued). The marina in Denerau is convenient to Nadi Airport for crew changes.

It seems we can never leave a place without declaring it another of our favorites, but that's the South Pacific for you. So what makes Fiji special? The friendly and outgoing people, for one thing. Varied landscapes (above and below sea level) are another, with a lot of superlative scenery packed into a relatively small space. Prices are good, too, especially for staples and the bountiful produce available in town markets. It's no wonder that some crews devote several seasons to Fiji, coming back again and again to visit old friends and favorite places. No matter how long you spend there, Fiji will provide memories for a lifetime.

# Chapter 45

# Fact File:
# Dispelling the Myth of Sevusevu

How often do you get an official audience with a real chief? Fijian custom dictates that visitors present themselves to village chiefs with an offer of yaqona, the root used to make traditional kava drink (available in dry bundles in all town markets). Not to worry; it's not as intimidating as it sounds. All it takes is stepping ashore and asking for the village headman (*Turanga ni Koro*). He will present you to the chief for what's usually a fifteen minute ceremony of chants and speeches. The only tricky part is clapping at the right moment and downing your kava in one swig. Kava is an acquired taste but only mildly heady; even a lightweight won't keel over from one bowl. Morning sevusevu might bypass the drinking part entirely, while afternoons sometimes turn into longer drink-a-thons.

Beware that an empty kava bowl will be refilled for a second (and third, and fourth) round unless you excuse yourself with a vital mission, such as visiting the local school or checking on your anchor. Coordinate with other crews for a group sevusevu, dress modestly, and ask before taking photos. The excellent *Mariner's Guide to Fiji*, a free booklet available in marinas, includes a detailed, three-page guide to all aspects of sevusevu.

A bundle of yaqona roots

# Chapter 46

# Southwest Pacific: Lessons Learned

Crossing an ocean on paper and on a boat are two vastly different exercises. In the years we spent dreaming about and then planning a Pacific crossing, we spent many an hour poring over charts, measuring and re-measuring distances, reading books and blogs. Foremost in our minds were the longest passages: 3,000 miles from the Galapagos Islands to the Marquesas, and 1,000 miles from Tonga to New Zealand. In comparison, the western end of the ocean seemed like a piece of cake. Only 500 miles from Fiji to Vanuatu, and a pesky 300 miles from Vanuatu to New Caledonia: mere stepping-stones that fall well within the span of a reasonably reliable weather forecast.

But the ocean is not made of paper; it's a liquid world that shifts and changes with every puff of wind, every change in air pressure. And the southwest Pacific, at least in our experience, is quite a different beast than its distant cousin to the east. We learned many a lesson along the way, one of which was that the southwest Pacific can be considered an ocean of its own.

## Westward Bound

Even with a three-year sabbatical, we are always mindful of a ticking clock in our cruising – particularly, the November onset of cyclone season in the Pacific. After two packed months of wonderful Fijian hospitality and scenery, it was time to move on for the last of our island landfalls: fascinating Vanuatu, then New Caledonia. Eventually, we would head on to Australia to sit out cyclone season out of the tropics. Leaving

Lautoka at noon one fine August day, we threaded through our last Fijian reef. *Namani's* bow pointed west into the setting sun for what would be a four-day passage to the island of Anatom in southern Vanuatu. We'd long since learned to treat GRIBs with a grain of salt, and sure enough, the wind was significantly higher than predicted. With twenty knots of wind from the south, we were humming along at six knots on a rhumb line course of 250°.

Nothing to complain about – except for a contrary southwest swell. We knew to expect that, too, but somehow hadn't imagined it being quite so uncomfortable, with regular dousings of our normally dry cockpit for the first forty-eight hours of the passage. Splish! One wave would try to sneak aboard from the starboard quarter. Splash! The next would bowl us over from port. All hatches remained sealed tight, the cabin a stuffy refuge from the elements. All the crews checking in on our informal SSB net were equally miffed. What happened to the pacific part of the Pacific?

It was the short period of the waves that did it, not the size (six to eight feet). Like the Inuit, who have multiple terms for different types of snow, I'm convinced that master Pacific navigators of old had a special name for this kind of swell: something with lots of vowels and a melodic Melanesian sound. My version, however, had just one syllable and four letters. The only way to achieve a more comfortable motion was to fall off the rhumb line by fifteen degrees. This is a recurring dilemma aboard *Namani*: whether to pay our dues early in a passage, or to gamble that we'll see easier conditions later. What to do? We gritted our teeth, hung on, and zipped our foul weather jackets tight.

By noon of the next day, the wind was up to thirty knots and we caved in, putting in a third reef and choosing a more comfortable westward heading in squally conditions. The slender arc of a beautiful crescent moon gave us something positive to focus on, its lazy lean a reminder of our latitude at 18°S. Back in Fiji, we had crossed the International Date Line and were now firmly in the realm of east longitude, another reminder of how very, very far we'd come from our starting point in Portland, Maine (70°W, for the record). Another sunny point in those cloudy days was the positive attitude of our son, who'd pop up on deck and declare it "not so bad!" before disappearing into his cozy quarterberth bunk. Back at age four, when we cruised the Atlantic for a year, he was the one most susceptible to seasickness. At the ripe old age of nine, he is practically immune.

The culinary arts pretty much went by the wayside on those first days, and we vaguely remembered the good old days, when passage-making meant a good book and the occasional batch of muffins. Now, we were in a constant game of Twister: right hand on the overhead rails, left hip bashing the corner of the chart table. Dodge flying cookie tin; spin again. A good thing to be said about short passages is that even when they get messy, the end is always in sight. Normally, we don't start our countdown until the last miles of a passage, but in this case, it kicked in as early as mile 262 of 489!

Conditions gradually eased over day three for a smoother ride on day four. The swell had gone on to bully other sailors in another part of the ocean, leaving us with a gentle bounce – a warning that further mischief awaited, perhaps. We opted to keep the main reefed despite wind down to fifteen knots to slow down for a morning arrival. It was with a sigh of relief that we lined up the range markers and entered reef-protected Anelcauhat Bay on the south side of Anatom (Aneityum). Crews who arrived two days later made it under gentler conditions but logged hours of engine time as the trade winds fell into a slumber. That's yet another trade-off of cruising: comfort and speed versus budget. We're not above kicking the engine on when we have no choice, but we generally try to spare diesel costs. In that sense, we certainly did pick a good weather window.

Making landfall on Anatom in Vanuatu

For the following month, we were enchanted by the people and landscape of Vanuatu, a magical place that earned top marks among so many Pacific highlights. We kept putting off our departure. One more island! Just one more! At the same time, we were digesting lessons learned. Continuing our intended course west to New Caledonia and Australia meant more south than west in our headings. The farther north we headed in Vanuatu, the less favorable the course to New Caledonia would be, given prevailing southeasterlies. For example, checking out of the islands at the capital of Port Vila would put *Namani* on a heading of 192°. Going as far north as Luganville on the island of Espiritu Santo would make it 182°. So we swallowed the bitter pill of compromise and ended our Vanuatu adventures at the midway point of the island nation. The next passage to New Caledonia was only 330 miles – but by now, we knew enough not to expect either quick or easy.

Dancers during a ceremony on Tanna

## Four's Company

It had been a long time since we had a friend aboard for an offshore passage, but we were happy to offer Danny, the twenty-something son of a fellow cruiser, a ride to New Caledonia. *Namani* now had a complement of four people. Hot-bunking and an extra plate to wash after mealtimes were more than worth the fine, fun company and an extra hand. With three adult crew, we now had the luxury of three-hour watches and a full six hours off, rather than our usual four hours on, four hours off. The extra rest time was well appreciated because our familiar companion, the sloppy swell, seemed determined to give *Namani* a wild ride.

We knew the first twenty-four hours wouldn't be pretty, but there aren't many nice options for the trip from Port Vila to southern New Caledonia's Havannah Pass. We decided to take the best from slim pickings and depart on an ESE wind forecast to go through the east and then to the north for a short time. The idea was to ride those winds for two days, then sit out a passing front and contrary winds with a pit stop in the Loyalty Islands. (Unfortunately, it's not possible to clear in to New Caledonia at the

294

Loyalties, so most sailors bypass the islands or make brief, discrete stops.) Once the headwinds moved on, we hoped to catch southeast winds on the tail end of the frontal passage for the last one hundred miles. Another great plan – on paper.

Of course, we'd learned to plan on the unexpected, so the plan was more of a vague hope, anyway. And a good thing, too, because things didn't develop quite according to the forecast. We did get twenty-five knot easterlies to blast us out of Vanuatu over the first twenty-four hours, along with the expected two meter, short period swell from the beam. *Namani* banged along on a close reach and endured sneaky below-the-belt punches of the competing swell lines. Our generally miserable crew hung on to the hope of better things to come – and if not, well, 300 miles isn't really all that far, not in the grand scheme of things.

Unfortunately, the frontal passage moved more slowly than anticipated, so that northerlies were still blowing when we hailed the island of Maré in the Loyalties. Without a good anchorage to shelter us from the north, we were forced to scrap our pit stop. The catch of a nice mahi mahi did much to boost crew morale as we pushed straight on for New Caledonia – and straight into the frontal passage. Flaky winds and intense lightning storms marked the front, making for an electrifying night. Markus called it "intense periods of light punctuated by brief flashes of darkness." Using the radar, we managed to sneak between the heaviest storm clusters and got through with nothing worse than jittery nerves.

Behind the front lay the southwest winds we had hoped to sit out in the Loyalties. Now tacking was on the menu as *Namani* inched toward a dawn arrival at Havannah Pass. The current there can reach four knots, so our timing was good for slack tide – with a little help from the iron genny. And once through – poof! – the slamming and grinding ceased; forward motion was no longer hard work but a pleasure. Having arrived on a Friday, we anchored in the quiet Bay of Prony for a little R&R before continuing on to Nouméa for a Monday clear-in.

Suddenly, we were in a completely different world. Having ducked under the curtain of clouds that cluster over Vanuatu, we emerged into a sunny new universe on the other side. Gone were the gray-blues of Vanuatu and the open ocean; this world was a startling aquarium of turquoise and pale blues. The lush, green heights of Vanuatu were replaced with the weeping red earth tones of New Caledonia. These testify to the island's rich mineral deposits, as well as man's greed in harvesting them. The tranquility and third-world charm of Vanuatu were behind us; we were back in France and a somewhat less endearing version of civilization. But New Caledonia's lagoon was a thing of wonder, and we were thrilled to spend many happy weeks exploring its reefs and sandy cays.

## Lessons Learned

So what ever happened to short and easy? A lesson we had long since learned had been reinforced: it's not distance but conditions that ultimately defines those terms. Our 3,000 mile passage between the Galapagos Islands and the Marquesas had been a dream of steady sailing in benign conditions, making those twenty-eight days the "shortest" passage in our wake. In contrast, these three and four day hops seemed much longer. Part of the reason was our heading: southeast winds can seem a lot less friendly when the bow is pointing SSW instead of west. Beyond that, the southwest Pacific consistently served up a different kind of ride – almost like an ocean of its own, where the long, steady swell of the eastern Pacific was replaced by a confused slop.

What accounts for the swell? This stretch of ocean is several thousand miles west of the carefree playground we left behind somewhere in the vicinity of Bora Bora. It's the home turf of the SPCZ and highly sensitive to the spillover of weather systems whisking by in the far south. The two can also gang up, for example, when frontal passages in the distant south connect with a branch of the SPCZ. Part of it may be a hemming-in effect: more islands, fewer swaths of open water to allow the swell to stretch out, plus an irregular underwater topography. No matter how much information we gathered on weather systems, convergence zones, wind and swell conditions, there was no predicting exactly how everything would align in terms of crew comfort. That's the ocean for you. If we wanted predictable, we'd never have left home.

The lesson, I suppose, is not to underestimate the sea – any stretch of it, no matter how short. But the rewards remain the same: the pride of having covered yet another inch of the globe, and the unique landscapes – cultural and physical – at either end of the trip.

# Chapter 47

# Paradise Unplugged: Southern Vanuatu

A Pacific crossing can bring the lucky cruiser to many pockets of paradise. But nowhere did we experience quite the raw, unadulterated version we found in Vanuatu. It's paradise unplugged: no power, no price tags, no Internet. Lush, green mountains where nature is king. A way of life that is both exotic and accessible. Visiting Vanuatu is like stepping into a photo spread of National Geographic magazine: we saw grass skirts, fierce face paint, and fiery volcanoes, all up close and personal. It's a place where some people worship a bizarre cargo cult and the national newspaper covers allegations of witchcraft in local sports competitions. What's not to love?

The south end of Vanuatu lies less than 500 miles WSW of Fiji, a four day passage for *Namani*. Heading for the southern end of the island nation and then working up the chain with the wind is a new privilege for cruisers: previously, customs and immigration could only be completed on Efate, in central Vanuatu. Many sailors skipped the hard slog against prevailing trade winds to the southern islands. As a result, the area doesn't have a cruised-out feel to it. Nowadays, the police in Anatom offer preliminary clearance. We found ourselves in a happy medium: neither pioneers nor too late to miss the real thing. As we worked our way north, we could also enjoy the thrill of open ocean sailing in small doses, either in long daily runs or quick overnights – a bonus for the mile-weary Pacific cruiser.

The minute we stepped ashore in Anatom, we realized that Vanuatu is different than its Melanesian neighbors. Our first impression was of a reserved population, particularly in contrast to the outgoing Fijians. Our reception in the village of Anelcauhat was polite but muted; people waved absently and went about their business, leaving us to go about ours.

## The Learning Curve

Lesson 1: Vanuatu Is Not Fiji. Nor is it New Caledonia, with its paved roads and first-world services. If Fiji made us feel like royalty and New Caledonia made us feel like tourists, the people of Vanuatu made us feel like neighbors. We were left to wander, pursue our own interests, and generally observe daily life like oversized flies on the wall. With time, we were also able to develop closer friendships with individuals, but nowhere else did we find the instant, easy acceptance that southern Vanuatu offered us.

It took us a while to figure all this out, however. On our very first shore expedition on Anatom, we hoped to hike to a distant waterfall. We were a little taken aback when we asked villagers the way.

"Oh, it's very far," said the first man, eyes on the ground.

"Um, it's private land," said the second, scratching his T-shirt.

"Er, it's easy to get lost," added a third, after a pause.

So which was it?

"The spirits could get you," chipped in a fourth man, genuinely concerned.

That, too?

We were starting to wonder whether they just preferred not to have strangers wandering around their island unaccompanied – a fair enough wish, after all. But then, it clicked. It was all of the above. Vanuatu has a complex belief system that can't easily be distilled into simple terms for the western mind. And that's part of the appeal: the mystery, the sense of always having something new to learn, no matter how much time you spend there. In that way, Vanuatu is much like sailing itself.

Eventually, we found a guide and thoroughly enjoyed a long day's outing to the waterfall, as much for the slippery rainforest trail as the cool cascade itself. The guide turned out to be a real bonus (and a fair deal, at US$5 per person). Young Elisha, like his fellow islanders, was reserved at first but more chatty as the day went on, teaching us about local customs and helping us trade for juicy grapefruit, plucked fresh from the tree.

We had spent the previous cyclone season in New Zealand, where outdoor activities are smoothly packaged and peddled. In Vanuatu, a minor tourist economy exists, but it's all in local, amateur hands. Advertising consists of a guy named Colin in a dugout canoe, inviting you to a roast pig feast. Which brings me to Lesson 2: There Is No Middleman. Doing "business" is like drinking from a pure mountain stream: the water trickles, clear and cool, straight from the source to the throat of the thirsty consumer. Delicious.

Call us slow learners, because it took us a while to catch on to this lesson, too. When Colin first approached with an offer for an evening of feasting and dancing – no hype, no hard sell – we nearly turned him down, feeling a little feasted-out after Polynesia. After all, there is only so much roast pig one can partake of. Or so we thought. The feast / cultural performance described in no-frills terms by Colin turned out to be one of the highlights of our stay. His extended family treated us to a delicious meal after explaining traditional ("Kastom") dances and costumes. Part of the night was devoted to Kava Drinking 101 (in brief: down-in-one, then "listen" for the effects of the drink). The evening was well worth the US$15 per person, money put toward paying school fees. The family elders see the program as a way of preserving traditional song and dance for the younger generation. It's a win-win for cruisers and locals alike.

After a day of snorkeling in search of sea turtles and reef sharks off nearby Mystery Island, it was time to weigh anchor and become sailors again. A quick afternoon's motorsail in the lee of the hills took us to the northern side of Anatom, where we secured the cabin for a brisk forty-three mile "passage" north to Tanna the next day. Even after a few days at rest, our sloop gets the look of a gypsy camp; "sailing" mode is very different than "at anchor." The trip north was a blustery beam reach in twenty knots and six foot seas. Navigation was easy, with a plume of "smoak" (as Captain Cook put it) from Tanna's volcano guiding us like a beacon. We struck the sails and puttered into Port Resolution, where the great Cook himself dropped anchor – on a bottom that has since been uplifted several feet by tectonic activity. Our chartplotter showed us anchored firmly on land, a clear warning as to the reliability of charts. Lucky for us, there are very few isolated dangers to mind.

## An Incredible Twenty-Four Hours

Tanna is a lot of things, but to us, it was the island of the most incredible twenty-four hours of our entire Pacific crossing. Things began on a Thursday at 3 p.m., when a rattling pick-up bounced us over hill, dale, and gully to visit the nearby hot spots – literally. First up was a village with steaming hot vents. The people there are members of a fascinating cargo cult set in motion by a mysterious 1936 foreign visitor named Jon

Frum (a bizarre story milked to the hilt by Jimmy Buffett in his novel, *A Salty Piece of Land*).

Next up: Mount Yasur, an active volcano. Very active! We climbed to the crater rim just in time for sunset and a spectacular nighttime sound-and-light show. Nicky called it the scariest and most amazing thing he's ever seen, and we adults agreed. The earth shakes and the mountain roars while the crater spews cow-sized chunks of orange-red lava into the sky. We were torn between staring into the mesmerizing red glow and fleeing for our lives. Is it safe? Kind of. Given the number of flip-flop shod tourists who make it home alive every year (entire families, including babies in little snuggle packs, all watching the pretty lava go up and down), it seems safe enough. Our guide assured us that the national park authorities enacted safety measures after two people died there in the early 1990s; visitors are no longer allowed as far as the rim if activity exceeds a "gentle" level two.

Mount Yasur was a spectacle of nature, and we were privileged to observe its cultural counterpoint early the next morning. A local boy was celebrating his coming of age, and the whole village was invited – including the crews of the eight boats in the bay. Think National Geographic Magazine: grass skirts, squealing pigs, ground-stomping dances. Yes, a bit of western culture has crept in: women use commercial dyes to color their grass skirts, and the master of ceremonies wore Nikes under his lavalava. But those are small distractions; the overall impression is of a timeless ceremony from the far side of the world.

But our busy social calendar was not yet complete, because we had agreed to a feast at noon. Our hosts, Nelson, Vivian, and Lea, explained that while primary education is free in Vanuatu, secondary school is extremely expensive – to the tune of US$500 per student per year. Hence the feasts they offer for a very fair $5, featuring traditional dishes like sticky laplap served on beautifully woven palm leaf plates, not to mention the obligatory roast pig. Did I say tourist economy? Scratch that. These family efforts have more in common with bake sales: honest fundraisers to bring in cash earmarked for a specific purpose. Our hosts were quick to point out that they live well off their lush land and rich seas. Their principal cash expenses are education and medicine.

By 3 p.m. Friday, we had enough impressions to last a week, and spent the next days decompressing in the familiar comfort of our floating home. It was during that time that we got to know Tom, a quiet local who paddled over asking to borrow tools. It's not something we do lightly when the nearest Home Depot is roughly 6,000 miles away, but Tom was good as his word, returning the tools the very next day. In return, Tom invited us to the late afternoon kava hour at the *nakamal*, the village meeting ground. That is to say, he invited Markus; it's a boy thing. (Sorry, ladies, you'll have to miss out on drinking mud-colored, mildly hallucinogenic liquid chewed and spit out by the

300

two guys over there. Shucks.) Markus described it as a hushed, ritual-heavy, Happy-Hour-meets-boy's-smoking-club and council meeting. After all, people who lack Major League Baseball and sports bars need their own release. Or do we North Americans have MLB and sports bars because we don't have kava? Lesson 3: It's All About Perspective.

## Island-Hopping Northward

Senses stuffed with rich impressions, we left Tanna for an overnight sail to the next island, getting spectacular night views of Mount Yasur in action. A crescent moon lay slumbering on its side as we crossed the line of 19° south latitude on our northwest course. Sailing along the windward coast of Tanna was slow and easy, with both wind and seas picking up as we broke into the open channel between islands. A sloppy swell seemed to dominate open water in this part of the Pacific, as it had on the entire passage over from Fiji.

Erromango, to our sensory-satiated relief, was a delightfully subdued experience. Even though Dillon Bay was a bit rolly, we enjoyed several days there. They don't get a lot of cruisers, but we were warmly greeted by two different villagers in dugout canoes. One, Donald, seemed purely interested in a little outside contact. The other, David, hopes to set up a yacht club on shore – a modest cruiser's hangout that would attract more boats if his long-range plan succeeds. It was a delight to make their acquaintance and we feasted on the fresh fruit they gave us for days.

Rather than slopping water to *Namani* to do laundry, we joined local women at the river for a washing spree. It turned out to be a delightful experience in which clean sheets were but a minor perk. The real joy was sitting on boulders among locals, our faces warmed by the sun, feet cooled by the water. The women whispered and giggled at our amateurish technique, then carried on. For a short time, we were just part of the gang. With thousands of gallons of fresh water rushing through our little eddy, our laundry has never been so clean. Our minds, too, were clearer for the experience, remembering that the majority of the world's population does not freshen their clothing with the press of a button. Yet another life lesson – and memorable experience – among many gained throughout a Pacific crossing.

One of our strangest Vanuatu experiences followed that evening, when we made a bonfire on the rocky beach to celebrate the eighth birthday of a cruising buddy. Out of the dark night came five men who peered at us from the shadows. Criminals? Cannibals, even? No, they were just five wetsuit-clad locals, drawn to the light between night dives for lobster. They seemed as fascinated by us and our rituals as we were by theirs, especially when the guitar came out for a few of the kids' favorites. Our new friends sang along to tunes familiar to all of us, including Frère Jacques and Old McDonald. Sitting under the moon by a bonfire singing E-I-E-I-O with a couple of burly Melanesians qualifies as one of the more surreal – and somehow touching – experiences of our three-year Pacific cruise. Lesson 4: Embrace Unlikely Encounters – as Markus did the next day when three armed men came out to *Namani* seeking help with a jammed hunting rifle. In short order, the problem was found and our new friends shown the source of the problem; wide grins flashed all around.

Erromango also provided Lesson 5: Every Island Is Different. And not just because there are over one thousand local languages. Land rights differ, too: on Anatom, we needed a guide for any walk outside the village. On Tanna, we could wander rough four-wheel-drive tracks to our heart's content, marveling at massive banyan trees and catching glimpses of tropical birds. On Erromango, villagers seemed confused that we even asked permission to walk. Had we taken a full day, we could have hiked as far as the sandalwood forest high in the hills. But with all that laundry, singing, and gun repair, well...

## Moving on to the Capital

Next stop: the capital "city" of Port Vila on Efate. Throughout the cloudy night, we counted down the eighty-five miles over rolly seas but made good time with twenty knots of SSE wind. No, there's no danger of losing your sea legs during your stay in Vanuatu! There must have been something in the night air, because we could see the glow of the capital from fifty miles away. In contrast, we couldn't pick up on any hint of New York City from that distance when we sailed past some years earlier.

Port Vila showed us the developed side of Vanuatu, with busy streets (cars, even!), shops, and a bustling port. The innermost harbor is very deep, so most cruisers take a mooring at Yachting World. There, we could (unenthusiastically) plug back into the outside world, making the most of the Internet, local restaurants, and services. We thoroughly enjoyed the national museum and its lively custodian, Edgar, who provided a lovely summation of what we had experienced thus far and what still lay ahead. We wanted to go everywhere, see everything: Ambrym, with its carvings, sand drawings, and giant tam-tam drums; Pentecost, home of land-diving; Espiritu Santo with its wreck dives; Epi and its dugongs; the Banks Islands, where few cruisers venture. And that's just the beginning of the list, all steppingstones for sailors bound for the Solomon Islands and beyond.

Alas, those heading west, like we were, face a difficult choice. The farther north one sails in Vanuatu, the tighter the wind angle to New Caledonia becomes. That and a prior commitment to meet family had us clearing out in Port Vila and setting a course to the SSW. You can't have it all, but as it was, our senses were near-saturated with so many rich experiences. And who knows? Someday, we might just be back for more.

# Chapter 48

# Fact File: Vanuatu

Clearing in: Anelcauhat on Anatom (preliminary), Lenakel on Tanna, Port Vila on Efate

Fees: Equivalent of US$60 to clear in for one month at Anatom, plus another $40 to complete the procedure in Port Vila; $70 to clear out. Extensions for a crew of four are expensive at about $250.

Money: Change cash (US / NZ / Fiji $ or Euro) for Vatu in the small banks of Anatom or Tanna (in Lenakel); ATMs in Port Vila.

Shopping: Come fully stocked until you can get to the very good supermarkets of Port Vila (Leader Price, Au Bon Marché). Fruit is plentiful and cheap.

Cruising Guide: The Tusker Cruising Guide to Vanuatu.[1]

Weather: The SPCZ practically hovers over Vanuatu. The general weather pattern we observed was clear mornings, clouding heavily in the afternoon, some showers, and steady fifteen to twenty knot SE winds.

Water: Jerry jug clean, fresh water from public water spouts in Anatom or fill at the fuel dock in Port Vila.

Health: The risk of malaria in southern Vanuatu is low during dry season. Many cruisers went without medication but were diligent about applying insect repellent.

Language: French and English are widely spoken in Vanuatu (carry-overs from colonial times that only ended in 1980), so it's joyfully easy to converse with locals. Bislama, a version of pidgin English, is one of the official languages. It's a logical, phonetic

---

[1] http://www.cruising-vanuatu.com

language that gave us many a hearty chuckle during our stay. In Port Vila, cell phone providers offer "*Laki Kash*" prizes and "*topup*" points so customers can have more time to "toktok." *Blong* is a word that means *for* or *of*; our favorite uses are in "*basket blong titi*" (bra) and "*mixmaster blong Jesus Christ*" (helicopter). It's *numbawan* (excellent)!

Dressed for the festivities

# Chapter 49

# Introducing New Caledonia's Idyllic Lagoon

Sailing New Caledonia? "It's horrible!" one sailor complained. "The water temperature today is only 25°C!" That's a frigid 77°F to us North Americans.

Yes, New Caledonia was spoiling us rotten with its balmy temperatures, French cuisine, and abundance of sea life. A dozen perfect anchorages within a startlingly turquoise lagoon, only a short sail away from first-rate provisioning in the capital city. Not to mention inland delights for those with the time and gumption to step away from the coast.

For two months, New Caledonia blessed us with "calendar" cruising: no matter where we pointed the camera, we had an award-winning shot. It was a different kind of cruising than we had experienced thus far in our Pacific crossing: short distances in a compact area with periodic runs to replenish supplies, meet visitors, or pick up parts. Refreshingly, charts are spot-on and aids to navigation well-maintained. At the same time, reefs and isolated dangers keep things just challenging enough. It's an aquatic wonderland accessible to part-timers and long-range cruisers alike, thanks to numerous charter bases operating out of Nouméa.

Every islet in the lagoon has its own charm, its own appeal. Many rival the most remote atolls of the Pacific in pristine beauty. And despite their proximity to the capital, we found ourselves blissfully alone at many a picture-perfect anchorage. Case in point: at the remote Cook Island of Suwarrow, we were one of thirty boats. In New Caledonia, we claimed entire anchorages for ourselves, time and time again. Of course, numbers swell on weekends when working sailors flee the mainland. That's when we the flexible head to the outermost islands or back to the capital for supplies.

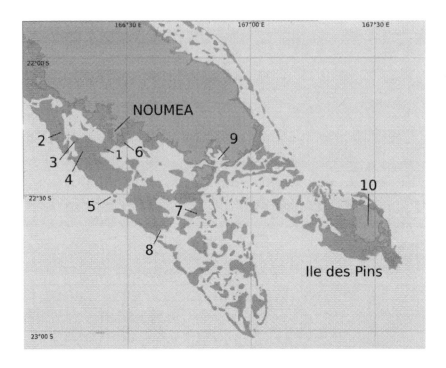

We arrived in New Caledonia with little idea of what to expect and left chock full of azure memories. May you do the same, with a little help from this introduction to the area's highlights. First, we'll have a look at the capital city, Nouméa; second, explore the islands on Nouméa's doorstep; and finally, move on to the true jewels farther afield.

## Nouméa

Call it ugly, call it busy, call it characterless; Nouméa is par for the course as far as South Pacific cities go. Like Tahiti's Papeete, it's a major boating hub with well-stocked grocery stores, chandlers, and yacht services of all types. Prices, like everywhere in the Pacific, are high, except for staples like the ubiquitous baguette. A few colonial-era buildings, the market place, and central park provide small doses of eye candy in an otherwise featureless cityscape. There are a number of interesting museums in Nouméa, starting with the outstanding Musée de Nouvelle Calédonie (with excellent, bilingual exhibits covering the breadth of Melanesia) and the Maritime Museum. Anyone waiting out a longer period in the city can enjoy beaches like Baie des Citrons and Anse Vata or take in hilltop views from Ouen Toro.

Between acres of anchorage room and the Port Moselle marina, you can always find a "parking" spot in Nouméa, although swinging space is tight. Clearing in and out requires some legwork, but most officials are friendly English-speakers, and the process is free. Port Moselle marina gives priority to overseas arrivals and will facilitate clearance procedures whether you're a guest or not. Generally, the visitor's dock turns over rapidly and it's sometimes possible to sublet a private slip there for a longer stay.

Nouméa was one of the few areas where we could reliably access the Internet, either through iNet (about $10 a week; buy at newsstands) or the marina WiFi. The snail-paced connection, however, pales in comparison to the excellent services back in Fiji.

Perfect sailing in New Caledonia's lagoon

## On Nouméa's Doorstep

Just a short sail out of Nouméa lies an embarrassment of riches in terms of anchorages – but even that hop is enough to transport the jaded city-goer to the wonders of the aquarium-like lagoon. Islands like Ilot Maître and Laregnère fall within protected marine sanctuaries and shelter the richest sealife. The turtles, sharks, rays, and occasional dugongs there are a confident lot and therefore much easier to snorkel among than the flighty denizens of unprotected areas. The marine reserves also provide free moorings – though it pays to check the line before trusting your boat to it.

For a quick escape from the city, nothing beats Ilot Maître, just four miles south of Nouméa (see map, #1). The proximity means weekend crowds of dozens, but the island falls back to an easy slumber on workdays. The water clarity and marine life are outstanding and dozens of mooring buoys await the lazy cruiser. Although the shoreline is marred by hotel bungalows, a drink at the hotel bar buys you Internet access, making Maître a good place to monitor weather reports for an upcoming passage while staying within spitting distance of the city for a final provisioning run.

Ilot Mbe Kouen, fourteen miles northwest of Nouméa, feels like a place on the edge of the world (map, #2). We shared this reef-encircled anchorage with just one other boat and spent days playing Robinson Crusoe on the sandy cay. It's also a reliable spot for dugong sightings; at least one regular spiced up our quiet days. On weekends, the "crowd" swelled to six boats, many of them kite surfers who put on a spectacular show. There's no wind shelter at Mbe Kouen, but the reef proved to be an effective barrier during a period of thirty-knot southeasterlies we sat out, comfortably anchored in fifteen feet over a sandy bottom.

Ilot Laregnère (map, #3) and Ilot Signal (map, #4) are neighboring islands and protected marine reserves with free mooring buoys seven miles from Nouméa. The wildlife is well accustomed to visitors; we were able to snorkel casually alongside sea turtles here rather than stealing furtive glances as in other areas. Another reptile well represented is the Tricot Rayé, New Caledonia's striped sea snake. They're fascinating creatures that move easily between land and sea. Though poisonous, these sea snakes are perfectly safe – the venom is located so far back in the throat, you'd have to force one of the poor creatures into biting you. A walk around either island provides an opportunity to stretch your legs, beach-comb, and observe nesting sea birds.

Phare Amedée (a lighthouse) is a New Caledonian landmark (map, #5). The tiny island and marine reserve are only fifteen miles from the capital, but feel like a different world. The slender lighthouse was built in France in 1862, then shipped and reassembled here. It's open to visitors for spectacular bird's-eye views over the lagoon (daily from 11:00 to noon – more or less – for a small fee). The island and reef offer only partial protection, so the mooring field can get rolly. Otherwise, it's a lovely place right at the edge of the ocean, and Boulari Pass is a perfect staging point for a passage west. Reef sharks, turtles, sea snakes, and sea birds are all plentiful here, drawing the occasional excursion boat from Nouméa. At those times, the island feels too busy with its snack bar and SCUBA center, but things settle down quickly in the afternoons. Overall, we reveled in the special atmosphere of the place, spending a magically calm night under the sweeping beam of the lighthouse.

Ile Uere is a horseshoe-shaped island just outside Nouméa, with excellent protection and holding (map, #6). It's a pretty spot with nice night views of the city lights, just outside the hustle and bustle of it all. It's the perfect place to ride out a storm or escape the city for a few days, and a great place for young children who enjoy calm water. Avoid weekends, though, when the watersports crowd takes over.

## Farther Afield

The following anchorages are either a long day's sail or a two-day hop from Nouméa and therefore attract fewer weekend warriors. Ilot Mato and Kouare are idyllic drops of green in the blue lagoon, while Prony offers a taste of an entirely different landscape in ochre and red. As for Ile des Pins – well, that gem is in a class of its own.

Ilot Mato is an excellent stopover point for those heading to Ile des Pins and an anomaly as one of the few high islands in the lagoon (map, #7). Its forty meter peak offers a lovely panorama of the southern end of the lagoon with its incredible aquamarine color palate. The reefs ringing the anchorage provide nice, if not spectacular, snorkeling, with glimpses of reef sharks along the way. There's space for dozens of boats, though we had this beauty all to ourselves in the middle of the week.

The best snorkeling we found in the lagoon was at Ilot Kouare (map, #8). Water clarity varies with the tide, but hit it just right and the craggy, colorful reef will amaze you with its variety, length, and multi-story structures. There are three different anchorages on all sides of the island, making it a safe bet in all but the hardest blow.

Baie de Prony is a wide bay from which several fingers branch out, a mini cruising ground in its own (map, #9). A winding trail leads from Bonne Anse, the southeastern-most arm of the bay, to the lighthouse and whale observation post on the top of the hill, with views all the way to Ile des Pins. At the head of the bay is Baie du Carenage, a hurricane hole of a creek with a natural hot spring. The landscape is harsh but beautiful in its own way, with red earth and the low scrub typical of the mainland.

Ile des Pins deserves a chapter in itself (map, #10). For us, this eight-by-eight mile island was one of the highlights of the entire Pacific for its laid-back character and variety. Baie de Kuto is the perfect place for an extended layover; we spent a happy ten days there in a picture-perfect bay ringed by the namesake pines. There's a boulangerie and small shop where you can stock up on fresh supplies. You can treat yourself to a meal at one of the hotels or just hide away from it all. And yes, there's even iNet Internet coverage out in the bay.

Back to back with Kuto is Baie de Kanumera with its gorgeous shoreline and pleasant snorkeling. A short walk brings you to the ruins of the jail that housed France's political exiles in the 1870s. For an active day out, hike the 262-meter Pic N'ga or rent a bike from one of the low-key resorts to visit the old town of Vao and pretty Baie de Saint Joseph, home port to many traditional pirogues (sailing canoes). The hardy can even circle the entire island with a stop at Baie d'Oro with its *piscine naturelle* (natural pool).

The catch? Kuto is a favorite of cruise ships, which visit as often as three times weekly and disgorge thousands of sunburned passengers at a time. However, these visitors herd at one end of the beach, leaving wide swaths of peace and quiet for those willing to walk a few minutes. The advantage of cruise ship day is that local families set up barbecue stalls along the beach, your opportunity for a break from standard galley fare.

Weather protection is another issue. While Baie de Kuto is a deep scoop in the island's shape, heavy westerlies will occasionally heave into the bay. That's the time to circle around to Kanumera. While Kuto may have a dozen or more yachts at a time (rest assured, the bay can hold many times that), other parts of the island see fewer boats, such as beautiful Baie de Ouameo. A number of off-lying islets offer good day or overnight anchorages, as well.

All the highlights described here cluster around the southwest end of New Caledonia. Sailors with more time can explore more of the lagoon, heading northwest along the leeward shore of the mainland, or better yet, overnight out to the Loyalty Islands to the east. Local sailors give Ouvea (the northernmost of the three Loyalties) top marks, thanks to its beautiful lagoon.

Still, most cruisers "confine" themselves to the southwest corner of the lagoon, an experience as liberating as any in the South Pacific. Again and again, we were amazed at how quickly we could get away from it all just in the compact area described. In fact, we postponed our departure for Australia again and again, drinking our fill of the lagoon's wonders for a full two months before bidding it a fond *au revoir* – until we meet again.

# Post Script: New Caledonia Fact File

## Inland Sights

Inland travel will reveal an entirely different side of New Caledonia: rugged red mountains sprinkled with sleepy Kanak (native Melanesian) hamlets. With a one or two day car rental (check Pointe Rouge near Orphelinat for the best rates), it's possible to quickly tour north to Bourail with its intriguing coastline and Sarramea for lush mountain scenery. The most spectacular coastal scenery is found in the far north, in places like Voh and Hienghène. Our top pick for an active day trip is Rivière Bleue, a provincial park located ninety minutes south of Nouméa by car. There, we exercised long-forgotten muscles with a combination mountain bike / kayak excursion (call ahead to reserve; see *www.sudloisirs.nc*). The hiking trails at Rivière Bleue are a good bet for spotting wild cagou, the graceful national bird of New Caledonia.

## Bits and Pieces

Money: The Cour de Franc Pacifique (CFP) is a currency tied to the Euro, familiar to cruisers who have visited French Polynesia (take a close look: every bill has a Polynesian and a Melanesian-themed side).

Provisioning: Carrefour and Casino supermarkets are both in walking distance of the Nouméa anchorages.

Cooking: Only butane is available in New Caledonia, and only approved bottles (the round blue type) will be filled. To fill any other type of bottle, you will need to gravity-feed using an adaptor.

Customs and clearance: Quick, easy, and free for a three month stay. Ask for the information sheet at Port Moselle marina that details the procedure and locations. Unlike French Polynesia, New Caledonia does not require a bond of visiting North American sailors.

Cruising guide: *The Cruising Guide to New Caledonia*, an excellent electronic guide, is available from cruising-newcaledonia.com. It is based on the 1996 print book and was updated in 2012.

Information: Check Julie Harris' outstanding English-language blog – with everything from tips on day trips to local culture to latest news and events.[1]

---

[1] http://www.newcaledoniatoday.wordpress.com

# Chapter 50

# You Can't Have It All: Comparing Two Routes from Vanuatu to Australia

Throughout our Pacific crossing, we were hounded by a recurring dilemma: which way to go? From the Galapagos Islands, we could set a course for either Easter Island or the Marquesas, but not both. It was difficult to choose between the widespread atolls of the Tuamotus, just as we later struggled to decide which of the Cook Islands to call at, or whether to sail to Tonga via Samoa or Niue. At every juncture, we seemed to face an either / or situation. You simply can't have it all, not without multiple seasons and a lot of upwind sailing.

So it was no surprise that a last set of choices confronted us at the westernmost end of the South Pacific, raising the inevitable conundrum once again. We'd already spent a month in the southernmost islands of Vanuatu. Should we devote several more weeks to exploring the fascinating island cultures of central Vanuatu or divide our time equally with New Caledonia? Visit remote reefs like Huon and Chesterfield en route to Queensland or sail a direct course for Sydney in New South Wales? Many questions, no easy answers.

Night after night, we of *Namani* and our friends on *Victoria* (Kay and Heike, with sons Hannes and Niclas, ages five and seven) hashed over the choices. Both boats were moored in Port Vila on the island of Efate in September, and both were ultimately headed to Brisbane, Australia to conclude our cruises. But which way to go? Compromise hung thick in the air like one of the daily rain showers we came to count on in Port Vila.

Ultimately, *Namani's* route was dictated by two factors. First, we were scheduled to meet a relative in New Caledonia, and second, the image of a spectacular New Year's Eve in Sydney (front-row seats guaranteed!) called to us like a siren. That meant less of Vanuatu and by-passing the remote reefs – a tough pill to swallow. On the other hand, we would get a good taste of New Caledonia's incredible lagoon, not to mention a lovely family visit, plus insight into French-Melanesian culture to round out our Pacific experiences.

*Victoria's* crew couldn't quite drag themselves away from Vanuatu. They also liked the idea of visiting remote reefs and breaking the passage to Australia into shorter chunks. Therefore the Vanuatu – Huon – Chesterfield Reef route seemed a natural choice. Since they were planning to tour Australia by land after putting *Victoria* on the market, a long sailing detour to Sydney didn't appeal.

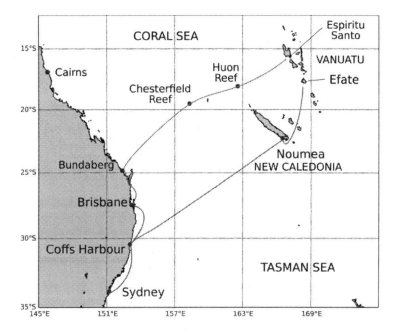

So when we bid each other farewell in Port Vila – *Victoria* sailing north to see more of Vanuatu while *Namani* looked for a weather window for her passage to New Caledonia – each crew wondered if they had made the right decision. When you've traveled halfway around the world, it can be hard to let enticing destinations slip past, closer than they'll ever be, yet oh so far. Only one thing was certain: we'd have a lot of stories to trade at our next reunion.

# Central Vanuatu and Huon Reef

Following the path less traveled, the crew of *Victoria* extended their visas (roughly US$250 for a crew of four) and devoted a second month to the fascinating islands of Vanuatu. Mask dances on Ambrym, land diving on Pentecost, and the dugongs of Epi provided one rich experience after another for parents and kids alike. When the time came to clear out in Luganville on the island of Espiritu Santo, they could do so knowing the next passage was relatively short (280 nautical miles) and on a comfortable heading of 240°.

Both families would later agree that the first twenty-four hours out of Vanuatu were the worst part of either passage, marred by the sloppy, confused seas that seem to haunt this part of the Pacific. The sea state gradually settled down as steady southeasterlies carried *Victoria* west, away from the islands and scattered undersea mounts. Only then could life on board fall back into the comfortable rhythm they knew from so many previous blue water passages.

The reef at Huon barely scratches the ocean surface, so the chart plotter came in handy as *Victoria* circled to enter from the leeward side – a far cry from places like Suwarrow where the atoll's outline was discernible from a fair distance. Within a mile of the entrance, however, isolated reef patches were clear to the naked eye and piloting in proved straightforward. *Victoria* was immediately greeted by legions of birds, almost Hitchcockian in number and tendency to swoop in for close fly-overs. As soon as the sloop was anchored, several birds took up watch, perching on the radar and even the anchor chain. Sea birds number in the thousands in this pristine area; leaving their mark on *Victoria's* solar panels became a daily ritual.

Going ashore on the lone, scrubby islet at Huon meant stepping carefully around scores of bird nests. October was also mating season for green sea turtles: three or four males queued up for every female and the sand was riddled with tracks of nesting females, who lay multiple clutches over several weeks. Having heard that male turtles can become aggressive at this time of year, the visiting sailors weren't too tempted to snorkel. They did, however, paddle ashore for hushed nocturnal visits, observing female turtles excavate nests and lay their eggs. Huon proved to be a natural wonderland shared by only two crews. Paradise, indeed.

The catch? While *Victoria's* anchor had a good grip on the sand bottom thirty feet below, a persistent swell worked its way over the low reef. Thus life at anchor was rocky and shuttling ashore with two children proved challenging at times. As the wind increased from fifteen knots to twenty and more forecast to come, Heike and Kay weighed their options. Although they could have safely waited things out at anchor (other sailors report no problems in even thirty to forty knot winds), they would have been boat-bound for several days. Not an enticing prospect with two energetic boys on board! Therefore the family decided to continue on to Chesterfield Reef after three days in Huon. For the fifteen ton, forty-three foot steel boat, that 280 mile passage would translate to three routine nights at sea.

Boobies on Chesterfield Reef

## New Caledonia

*Namani* set off for New Caledonia in early September, guts wrenching not only at the thought of what we'd be missing in Vanuatu, but also at the rough seas. Twenty knots on a close reach and sloppy seas do not a pleasant passage make, short though it may be at 330 miles. We consoled ourselves with the knowledge that our heading of 192° from Efate still beat the grittier 182° from Luganville to New Caledonia. When the weather didn't develop quite as expected, we found ourselves right in the path of a messy frontal passage, marked by a rather (ahem) exciting night of lightning. With the wind on the nose at our arrival at Havannah Pass, *Namani* – all thirty-five feet, six tons, and thirty-five horsepower of her – chugged slowly in toward her destination.

If the passage left much to be desired in terms of comfort, New Caledonia surpassed all expectations. Our memories will forever be saturated with the aquamarine hues of the incredible lagoon, where we claimed many a lovely anchorage for ourselves. For two months, we savored idyllic, short-distance sailing from tiny, uninhabited islet to islet, not to mention plenty of water playtime – drinking our fill, so to speak, before heading on to the crocodile, shark, and jellyfish-infested waters of Australia. Often, we felt as remote as we've ever been, despite being within a day's sail of Nouméa. We were also delighted to find sailing friends, old and new, in New Caledonia – and set about a full schedule of dinner parties and beach outings with up to six kids.

Throughout the month of October, we had our eyes open for a weather window west. Without an intermediary stopping point along our 865-mile route, we wanted a good, stable window on which to depart. Our chance came on October ninth, when we slipped the public mooring at Ile Amedée, waved goodbye to the historic lighthouse, and headed out Boulari Pass for the Coral Sea.

## Chesterfield Reef to Queensland

*Victoria* was ahead of *Namani* in continuing her trip west, first from Huon to Chesterfield Reef and then on to Australia. The only uncomfortable part of the passage from Huon to Chesterfield was an awkward morning arrival, which meant circling the reef, then squinting into the sun while the boat bucked the contrary wind and current to reach the shelter of the reef. Ultimately, however, Heike judged both Huon and Chesterfield to be easier to approach than many of the reefs we'd run back in Fiji. The fact that both Chesterfield and Huon Reefs have wide approaches that can be run at virtually any time is also a bonus.

While most of Chesterfield Reef lies beneath the surface, sailors can orient themselves by a tiny chain of islands that can be traversed on foot at low tide. The long reef provides extended anchoring possibilities, meaning any boats (all three of them, at the time of *Victoria's* visit) could spread out as far as they wished. Chesterfield's vibrant colors delighted both the eye and camera lens: white sand, green-blue shallows, fair blue skies. There were sea turtles aplenty, if not the same bustle of activity witnessed at Huon. Snorkel expeditions revealed nice, if not spectacular, coral and fish (standards by this point in a Pacific crossing being fairly high), and though Heike and Kay longed to visit the outstanding dive sites they read about, they couldn't quite fit SCUBA diving into their six day stay.

In Chesterfield as in Huon, the family marveled at their pristine surroundings. With good holding in thirty feet of sandy bottom and better protection than at Huon, crews with sufficient provisions can linger in this aquatic Garden of Eden for weeks. But sooner or later, the time comes to move on. Heading west to Australia means negotiating a different pass with a favorable tide; nothing this experienced crew hadn't handled before. Rather than heading directly to the shallows of metropolitan Brisbane, *Victoria's* crew decided to clear in to Australia in Bundaberg, a quiet port of entry with an easy approach. Giving intermediate reefs a wide berth, they set a course of 225° for Bundaberg, 450 miles away.

It was to be their last ocean passage: four relaxed days and nights of pleasant sailing aboard the floating home that had carried the family halfway around the world. Landfall was a muted event, since the low coast was not visible until a few miles away. The approach was easy and customs officials extremely friendly – and thorough. Even the deepest nooks and crannies of *Victoria* were checked with the help of flashlights and mirrors. A good thing this crew had nothing to hide! After a week spent decompressing in Bundaberg, *Victoria* day-tripped her way 185 miles south to Scarborough (a suburb of Brisbane), where the steel sloop would find a buyer within six weeks of arrival.

## New Caledonia to New South Wales

After balking at several weather windows not quite stable enough for our liking, we on *Namani* finally dragged ourselves away from New Caledonia. And a good thing, too, because the pronounced high-pressure system we rode turned out to be the last chance for several weeks. Waiting any longer would have pushed us into cyclone season (at least, the insurance company's definition of cyclone season). Having spent two months in sheltered waters, we needed twenty-four hours to find our sea legs again, but smooth seas and sunny weather made for a pleasant start. *Namani* herself had no such issues, romping into blue water at a six knot pace.

Our log book reports all the hallmarks of a comfortable passage: reading, baking bread and brownies, home schooling, not to mention the occasional bucket bath and dolphin sightings. For once, wind and seas direction matched, both abaft the beam. Our only concern was how long the fair conditions would hold. The forecast called for a trough and a low to sweep over the coast of east Australia about eight days after our departure from New Caledonia. We'd have just enough time to squeak in ahead of it – if the trough developed as foreseen.

Weather was just one of several "invisible" factors influencing our trip. Another was the current: not only the mighty East Australian Current, but also the large eddies swirling through the Coral and Tasman Seas (delineated roughly along the line of 30°S). Even half a knot of speed could make the difference in avoiding the trough, so we made several course alterations to skim contrary eddies along the way. Finally, there were also seamounts to dodge, not for any solid danger but for the lumpy seas they can kick up.

Taking the south-setting East Australia current into account, we took aim for a way point well north of our destination, Coffs Harbour. But as *Namani* approached the coast, so too did the oncoming trough, along with high wind warnings and an increasing swell. If we didn't make it in to port by about noon on Saturday, we risked hitting thirty knot headwinds. And so the race was on for the last forty-eight hours of our passage. By Friday night, the wind was a mere puff and the sky alive with lightning, heralding the arrival of the trough.

Thus all the action in our week-long passage was squeezed into the last twelve hours, which went by in a flurry of sail changes and anxious skyward glances. The wind waffled, puffed, and suddenly roared to a hefty thirty-plus knots on the beam. We hastily reefed both sails and held on in building seas. As *Namani* paralleled the coast south, we ticked off beacons and steeled ourselves for an unpleasant finale. But luck was on our side: the wind mellowed just as quickly as it came, leaving us to cover the final twenty miles on a gentle beam reach.

Having sailed 916 miles in eight days, we made landfall just in time: 10:00 on Saturday, November 16. Two hours after our anchor bit in, a hailstorm shot holes straight through our dodger and vicious winds howled throughout the night. We were pleased to play turtle in *Namani's* snug shell and grateful that Coffs Harbour customs agents allowed us to anchor out and wait for a Monday clear-in. At this point in our seafaring careers, an extra thirty-six hours on board was far preferable to the high cost of a weekend check-in.

For us, Coffs Harbour was a manageable port of entry that cut 185 miles off a direct passage to Sydney (1,050 miles) – a difference that would have found us taking the brunt of the trough's effects at sea. Once the trough passed, we headed south from Coffs Harbour in favorable conditions and spent an unforgettable month in Sydney. Few sailors had as much cause for celebration at the incredible New Year's fireworks as the crew of *Namani*! Once the holiday revelry settled down, it was time for us, too, to set course for our final 500-mile passage to Brisbane. For us, the detour to Sydney was well worth the effort, rounding out an incredible Pacific crossing with a bang.

## Reunion in Queensland

Four months after parting ways in Vanuatu, *Namani* and *Victoria* were reunited in Queensland. Having shared so many difficult decisions, we could now compare notes on the two different routes. So many stories to share, so many pictures to admire! It was also time to set a new course for the future, as both families wrapped up their cruises and slowly packed for home. Sadly, the time had come to sell our floating homes and ease ourselves back into "real" life.

Which crew chose the better path? In the South Pacific, there's no such thing as a single "best." We'll all look back on incredible places, cultures, and experiences. We'll all treasure the days of good health, dear friends, and fair seas. And yes, we'll all dream of someday, maybe someday, coming back for more.

# Part X

# Australia

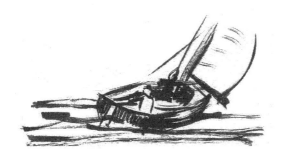

# Australia

For many sailors, Australia is more of a practical place for a layover than a place to cruise. For some, it's just a convenient pit-stop before heading on to Indonesia, Asia, or the Indian Ocean. For others, it's the end of the line – including crews like us, who concentrate their sailing time in the Pacific and then sell the boat Down Under.

But what about actually sailing in Australia, just for the sake of it? What we discovered was a mixed bag. Sailing the east coast of Australia is a lot like visiting the Outback: you'll find a couple of attractive hot spots separated by long stretches of open country – or in this case, challenging coastal passages that will keep you on your toes. But just like the Outback, the exceptions make the journey more than worthwhile.

This section covers both the exploration and the business sides of sailing in Australia, with chapters describing stunning Sydney and its multi-faceted neighbor, Pittwater. Then we zoom the focus out to cover a coastal passage to Brisbane and the island-hopping route up the Queensland coast to Cairns and the Great Barrier Reef. Last but not least, we provide a primer on selling a boat in Australia for the sad day when it's time to part ways with your floating home – a process that's not as complicated as the coconut grapevine sometimes makes it out to be.

# Chapter 51

# The Pot of Gold at the End of the Rainbow: Sailing Sydney

When we left Portland, Maine in September 2011 for points south, we programmed two way points into the GPS: one for the Isles of Shoals, sixty miles away, and another for Sydney, Australia. That's 8,954 nautical miles, as the albatross flies. That way point mesmerized us, the pot of gold at the end of the rainbow. Not that we wanted to rush through the bands of colors along the way: the incredible islands, cultures, and experiences of the Pacific. But since our cruise had to end sometime, we wanted it to end with a bang. Where better than under the New Year's Eve fireworks in Sydney Harbor?

Two-and-a-half years later, we sailed under the Harbour Bridge aboard *Namani*, a dream come true. But we quickly realized there's more to Sydney – much more – than "just" the iconic sights of one of the world's greatest natural harbors. This superlative city exceeded our expectations – in variety, for one thing, and in manageability, for another. We'd expected expensive marinas; what we got were frcc anchorages and public moorings, both within the bustling central harbor and in the quiet pockets of bushland right around the corner. All with fantastic sailing conditions, to boot. Sydney truly is a place where sailors can go walkabout for weeks, even months.

Visiting during the holidays made the occasion even richer, with concerts, Christmas lights, New Year's celebrations – all in summertime, no less. Throw the start of the famed Sydney-Hobart race under the Christmas tree and you get ten days of nonstop highlights – plus a stocking stuffer: the option to hide away from it all in a quiet nook of your own.

# A First Glance

Our pulses were soaring as we rounded the cliffs of North Head and steered *Namani* into the city for the first time. The initial view isn't striking; with a tight corner hiding the inner bay, we could forgive Captain Cook for sailing straight past, making only a passing note about "a Bay or Harbour wherein there appeared to be safe anchorage which I call'd Port Jackson." It wasn't until 1788 that convict settlers of the First Fleet stumbled across the inner harbor and laid the foundations of what would become a spectacular city.

The moment we turned that tease of a corner, iconic views of modern Sydney were ours, there for the taking in the form of several hundred camera clicks. The Opera House, the "coathanger" bridge, the contrast of a high rise city with peaceful swaths of green. Having been to Sydney before, it was all familiar, but arriving aboard our own boat was still thrilling – especially after sailing from halfway around the world.

Inside the sentinels of North and South Head, the harbor immediately splits into three parts: North Harbour, with the beachside city of Manly; Middle Harbour, an oasis of green; and the inner harbor, which narrows, then splits again into the Lane Cove and Parramatta Rivers. Each of these sections is a sailor's paradise, scalloped with smaller bays. So where to begin?

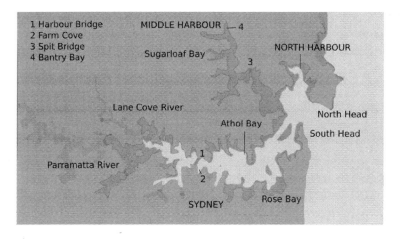

Our first instinct was to head for the center of action, and we spent two nights anchored directly across from the Opera House in Athol Bay, practically choking on the views. The immediate shoreline, part of Sydney Harbour National Park, proved perfect for extended walks in the shade. It's also the home of the Sydney Zoo, with close-up views of koalas, platypus, and echidnas, and an easy place to hop a ferry downtown. While it takes luck to snag one of the few public moorings in Athol Bay, we were happy to drop

328

the hook amidst a fleet of pleasure craft, large and small.

However, the downsides of Sydney are twofold: the density of water traffic means that the water is always churning, and almost every bay is packed with moorings. Although Athol Bay is clear of the latter, it's plagued by wakes, and the constant roll had us thumbing through our cruising guide for some escape. We quickly discovered a number of bays with enough space – plenty of space, in fact – to anchor in reasonable depths (thirty feet, give or take), both in the inner harbor and in the side branches. Who needs a $250 / night marina when you've got sturdy ground tackle? Over our entire month's stay in the greater Sydney area, we anchored for free. When the wind chased us around the harbor, we could always duck into another corner of the maze.

And the wind did shift – constantly – during the month of December that we lingered in and around Sydney. Tired of the constant roll and expecting an imminent southerly change (the abrupt wind shift that comes with a passing of a Tasman Sea low), we moved to Rose Bay, just a little farther out from the center of action. There we enjoyed unobstructed views of the city skyline with a fraction of the wake wash. Rose Bay offers good protection from the south and east with a good mile of shoreline free of moorings. Local amenities include a supermarket, a beautiful public library, waterside parks, and easy connections downtown, just twenty minutes away.

When a high pressure system piped in wind from the north, we'd head out as if to sea, then pull a hard left into Middle Harbour. It's a quick six-mile trip that we learned to time just right for the opening of Spit Bridge. Once through, we'd circle into either Sugarloaf or Bantry Bay, serene backwaters encircled by nature preserves. The area is all bushland, full of walking trails where keen eyes might pick out the occasional echidna or swamp wallaby. At night, cockatoos squawk and preen. All in all, it's a world apart from the city, yet still within city limits. Sugarloaf Bay is a place where you really can have it all: a peaceful day in a perfectly placid anchorage, or a day out on the town, thanks to nearby bus routes. Where in the world can you find the same? It's there that we spent a lovely Christmas, hermited away for one special day.

Soon, we established a pleasant rhythm of two or three days in the splendor of the city, then two or three relaxing in the peace of the bush. With the holidays upon us, every second day brought a special event. It started with a night at Carols on the Domain, a free city concert with big name entertainment, and continued with engagements with friends. Making up for the lack of a white Christmas were Christmas barbecues and beach outings – not quite what we're used to back home!

## Holiday Fun, Holiday Madness

Boxing Day, December 26, is not just a day to sort through crumpled wrapping paper – not when you're in Sydney. This day sees the start of the 630-mile Sydney-to-Hobart race in the inner harbor. Entrants range from professionals aboard hundred-foot maxi yachts to amateurs on thirty-five footers – all madly circling the starting line as a fleet of spectator craft attempt to avoid collision. We opted to stay away from the melee and climbed the heights of South Head for an overview instead. There we could observe not only the start but also the fleet's progress into the open sea.

Given the weather forecast, we watched with the sick fascination of spectators waving gladiators off to the arena, wondering what fate they might meet. The 2013 event headed straight into a gale predicted to bring seventy-knot gusts and thirty-foot waves. Over the next few days, newscasts showed sobering images of huge racing yachts sporting tiny orange storm sails in a neck-to-neck race for the finish. Eventually, ten of ninety-four yachts retired, including one dismasting and a broken rudder.

The next big event was one that had us wondering what damage our own hull might sustain: New Year's fireworks over Sydney Harbor. We'd long dreamed of having front-row seats from our own floating home, but we were spooked by stories of mayhem on the water. Were we willing to risk it? If so, where, given the armada of pleasure craft (in various degrees of seaworthiness and sobriety) all vying for prime views? Minding the official exclusion zones, we whittled the choices down to three. You can't get any closer to the action than Farm Cove, beside the Opera House. However, that close seemed a little too close. (Indeed, sailors later reported a nightmare of boats anchored on too-short scopes, dragging and bumping all night.) The second option is Athol Bay, but that's not only next to the zoo, but a zoo of boats on New Year's Eve.

We opted for the third choice, Rose Bay, where we could sit back and relax until the fireworks started – all three rounds. Sydney puts on a family show at 9 p.m. as appetizer, offers a brief 10:30 palate cleanser, and finishes with a main course at midnight. It's a show that capitalizes on both the lovely harbor setting and city architecture. That night made our 500-mile detour to Sydney (off a course to our eventual destination, Brisbane) completely worthwhile.

Between the special events and quiet days at anchor, we thrilled in great sailing in brisk winds, yet protected waters. What can beat tacking from the Opera House to South Head, or gliding downwind under the Harbour Bridge? It's thrilling, too, given the traffic on the water, from high speed ferries (who always, always, have right of way) to navy vessels and pleasure craft of all sizes skippered by the brightest and dimmest of bulbs. The good news is that commercial shipping and flights are all concentrated in Botany Bay, well south of Sydney. It would be hard to imagine the harbor getting any busier, especially around the bottleneck off the Opera House. Still, I wouldn't trade a minute's worth of winching in the sheets in this setting for an hour of sailing any other city in the world.

Enjoying a sail in Sydney Harbour

## The Third Half: Broken Bay

For all the city bustle and quiet getaways, there's even more just around the corner. I'll borrow a line from Yogi Berra and call it the "third half": the waterways that fan out from Broken Bay, twenty miles north. That's where you'll find Pittwater, where moorings fill every inch of coveted shoreline and several charter companies base their fleets. The narrow bay explodes with sailboats during weekend and weekday evening races, in which participants fly everything from custom-sewn Kevlar to patched scraps of canvas. Some days, we watched the races from the shade of our cockpit while kicking around at anchor. At other times, we mimicked them with our own maneuvers, tacking up, then gliding back down the bay.

In spite of the startling number of boats in Pittwater, we always found a place to anchor. Morning Bay provides shelter from the west and has enough space outside the moorings for several transients to anchor in mud at depths of thirty feet. When the wind went around to the southeast, we'd anchor at the edge of Careel Bay, where we could practically walk ashore through the tightly packed mooring field. Of course, it was a long dinghy ride to the head of the bay, then a healthy walk to the nearest supermarket in Avalon – but that's what vacations are for. We had all the time in the world – enough for day hikes like the one up Barrenjoey Head with its namesake lighthouse and Tasman Sea views.

Pittwater is just one of several arms that branch off Broken Bay and cut a lightning-bolt pattern into the surrounding countryside. The Hawkesbury River is another and popular with houseboaters, though a twelve meter bridge at the head blocks most sailboats out. Instead, we headed up Cowan Creek and the primal world of Ku-ring-gai Chase National Park. Cowan Creek gave us a glimpse of Australia before the arrival of Europeans: green, thick, wild. A deafening chorus of cicadas strikes up every dawn and dusk, when it's the kookaburra's turn to laugh.

Dozens of free public moorings line every deep-water branch of Cowan Creek. These fill quickly on weekends, but at mid-week we had no problem snagging one – then another, and another, working our way through the area in short hops. Just when we thought the steep hillsides ahead would pinch to a close, a sharp turn revealed yet another twist in the maze.

The only drawback was not being able to take more than a very quick dip in the water, and that, with a very sharp lookout. The threat of sharks seemed secondary to the blooms of jellyfish that floated past with the eerie silence of an alien invasion. On the other hand, we delighted in kayaking, poking around orange-brown rock ledges and imagining life as it might have been in the Dreamtime days of Australia's first people. This was another side of Sydney, and a lovely one, too.

When the time came to sail to Brisbane, we could leave Sydney with a deep sense of satisfaction. There's a special thrill to big city sailing, that wow-I'm-really-here factor, which doubles when experiencing it all from the deck of your own boat. And city thrills were only part of the fun. The unexpected gift tucked far behind the others was the option of quiet bushland retreats within city limits. It's as if some sail-friendly god took the best parts of the best waterways in the world, partnered them with fair weather and a friendly population, and created something nearing perfection. For us, the pot of gold at the end of the rainbow.

## Post Script: Sydney Fact File

Cruising guide: Alan Lucas' excellent *Cruising the New South Wales Coast* quickly paid itself off as it guided us to night after night of safe (and free) anchoring.

Services: Fuel, water, and pump-out available at the marinas that dot the shores of these waters. A conveniently located chandler in Pittwater is the Bosun's Locker, at

Royal Prince Albert Yacht Club (use visitors' dock or an unoccupied mooring for short stops).

Customs: Overseas arrivals report to Customs in Neutral Bay (west of Athol Bay); note mandatory ninety-six hour prior notification.[1]

Sugarloaf Bay: Walk fifteen minutes to Eastern Valley Way to catch a bus[2] downtown.

Events: Times and exclusion zones for the Sydney-Hobart race start and New Year's fireworks are detailed at *rolexsydneyhobart.com* and *www.sydneynewyearseve.com*.

---

[1] http://www.customs.gov.au/site/page4360.asp
[2] http://www.transportnsw.info

# Chapter 52

# Going With the Flow: Navigating the East Australia Current

Funny how the beginning and end of a voyage can parallel each other, even when they're three years and thousands of miles apart. In 2011, when we set off from the US East Coast for Panama, the greatest complicating factor for our Caribbean-bound trip was crossing the Gulf Stream. When we set off on our final offshore passage from Sydney to Brisbane in 2014, the East Australia Current posed a similar challenge to *Namani*. By then, we knew enough to go with the flow when forces of nature were concerned, but it seemed that we were in for a little reminder all the same.

Why Sydney to Brisbane? After three years of magical Pacific cruising, the time had come to sell our boat and head back to work, and Brisbane has a reputation as a hub of boat sales. After a month of fun and games in Sydney, it was time for us to get down to business and head north.

## In the Teeth of the Current

We'd gained firsthand experience with the East Australia Current (EAC) six weeks earlier, having made landfall midway along the coast in Coffs Harbour, then sailed south to Sydney. We had observed the south-setting current race at three or more knots and knew its effects can be felt well offshore. The tricky thing is that the EAC is not a simple one-way flow but a series of eddies that are constantly in flux. Generally, the south-setting current stretches about 250 NM offshore, but there are patches and even entire corridors of north-setting current in between. The chances of catching a north-setting ride are also good on the eastern side of the EAC, especially once you get 150 NM or so offshore.

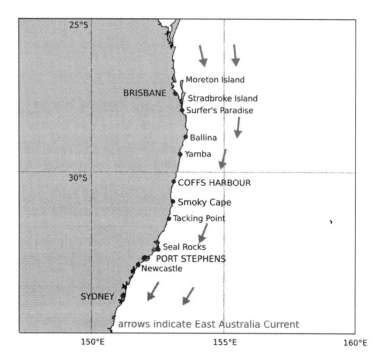

With this in mind, we developed a plan – a good plan, or so we thought – for heading north. The idea was to head well offshore and ride eddies to our advantage over the 500-mile passage. In doing so, we'd be bucking conventional Ozzie sailing wisdom that calls for sailing north with "one foot in the sand" – that is, skirting the coast where the contrary current is at its least or even reverses. We weren't keen on that idea, having observed how closely freighter traffic hugs the coast. By heading offshore, we reasoned, we could find north-setting eddies and avoid the inshore shipping that had given us so many headaches on our previous trip south – well worth the price of a detour. We'd had weeks to observe the weather and wait for the leading edge of a stable high pressure system to move in, providing a steady flow of southeasterlies so that we could make the trip in one six-day run.

It was a beautiful plan – except it didn't work. Once we had our weather window, we set off, confident in our logic. But the forecast southeast wind had a lot more east than south in it. So much, in fact, that at times it even tended ENE – not a good thing along this northeast tending section of the Australian coast. Combined with an adverse two knot current, the wind was such that all *Namani* could manage over ground was a two knot crawl of a close reach. Blue skies gave way to gray and the swell grew throughout the day, inching toward the three-meter mark. The only good news was that our stomachs were handling the transition back to blue water well.

Several frustrating hours later, we had to admit that another great plan had gone to the dogs. We were neither inside nor outside the EAC: we were smack in the teeth of the beast with easterly winds blocking any prospect of making it to the other side. That's when we decided to call it quits and head to Port Stephens, ninety miles north of Sydney, where we could mentally regroup and form a new plan. By this point in our sailing careers, we'd learned that flexibility comes ahead of stubbornness every time. We still had a frustrating night of tacking and cursing ahead of us as we dodged one ship after another. The main obstacle was the shipping off Newcastle, a bustling coal harbor. Little good our AIS receiver did us with a dozen ships in close quarters! A handful were anchored, while others drifted, awaiting the harbormaster's summons, and still others steamed to and fro. At one point, I was forced to put *Namani* on a port tack and head 195° to avoid one. That meant heading away from our destination at a clip of four knots, well above our speed made good in the desired direction!

Reefing in a squall while dodging traffic

## An Unscheduled Stopover

Twenty-four hours after departing Sydney, we finally reached Port Stephens, one of the few all-weather ports of refuge along an inhospitable coast. Inside its bold headlands, Port Stephens cuts a deep cleft into the mainland, branching into several arms that offer excellent shelter. We'd already visited the area on our earlier trip south, when we'd taken refuge from a Tasman Sea gale in North Arm Cove. This time, conditions were moderate enough for us to simply duck into nearby Shoal Bay, drop the anchor, and give ourselves a night to sleep on things. Happily, there was no need to rush into any decision, since we could count on the stable weather pattern to provide moderate southeasterlies over the coming days.

Morning and a good night's sleep brought clarity to our minds, and we resolved to grit it out on the inshore route despite the heavier shipping traffic. We did hang on to our original hope of tackling the remaining distance in one shot if possible. While there are a number of small harbors between Sydney and Brisbane, most lie behind shallow bars, making entry a tricky proposition in all but the most favorable points of tide. This point was dramatically illustrated in our cruising guide (Alan Lucas' excellent *Cruising the New South Wales Coast*), with its images of fishing boats floundering in massive standing waves after missing the tide. Lucas also makes a point of detailing every shipwreck along this coast, with long lists of macabre facts that fill the margins of nearly every page. We took his point to heart and resolved to make as few stops as possible for simplicity's sake. After months on the go, Markus and I could slip in and out of our four-hour watch-keeping schedule easily. Nicky had no qualms about blue water, either, so we set off again, somewhat wary of what our new plan might bring us.

The strongest flow of the EAC usually occurs between Sugarloaf Point (twenty-five miles north of Port Stephens) and Smoky Cape (another 100 NM to the north), so we'd have to keep closer to shore than we would have liked – within three miles, give or take. At least the swell had settled back down, giving us an easier ride. Geography was on our side, too: as soon as we rounded Sugarloaf Point, the coastline angled slightly more north. We'd still be heading northeast, but even a few degrees gained would make our course more tenable, especially with the wind slowly backing from east to east-southeast.

Soon, things were looking up, and we were feeling good about our decision to stay inside the 100 fathom line. Our unplanned stop in Port Stephens helped us make the mental shift needed to embrace the inside route, and a sunny day didn't hurt, either. Now *Namani* was sailing a good six knots to windward, practically racing along the coastline in comparison to the previous day. We passed Captain Cook's Tacking Point, relieved to be able to clear the cape in one try. Although the idea of staying inshore felt claustrophobic at first, I came to see it as an advantage. The land side was predictable and our route well-charted; it was the ships that were a problem, and staying inshore left them all to starboard, keeping our port side clear.

# Getting Ahead of Ourselves

*Namani* made such good speed that we realized we might get ahead of ourselves. If the good times lasted, our eventual arrival in Brisbane would be at nighttime – not an enticing proposition given the shoal-ridden approach to Moreton Bay. In the second snap decision of the trip, we hung a sharp left and pulled into Coffs Harbour thirty-six hours after leaving Port Stephens, just beating the setting sun in. We much preferred a night at anchor to a night heaving-to among ships, so we grabbed the chance at a solid night's sleep before continuing on to Brisbane, 235 miles away. We knew the layout of Coff's Harbour by heart, having initially cleared in to Australia there: the jetty, the breakwater, and the marina to one side. We dropped the anchor in eighteen feet and immediately treated ourselves to a quick dip in the water, followed by a fresh water shower and a hearty dinner. Our one regret is that we couldn't go for a rejuvenating swim. Just six weeks earlier, a surfer had been killed by a shark in the immediate area.

On our last visit, we'd spent two weeks in Coffs Harbour waiting for a weather window to head south to Sydney. Then, as now, we ended up tackling the distance in several hops. This time, we had the luxury of a stable weather system, unlike the very short windows of opportunity of our previous trip. Still, we made it a quick pit stop and headed out early the next morning for a final push north. In contrast, leaving Sydney had been a much harder proposition, at least mentally. I always get a case of the nerves about heading offshore after a few weeks close to land. The minute I head out, however, the butterflies are gone with the wind.

Thus far on this trip, we'd sailed twenty-four hours, stopped for a night in Port Stephens, then sailed another thirty-six hours before stopping for another night off – quite a comfortable schedule, as it turned out. We did, however, hope to make the remaining distance in one long hop, although we did note alternative pull-in points such as Yamba, at the mouth of the Clarence River, and Ballina, on the Richmond River. We were in no rush to conclude our final voyage afloat, but neither did we want to drag out the inevitable.

As we bid goodbye to New South Wales and watched southern Queensland slide into view, it seemed as if shipping traffic thinned. Fishing boats were out in full force, though, including slow trawlers that slalomed left, then right, then left again. By day, their movements were easier to predict. We could relax more and watch the coast roll by, thinking of Captain Cook discovering this continent and its people for the first time. It's not the most inspiring coast, however, with dun-colored hills marked only by the odd beacon or jutting cape. At night, the mainland was as dark as the sea, with only occasional clusters of light marking lonely outposts at the edge of civilization. The view above was more interesting: the Centaur reared, almost trampling the Southern Cross, while Orion cartwheeled overhead. We watched their antics with renewed interest, knowing our southern hemisphere sojourn was gradually coming to an end.

## Ticking off the Milestones

Now that we had found our rhythm again (and were making good speed as long as we remained inshore), it was a pleasure to watch time tick by, so unlike the rushed hours of our lives on land. With our sturdy boat, a cooperative wind, and each other, we felt we had it all. The moon was gradually waxing from quarter phase to a plump gibbous shape; that and a good book was all the entertainment we needed over the next two days and nights. Land provided fewer distractions, except for a few more distinctive mountains and the stiletto skyline of Surfer's Paradise, a Queensland milestone. Each mile brought us closer and closer to Brisbane. Soon, it was time to plan our approach.

The city of Brisbane lies behind two barrier islands, Stradbroke and Moreton Islands, which protect Moreton Bay, an area of sand banks and shallows. Although a narrow cut between the islands tempts some sailors to shortcut into the bay, we took *Namani* and her six-foot draft up and around both islands to follow the marked shipping lane into the bay. We had to fight a two knot current on the way, but by this point, we had hours of daylight on our side. One by one, we ticked off the buoys marking the channel, keeping red to left as is the rule throughout most of the Pacific. What was unusual was having navigation aids at all. In most places we'd visited since departing Panama, a crooked pipe stuck into the corner of a reef had been enough of a navigation aid to celebrate – here, we had real buoys to steer by.

We wound our way through ribbons of pastel greens and shallow blues, astounded at the size of the freighters maneuvering through the aquamarine maze. To make the most of our remaining hours at sea, we took to hand steering. It had been our plan all along to sell *Namani* in Australia, but the reality was truly upon us now. Soon, we spotted a forest of masts of boats within Scarborough Boat Harbour, located in a suburb of Brisbane. When we made *Namani* fast in her berth, we knew that our days of calling ourselves sailors were numbered. The following week was a flurry of beautification work to present the boat at her best, and we found a buyer within a few weeks. That part of the trip, at least, had gone according to our original plan.

If nothing else, three years aboard *Namani* has taught us to be flexible. This start-and-stop passage from Sydney to Brisbane wasn't the first to bring a few surprises. Our battle with the EAC proved more complicated than our Gulf Stream crossing several years before, but without the specter of adverse weather breathing down our necks, we had the luxury of time. A few days later, the prevailing high pressure system gave way to a troughy mess, so we were happy to have made the trip when we did – especially as the EAC intensified, sweeping south at three and even four knots. That would have been hard to beat!

One final, welcome surprise awaited us at the end of the passage – a story you'll find in the next chapter. Read on!

# Chapter 53

# Coastal Cruising Meets Passage-making: Along the East Australian Coast

Throughout our time in Australia, we had been steeling ourselves for a sentimental goodbye. Sailing into Brisbane's Moreton Bay, where we planned to sell *Namani*, had been our last hurrah – or so we thought.

In preparing the sales listing for our boat, we had tacked on a comment: "Will deliver." During the month we spent in Brisbane awaiting a sale, we'd all but given up on the possibility of extending our time aboard. But along came Janet with an offer we couldn't refuse: a good price for the boat, along with a deal that gave us two months to deliver the sloop to her home port of Cairns, 800 miles to the north.

## The Catch?

The only catch was the timing: March and April fall into the shoulder cyclone season. Over the past three years, we'd been avoiding cyclones like the plague, taking thousand-mile detours to stay out of their way. Australian sailor friends we asked advice of, however, had no reservations about sailing north. "Oh, you'll be right!" they declared in their happy-go-lucky way. The chances of a cyclone were small, they said, and there are plenty of creeks to seek shelter in along the way. Even so, we decided to wait until April before departing to reduce the statistical risk of encountering a cyclone. Our excitement grew as departure day approached, thanks to the promise of enticing cruising grounds ahead. Much as we'd enjoyed Australia thus far, East Coast sailing had consisted mostly of long dashes between the few easily accessed harbors along an uninviting coastline. By sailing on to Cairns, we'd be exploring real cruising grounds again: island groups with nooks and crannies that invite a sailor to linger and explore.

And so we set out on a month-long trip that was equal parts ocean passage-making and coastal cruising, alternating between overnight passages and easy days at anchor in choice locations. Theoretically, a boat can day-trip all the way up the Queensland coast, but with "only" five weeks to enjoy it all, we decided to start the trip with a 72 hour / 300 mile run to make a dent in the overall distance. Thanks to prevailing southeasterlies, finding a window to head north was an easy enough exercise. We set off in early April, delighted to have one last encore at sea.

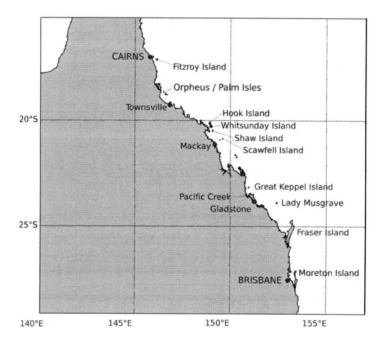

It was a relief to leave the single-digit shallows of Brisbane's Moreton Bay behind and head into open waters, where our main navigational challenges were monitoring shipping traffic and riding a contrary current. Six-foot seas from the stern quarter reminded our stomachs that we'd spent too much time on land, but we knew that initial three-day passage would get us into the swing of things again. On a goodbye sail, the brush of sentimentality paints everything in a special light: the exhilaration of the sails filling, the grandeur of a solitary watch under the southern night sky, and yes, even the feeling of a queasy stomach.

Given our schedule, we opted for the outside route around the long finger of Fraser Island, which didn't hold the same appeal as smaller islands farther north. This put us right into the teeth of the current. Progress slowed to a two knot crawl – until the moon pulled the tide around to a more favorable direction and bumped our speed up to as high as seven knots. Queensland's central coast has some of the most extreme currents and tides observed Down Under, the latter topping out at six meters around Mackay. We quickly learned not to despair when *Namani* turtled along, knowing she'd be speeding ahead a few hours later.

The difficulty lay in deciding how close to cut the corner of Fraser Island. Too close and the contrary current would only intensify. Too far, and we'd be shoulder-to shoulder with the steady parade of freighters paralleling the coast. Eventually, we decided on tiptoeing along the one hundred meter contour about ten miles off Fraser Island and spent the night keeping a sharp eye out for steaming lights. Having our AIS receiver to help predict their movements was a welcome novelty. For most of our Pacific crossing, the AIS was of little use since so many ships and fishing boats operate without it. Off Queensland, just about every vessel transmitted a signal we could pick up from as much as thirty miles away, and there were only a handful of smaller vessels without AIS to track.

En route to Cairns

## So Close Yet So Far

We'd spent so long sailing wide open swaths of ocean that traveling along an extended coastline felt strange. On one hand, we felt very much in blue water mode, with the open ocean on our right and a four-hour schedule of watch-keeping day and night. To port, however, lay the slumbering coast, and the depth sounder never dropped below one hundred feet. It was a confusing, "so close yet so far" sensation. At one point thirteen miles offshore, *Namani* was overwhelmed by the scent of eucalyptus wafting offshore like the mother of all throat remedies – a special memory to add to a collection rich in sights, sounds, and experiences.

With sunny skies, balmy temperatures, and good wind, our final voyage was off to a good start. The only disappointment was having to bypass Lady Musgrave Island, an enticing coral cay with a navigable lagoon. That is, it would have been navigable if the sun had been overhead, but not at sunset, when we sailed past. The good news was that we had reached an important milestone: the southernmost end of the Great Barrier Reef, which begins far offshore and squeezes closer to the coast farther north.

The bad news was the latest forecast. Less than a week after weather authorities like Bob McDavitt declared a definitive end to cyclone season, a low built over the Solomon Islands that would eventually spawn Cyclone Ita and hurl it right at the Queensland coast. Although the storm's development was still uncertain at that time, we went on red alert. With a period of strong southerlies forecast to blow in the intervening time, our best chance to seek shelter would be over the next couple of days while pleasant conditions prevailed.

By the time we anchored off Great Keppel Island the next morning, we knew we wouldn't be settling in for long. That was a pity, given the island's gorgeous beach, green hills, and quiet anchorage. A massive eagle's nest in a treetop near the beach was the only sign of habitation in this echo of Eden. We spent two nights in this lovely location, playing on the beach but keeping our dips in the water brief. That's the agony of cruising in Australia: the ever-present threat of sharks, crocodiles, and deadly jellyfish tends to spoil the attraction of the sparkling tropical waters. We settled for beach combing instead – between downloading weather reports, that is.

The only thing the various forecast models agreed on was that a cyclone would develop and strike the north/central Queensland coast – somewhere. Some models had the cyclone dissipating over land, while others had it bouncing down the coast, right at *Namani*. In any scenario, heading any farther north would be folly. We decided to hunker down amidst the mangroves of Pacific Creek, a half-day sail south of Great Keppel Island. Timing our arrival carefully for high tide, we eased our six-foot draft over the bar at the creek's entrance (charted at three feet at low water). When depths dropped off to a healthy twenty-plus feet, we set our anchor in the muddy bottom of the creek. Then the waiting began.

It was a week to be endured more than enjoyed. We were sitting ducks to the mosquitoes and no-see-ums of the creek, and Nicky proved the tastiest of us all, racking up one hundred bites within forty-eight hours despite doses of insect repellent and netting on all hatches. We took to wearing pants and long sleeves despite the heat and burned mosquito coils all day, every day. If nothing else, we made good progress on our pet projects: Markus was busy programming a weather data program for sailors called Slocum,[1] Nicky made a 3D model of our boat[2] (with a little home schooling on the side), and I had plenty of time to write.

A week after our arrival in Pacific Creek, Cyclone Ita pounded the northern Queensland coast near Cooktown, then swept south, curving out to sea one hundred miles east of our location. The worst we registered deep in Pacific Creek was a occasional burst of forty knot winds. Had the cyclone hit more directly, we were confident that we would have weathered it well in the narrows of the creek. The experience lent a touch of symmetry to our three-year Pacific cruise: when we initially set out on the trip from Maine, Hurricane Irene put a similar monkey wrench in our plans.

## The Cumberland Islands

With the coast finally clear, we were eager to press on to the real highlight of our cruise, the Cumberland Islands. After a brief re-provisioning stop in nearby Keppel Bay (the only such stop during the five-week trip), we slipped back into passage-making mode and made a quick thirty-six hour run to Scawfell Island. Another night of stars, another day to contemplate our futures. We savored every moment, in no rush to leave our comfortable home and the quiet sailing life.

Or the quiet motorsailing life, as things turned out, given light, fluky wind from the east. Now inside the Great Barrier Reef, we had an easy time staying clear of shipping, which followed a well-defined lane that we paralleled at a safe distance. After so many miles of following a relatively bland coast, it was a joy to sail among islands and islets again. We counted one after another until the following sunset, when *Namani* slipped into the anchorage at Scawfell Island and settled in for the first of two nights. The orange light of Mars rose over the hulk of the island, the Southern Cross hung tenuously between the hooves of the Centaur, and Scorpio crashed the party, too, climbing high into the sky along with the flash of a shooting star.

[1]https://github.com/akleeman/slocum
[2]http://www.namaniatsea.org/nicky-page/namani-goes-3d

Over the next week, we switched back to day-hopping mode. Short daylight hours in these tropical latitudes kept us on our toes as we planned a route that would take us from Scawfell and Shaw Islands in the less-frequented southern Cumberland Islands to the Whitsundays farther north. Though small in area, the Whitsundays are the most frequented cruising grounds in Australia. The anchorages were packed with dozens of boats as a period of troughy weather settled over the area. We sat it out in Cid Harbor, where pines carpet the hillsides and sea eagles pluck fish straight from the water. Two fjord-like bays on Hook Island offer good protection, as well. At lovely Nara Inlet, we hiked a short path to a cave with Aboriginal rock art, then moved over to Macona Inlet for a little more solitude from the Easter vacation crowds. Having visited the gorgeous white sands of Whitehaven Beach some years earlier while chartering, we decided to give it a miss this time around and concentrate on our next overnight trip to places off the beaten path.

# North to Cairns

North of the Whitsundays, the coast takes a northwest bend, making for a more pleasant wind angle under prevailing southeasterlies. Sailors in Maine go Down East; in Queensland, it's Up West as we set a course of 300° toward the setting sun for yet another overnight passage. The rolly downwind sailing reminded us of our trade wind passage from the Galapagos Islands to the Marquesas – except that we had a continent on one side, the world's longest reef on the other, and only eighty feet of water under the keel.

Once underway under a new moon, we were reminded of how much light the stars provide – including our old friend the Big Dipper, peeking above the horizon. Thanks to the stars and several beacons, we had the visual reference of the mainland coastline and low-lying islands – a welcome sanity check for sailors like us who are never truly comfortable relying on electronic charts. We'd been warned against night sailing off shipping ports like Gladstone and Townsville, but the only real traffic we encountered was off Abbott Point, where seven ships lay at anchor waiting to load up with coal.

Daylight hours were peppered with Coast Guard bulletins coming through on the VHF, including weather bulletins and warnings of live ammunition exercises at Rattlesnake Island. But we on *Namani* carried on unperturbed in our own quiet bubble, just the three of us and the faithful boat that had carried us two-thirds of the way around the world since our earliest days in the Mediterranean. The days of that bubble were numbered, so we made sure to appreciate every quiet minute, every peaceful view.

Halfway between the Whitsundays and Cairns lies an island group known as the Palm Isles, the perfect place for a last stopover. We passed one small resort and a research station before grabbing one of two visitor's moorings in Pioneer Bay on Orpheus Island. After the relative crowds of the Whitsundays, it was a pleasure to have an anchorage to ourselves once again, and we enjoyed our solitude for another two days.

That left a mere 120 miles to our final destination. We couldn't have asked for much more for our last overnight passage aboard *Namani*: calm seas and steady wind to fill the sails, plus a tropical landscape to fill our senses. We drank it all in, eking everything we could out of the dying wind before switching the motor on in the wee hours of morning. In contrast to the relatively open waters of our previous passages, this one had *Namani* tiptoeing past tiny islets and reefs in an area where the Great Barrier Reef creeps close to the coast. Detailed charts and a series of beacons guided us through the night until we honed in on Fitzroy Island's powerful light. At dawn, we rounded Cape Grafton and gained our first view of Cairns.

Arrival was a bittersweet affair. We were sad to face the conclusion of a wonderful chapter in our lives and to say goodbye to the floating home that had brought us so far. But it was a time to celebrate as well. With so many magical experiences to look back over, we just couldn't complain, least of all after this unexpected delivery cruise along east Australia's most scenic coast. We were heartened to know that *Namani* would now reside in a beautiful corner of the world with an energetic owner who will lead her over many romps in her watery playground. As for us, well, the end of one adventure signals the start of another. Who knows what it will be?

# Chapter 54

# Sail to Sell Down Under

Years before we even contemplated a Pacific crossing, we had heard the rumors. Buy a boat in North America and sell it – maybe even at a profit – in Australia. The idea of a one-way Pacific crossing certainly has its appeal: all those idyllic islands, all that enjoyable trade-wind sailing. And so we started to plan and scheme, though concrete information on selling a boat on the other side of the world was hard to come by. By the time we set our plan into motion and transited the Panama Canal, we found ourselves in good company with several other crews who had the same idea. But no one had anything better than anecdotal evidence to go on. How easy would it be to sell a boat in Australia? What are the myths, and what are the realities?

Now that we have the experience behind us, we and our fellow cruisers are happy to report a smooth, easy process. Most of us were able to sell our boats within two months of putting them on the market, and at reasonable prices, too. Cruisers hoping to do the same can certainly take heart, if not entertain fantasies of netting huge profits.

## What Sells

What type of boat sells well? What is the Australian market looking for? I asked Anita Farine of Farine Yacht Sales in Brisbane, who speaks from fifteen years of experience. In general, she says, the most sought-after boats are solid fiberglass monohulls in the thirty to fifty foot range dating from the mid-1980s to the mid-2000s. Older vessels also sell, she says, but for much lower prices. To illustrate the range of possibilities: Anita once sold a fifty foot Halberg-Rassy for AUD$500,000 back to back with a Westsail thirty-two for AUD$60,000. "If it's a boat," she says, "I can sell it!"

What about multihulls? South African-built catamarans in the forty to fifty foot range get a lot of attention, though many of them price beyond the reach of the average buyer. The Australian market sees a lot of domestically built and homemade cats, whereas the population relies more heavily on imports when it comes to cruising monohulls. Still, Anita stressed, given a realistic asking price, just about any type of boat, rig, or hull material can sell.

There seem to be two groups of buyers in Australia: the first are pleasure sailors, who appreciate well-equipped cruising boats. Much of Australia's coast is rugged and exposed, so they look for good sail inventory, safety equipment, and a full range of electronics. The second group is primarily looking to save costs by living aboard. These are often people who work in remote mining camps for several weeks at a time before returning to a home base. For them, life rafts and watermakers are far less important than comfort and livability.

Price is obviously a major point for buyers, and it's a savvy market. Buyers will hunt widely for good deals even if import fees mean that most boats list for higher prices in Australia than they would in North America or Europe. Beware of pricing your boat significantly higher than others in its class, citing extras like electronics, life rafts, and a wide inventory of sails. These are highly negotiable points, and you don't want to price yourself out of the market. With plenty of reasonably priced boats available, any vessel that seems overpriced – regardless of how well-equipped it may be – is unlikely to attract a buyer.

Lesson number one: don't aim for the stars in an asking price. One boat we know that listed at a very optimistic price languished in a marina berth for months before eventually selling for nearly half the asking price. Reasonably-priced boats, on the other hand, attracted potential buyers quickly and sold within two months. Of course, you don't want to list too low, either. It seems that just about every buyer's first offer was AUD$10,000 or more below the asking price. That's the time to consider taking the deal, possibly stripping down extras to sell separately on eBay (or its popular equivalent, gumtree.com.au).

So how much might your boat sell for? The "Case Studies" section of this chapter, below, lists five concrete examples as a starting point. I recommend following website listings over an extended period of time to see how boats similar to yours price and move. The future is impossible to predict, and no market is immune in today's economy. Although Australia has managed a smoother ride through recent years than many other countries, their high-riding dollar has lost a little of its brilliance in recent times.

When it comes down to details, one thing many buyers focus on is the age of the rig. In the state of Queensland, for example, insurance companies will not cover boats with rigs more than a decade old for anything but third-party liability. If your rig is aging, it may well pay off to get new rigging before your Pacific crossing. That way, you'll benefit from the investment yourself and find selling easier.

Buyers also pay attention to engine hours and boat draft. Boats with drafts over six feet strike out with many potential buyers; long keels, on the other hand, are fairly popular. Boats wired for the Australian standard of 220 volts are preferred over 110, though that shouldn't be a deal-breaker. Sailors here will do their homework, too, looking for models that have proven themselves over the years. And if your schedule is flexible, it may help sweeten the deal to offer to deliver the boat yourself. We were based out of Brisbane and our offer to deliver to Cairns gave us the edge over other boats the buyer was considering.

Good presentation helps a sale, too. Months before arriving in Australia, we spent a few busy days taking sales photos. In order to make the boat look as spacious and attractive as possible, we shifted huge amounts of gear from cockpit to forepeak and back again. Upon arriving in Australia, we spent several weeks making the boat picco bello before showing it – that meant rebedding hatches, touching up varnish work, and scrubbing the deck. Watch for details that hit the eye, like worn upholstery or rusty spots. The trick is to make sure your boat gets its official valuation done before you make any improvements (more below).

Getting *Namani* ready for sale

353

# When to List and Where to Sell

We were hardly halfway across the Pacific before the issues of when to list a boat and where in Australia to sell cropped up as discussion topics in beach potlucks. While it's helpful to make contact with a broker as early as your departure from North America, it only really makes sense to list a boat once you reach Fiji, a few months prior to your arrival in Australia. That's close enough for the Australian buyer to conceive of the boat as being nearly there. Some buyers, of course, will travel offshore to see a boat. One Jeanneau we know of attracted an Australian buyer and signed a contract before they even left New Caledonia. We nearly had a buyer come visit us in Vanuatu, though he eventually pulled out to buy a Sydney-based vessel.

The next question is what port in Australia to sell out of. Boats generally sell best in easily reached locations, meaning a marina berth in an area served by domestic airlines. High marina fees put Sydney out of the question for us. We headed to Scarborough, a suburb of Brisbane, to base our boat in a marina with reasonable fees (AUD$500 a month for our thirty-five footer, AUD$600 for forty-three feet). Brisbane is the second biggest city in Australia with a high concentration of boats, and frequent air connections allow buyers to fly in from any part of Australia.

Another place frequently cited as a good selling base is Bundaberg, 200 nautical miles north of Brisbane. Several crews reported making profitable sales here in years past. However, this trend may be on the wane. For many years, Bundaberg's reputation rode the coattails of the popular "Port2Port" cruising rally which helped stock the local market. The demise of the rally might well mean the demise of the market in Bundaberg, especially given that connections in and out of the regional airport are limited. Still, a handful of sailors swear on Bundaberg, and who's to argue with success?

# Regulations and Import Duties

Importing a boat into Australia can be surprisingly easy. It seems that many of the wild rumors surrounding importation are patently false. For example, fumigation is rarely required. In fifteen years of assisting boat owners to import, Anita Farine reports that only one required fumigation – and that was a seventy-five year old wooden hull. There is no required certification for rigging, nor proof of recent antifouling for boats under twenty meters – just make sure your hull isn't sprouting a dense beard of mussels when you arrive. In the worst case, you'll be required to haul out and clean the bottom. It will be necessary to certify refrigeration and gas systems, but these can be arranged locally with little difficulty (approximately AUD$200 each).

Unfortunately, there's no way around the 10% import tax. Most boats also pay an additional 5% duty, though this is waived for US-flagged vessels thanks to the Free Trade agreement. These duties will take a significant chunk out of your take-home cash. I suspect that the stories of people selling a boat in Australia for a higher price than they bought it in North America does not figure in import duties. Some sailors try to bypass this by selling duty-free in New Caledonia, though the market there is limited (see *Post Script: Other Pacific Marketplaces* on page 357).

A critical point for importation is the official valuation of your vessel. The lower the value of your boat, the lower the import duty you must pay. Therefore, make sure you hold off on touching up that scratch in the varnish or that nick in the gelcoat until after the valuation has been made. It doesn't make sense to make major boat improvements in New Zealand or New Caledonia to increase the sales value of the boat in Australia since that will drive up the import value of your boat. Valuation is done by a surveyor or certified broker and is generally 50% less than the sales price of the boat. It is not possible to have valuation based on a bill of sale older than twelve months (not to mention that this is generally unfavorable, given that a bill of sale is likely to show a higher value than a local valuation will show).

Anita Farine recommends keeping receipts from as early as Panama for anything that could be construed as a boat improvement. For example, we were able to deduct the new rigging we had installed in Tahiti from the import value of our boat in Australia. Keep all major receipts – equipment, charts, antifouling, even marina fees. You never know what might be accepted as a deduction. Above all, talk to a broker well before your arrival in Australia for his or her advice on all importation requirements, including how and when to declare your intent to sell.

Foreign boats may remain in Australia for up to three years before facing importation. Once a boat is listed for sale, however, a so-called Restriction to Port comes into effect. This means that you're limited to local cruising once your boat is imported. Keep this in mind when choosing a location. I originally entertained the fantasy that we could continue cruising Australia to our heart's content until a buyer appeared. Our broker dissuaded me, explaining that it is much more difficult to sell a roving boat than one with a fixed location. This proved true, as many buyers ask to see boats on short notice.

Most of us awaiting a sale in Australia opened a local bank account, both for ease of daily transactions and for the eventual sale. Don't delay in opening a bank account because a strange regulation prevents foreigners from opening an account more than six weeks after their arrival.

# Case Studies

There is no magic formula for calculating what price your boat might fetch in Australia, and certainly none for predicting the future behavior of the market. I can, however, provide several case studies for a range of boats that sold in 2013 to 2014. The following boats are all well-equipped (if not luxuriously appointed) offshore cruisers that sold to local sailors. All were presented in perfect working order (with the exception of the Wauquiz Amphitrite which had some systems seize up during its long wait for a buyer). The prize for a quick sale among our cohort went to a 2001 Jeanneau Sun Odyssey 43: the new owner slapped down his payment before this vessel even reached Australia! (Apologies, but the owner does not wish to disclose details other than to say the boat listed in the AUD$150 to $200,000 range). Another vessel, a 2003 Beneteau 423, listed for AUD$160,000 and sold for $150,000 within six weeks of arrival. During that time, it hosted three prospective buyers before eventually going to a Queensland sailor planning on coastal sailing.

Our sloop, a 1981 Dufour 35, listed for AUD$70,000 and sold for AUD$60,000 within six weeks of arrival, plus an additional $2500 for the Parasailor, negotiated separately. Two serious parties came to view her in this time. The new owner is an Australian planning on coastal cruising in Queensland.

Another older vessel, a 1975 Wauquiz Amphitrite 43 ketch, was listed ambitiously at AUD$120,000 and waited six months before eventually selling for AUD$73,000. This vessel is a solid build but needed new rigging and other improvements. The new owners plan to cruise locally and hope to someday cruise overseas.

A 1989 steel Reincke 42 that was listed for AUD$80,000 sold within six weeks for AUD$74,000. Three serious parties came to view the boat. The owner stripped the boat of extras such as a Parasailor and SCUBA tanks to sell separately. The decade-old rigging was a cause for concern but did not ultimately hinder the sale. The new owner intends to use the vessel as a liveaboard in Queensland.

For all of us, the process was similar. After viewing the vessel, serious buyers paid a 10% deposit and arranged for haul-out and survey (paid by the prospective buyer) as well as a brief sea trial. As long as everything checked out, the rest of the payment was made and the importation / sales process went through in roughly ten days. This process was greatly smoothed by the services of our broker, who took a 10% fee for her work. Other cruisers report handling the work themselves without complaint.

We all went through a period of hopeful waiting, some longer, some shorter. No one struck the lottery, but most were satisfied with their sales. All agreed that the potential buyers we encountered were a bargain-seeking lot. In most cases, buyers were patient, too, suggesting that the onus is on the seller to accept a lower offer rather than lose a potential sale. It can be a nerve-wracking game of just how long you're willing to wait before accepting an offer. Ultimately, we were all sad to let go of our floating homes, yet relieved to have found a buyer after the voyage of our dreams.

For an idea of the current market, check out these online listings:

*www.yachthub.com*

*www.boatpoint.com.au*

*www.boatsonline.com.au*

Anita Farine Boat Sales: *www.farine.net.au*

## Post Script: Other Pacific Marketplaces

Of course, Australia isn't the only place to sell a boat. To us, however, it seemed like the most robust market with the largest number of potential buyers. There's a concentration of boats for sale in Tahiti, but that was only a fraction of the way across our dream route. From what we observed in Tahiti, it's more of a buyer's than a seller's market. Fiji has a much smaller market, plus there's the issue of cyclone season storage. New Caledonia, meanwhile, is no longer the seller's paradise it once was. A broker I approached for an interview there gave this simple advice: "Go to Australia instead."

New Zealand is the next biggest market where boats do move – but with a population of four million to Australia's twenty-three million, the potential customer base is that much smaller. Foreigners do fly in to view boats in New Zealand, but boats can wait for longer periods before finding a taker. It's not impossible to sell a boat in any of these places, but overall, Australia is your safest bet. Cruisers with flexible schedules might also consider giving New Zealand or New Caledonia a try for one season before moving on to Australia.

# Chapter 55

# Selling Your Boat: Practical Considerations for the Return Home

So what exactly does the boatless sailor do with all of his or her gear in a foreign port? As one of five crews to sell their boat at about the same time in Brisbane, we learned that it's not as complicated as it may seem to move on.

We were lucky in that we had a flexible schedule and a flexible buyer who asked us to deliver the boat 800 miles north to her home in Cairns within three months of the sale. That gave us time for a last hurrah on our floating home as well as time to think about what things we wanted to keep. We booked our flight home at that time (three months ahead of our actual departure). Once we reached Cairns, we spent a final two weeks on board. Since we used evenings and weekends to orient the new owner to the boat, she let us continue to live aboard and split marina fees with us – a very amiable arrangement for both parties.

We had already culled down our belongings when preparing the boat for viewing in Brisbane. At that point, we threw or gave extras away and shipped three boxes of personal goods home (a pricey proposition at AUD$5 per 500 grams even for sea freight). Once we reached Cairns, we shipped another two boxes home (foul weather gear, sextant, log books, Lego, other personal gear) and packed the luggage we'd fly with (including two suitcases bought at a second hand shop). Those were a fairly intense three days, during which time Markus managed to inflict the worst injury of our entire trip on himself – a broken collarbone sustained in the local playground where he was goofing around with Nicky! Then the new owner's friend gave us a ride to the airport, and we were off (hiding our tears at saying goodbye to our trusty *Namani*).

The other crews we knew had much quicker moving-off experiences, though all followed the same pattern: throwing or shipping out gear before showing the boat, then taking their remaining belongings as flight luggage. One crew paid to stay in a nearby motel during that time so as not to have the complication of living aboard the vessel while packing and cleaning, but the rest of us avoided this extra expense. These crews spent a maximum of one day interacting with the new owner, showing them the idiosyncrasies of their boats.

However, everyone had a fair period of forewarning, given that buying/selling a boat is a step-by-step process. Once a serious buyer shows interest, it takes another week to two weeks to set up a sea trial and survey. That gave us lead-up time to get serious about packing and shipping the last items. Even after a contract is signed, it takes a few days for money to transfer. Therefore, it was a lot of work, but none of us were ever in the position of being left on the dock with a mountain of gear and nowhere to go. We rented a car for one day to transport our boxes to the post office in Brisbane, and hitched a ride to do the same in Cairns.

Many of the crews we knew had scheduled in a period of land travel after arriving in Australia, so when they moved off the boat, they moved their remaining belongings into rental cars or campers as an intermediate step. One crew used a shipping agent to send a larger quantity of goods home in a small container. That may make sense for sailors with much to ship and the budget to pay for it, though not for penny-pinching sailors like us.

All of the above crews traded one to two months of cruising time for a cushion in terms of a sales window. Others cruised right up until their firm go-home date and allotted themselves only two weeks after arrival in Australia to get everything prepared: cleaning and repairing the boat as well as packing their things. Then they departed for their home countries, leaving the boat in the hands of a broker. Some were lucky; their boats sold fast. A 2001 Jeanneau Sun Odyssey 43 we know sold sight unseen even before arriving in Australia, and the family flew home within a week of arriving in Brisbane. This approach did not work well for a 1975 Wauquiz Amphitrite 43 ketch that was priced too high. It ended up languishing on the market, and with no one to keep her up, systems started seizing. That ultimately drove the selling price down to nearly half of the original asking price eight months down the road.

Many sailors bridge their time between living on board and heading home with a period of land travel depending on when and where the boat sells. We booked a multi-leg series of flights home to be able to visit friends and places along the way. Over a period of six weeks, we enjoyed stops in Indonesia, Japan, California, Vancouver, and Calgary. We then spent six weeks with family in Maine before flying on to our home in Germany. The price of that entire ticket was about US$3,000 per person, whereas a direct flight would have cost about US$2,000. We feel the extra was well spent and we were able to keep our costs minimal thanks to various friends who hosted us at each stop along the way. It was a lovely reunion trip, and a great transition time for us: we were still footloose travelers, but had the chance to get used to land life at the same time.

Taking good-bye pictures

# Part XI

# Tributes

# Tributes

It's a lucky sailor, indeed, who has not only a source of inspiration – the person who helps you cast off your mental bowlines – but also a friend who can be counted on to come through when the going gets tough. Being that lucky, I've penned a few sentimental lines to show my gratitude to two special sailors. I owe them as much as I owe the friendly islanders and the explorers who preceded me in the Pacific. Thank you, Dad, and thank you, Markus, for helping me forge and realize my dreams.

# Chapter 56

# In Search of the "Polish Navy"

Listing hulls, ugly figureheads, and unconventional ballast ratios: these were the hall-marks of the "Polish Navy" – my mother's name for the sincere but sometimes mis-guided attempts of my Polish-born father and his friend to launch their sailing dreams. Her stories were always guaranteed to work us into side-splitting hoots of laughter. Now an adult and a boat-owner myself, I have a new appreciation for what the Polish Navy was all about – and I can't help but wonder what became of the bold venture launched so long ago in New Jersey's Raritan Bay.

It was the late 1960s, and my father was a young man who had recently escaped from behind the Iron Curtain and found asylum in the Land of the Free. He had always harbored sailing dreams, and in America, he struck up a fortuitous friendship with a fellow Pole who had recently purchased an unfinished mahogany vessel. It was more hulk than hull, but Jan Skarbek (formally called Pan Skarbek, or Mr. Skarbek) saw its promise. Newspaper reports of the sale, on the other hand, describe a "modern day, misplaced Noah's Ark."

To complete his project, Pan Skarbek enlisted the help of friends, most of whom quickly retired to the cockpit for drinks. My father distinguished himself as someone who actually worked long hours alongside the visionary owner in South River Marina (which isn't to say he didn't down a fortifying vodka along the way), and was soon enlisted as crew for a Grand Voyage.

The problem was that the Polish Navy suffered from financial difficulties and therefore certain compromises had to be made. Skarbek couldn't afford lead ballast, so he made do with bits of scrap metal, poured by his untrained hand. The result was an inconve-nient but not insurmountable list to port. The boat was originally designed with a single mast, but the innovative Skarbek eyeballed two smaller (and cheaper) masts into place instead. The entire enterprise was a glorious example of amateur effort, equal parts willpower and faith in Lady Luck.

The vessel went through a series of name changes, mirroring the ebb and flow of Skarbek's love interests. Hence "Nina" was re-christened "Nonna" and eventually stumbled along to "Yolanta." One of Pan Skarbek's flames was my aunt, a striking, Jackie Kennedy look-alike, and my father put his artistic training to work by carving a figurehead in her likeness (with an enhanced bust for good measure). Unfortunately, neither portraits nor sculptures were my father's specialty. The ill-fated result had more resemblance to Medusa than my aunt, who reacted to the compliment by screaming, throwing a fit, and banishing the sculpture to her dimly lit basement (where, legend has it, she later mistook it for an intruder and screamed again). A fringe character in the tale was Skarbek's vengeful ex-wife, who would drop their sons off at the boatyard and floor the gas pedal on her way out, covering anyone busy in delicate varnish work in a cloud of dust. Whether the effect was intended for Skarbek or the general boating public remains unclear.

But no matter! Our good men shared a common vision! The grand plan was to work on Nina/Nonna/Yolanta in the spring and sail to Europe in the summer. As things developed, the cruising plan was drastically whittled down; my mother recalls only an hour-long outing in sheltered Raritan Bay. Since it would take a gale to move that colossus, it must have been a slow, stately affair. And what then? With a baby on the way (that would be me) and the hope of an imminent adventure fading, my father dropped out of the venture. He went on to own a series of small day sailors until cancer took him at age forty-seven. We never learned what became of Pan Skarbek and the Polish Navy.

Now, forty years later, I can appreciate the untold parts of this story. I know the feeling of being dog tired after a weekend of contortion acts below decks, and the satisfaction of crossing jobs off a seemingly endless list. And although the misadventures of the Polish Navy were the subject of many a hearty laugh in my family, I have to admire the effort. Despite limited means and know-how, my father and Pan Skarbek put their hearts and backs into hauling in a dream, one handful at a time. They weren't content to simply start a new working life in a new country; they pursued even more ambitious goals. Not every American dream ends in success – but that doesn't mean they end in failure, either.

I wonder whether sailing was a metaphor for freedom to my father and Pan Skarbek, more so than it will ever be to me, a girl with the luxury of growing up believing that dreams are a right and not a privilege. Or were they simply in it for the joy of working in fresh seaside air, leaving the nitty-gritty of everyday life behind? Either way, I salute them. Here's to you, Dad, and to Pan Skarbek, for daring to pursue your dreams.

368

Here's to your story becoming part of another generation's oral history. Thank you for the laughs – and for the inspiration.

Aboard the 'Polish Navy'

# Chapter 57

# My German Engineer

Lucky me: I have my very own German Engineer husband. He's very sweet. He never barks orders. He's the man on hand for anything that goes kaput – or doesn't, thanks to his diligent preventative measures. Just what you need for cruising!

Here's a guy who can ground the SSB to the water tank in an afternoon. Who can not only install a charge regulator, but can understand the need for one, too. Ham radio license? Got it! Knot for every occasion? Goes without saying!

You can imagine this has its advantages, like the time the Wind Pilot broke in mid-Atlantic. And yet, there are compromises to be made, such as witnessing the over-engineering of straightforward tasks. You want to build a simple toy raft for Junior to tow behind the boat? Not possible. Buoyancy, balance, displacement are all accounted for in his creation. If necessary, we could abandon ship to it.

Well, I'm exaggerating, and also suffering from an inferiority complex. While I admire his successes, they make me shirk from attempting anything less than a graduate level project. I'm a person who approaches repairs with a roll of duct tape. If that fails, I hit the broken gadget. The Engineer, on the other hand, makes calculations, sketches, and drafts.

Take the ingenious system he rigged up after a broken fuel injection pipe started spewing diesel into the bilge, one hundred miles offshore in a calm. Markus managed to rig a hose from the cracked pipe to an empty jerry can so that the engine could run on two of its three cylinders. The hose ran neatly through a cork trimmed to match the jerry can's mouth. Not a drop spilled! (Too bad I was the only one there to appreciate his handiwork.)

As for me, I track water consumption. Snap sunset shots. Identify whales. I carefully calculate the number of cookies needed for passages – always with a comfortable margin of safety! I make lee cloths and hammer in grommets.

He downloads GRIB files.

This is not to say that I don't do any of the technical work. I once managed to take apart and reassemble the toilet pump, but I'm more in my element engineering full sentences in foreign languages.

Our priorities differ vastly. After a slow Atlantic crossing, we finally arrived in Antigua. My thoughts: *Shirley Heights reggae night! Must check time!* His? *Must check steering cables!* Despite occasional teeth gnashing, our characters complement one another well. Often, we are both right: the steering cables were threadbare, and Shirley Heights reggae night was an awfully good time. *Vive la différence!*

Without me, he'd still be chained to The Firm. Without me, all we'd have seen of Lanzarote would have been the chandleries. So we've each evolved into our own niches, like Darwin's finches.

Reading these lines, Markus threatens to write an exposé on sailing with a teacher/archaeologist. Uh-oh. Did I mention how much I appreciate my German Engineer? Without him, I might never have realized my dream.

Nadine's very own German Engineer

# About the Authors

Nadine Slavinski is a teacher, writer, and erstwhile archaeologist with a penchant for blue horizons. She holds a Master's of Education from Harvard University and has been teaching in international schools since 1996. Markus Schweitzer worked in the tourism, logistics and aviation industries before casting off the shorelines. His background is in engineering and computational mathematics. Their son Nicky crossed his first ocean at age four and later completed grades two, three, and four while sailing the Pacific Ocean aboard *Namani*.

Please consider leaving a review of this book on Amazon and/or Goodreads. Not only do reviews help other readers judge a book, they also help the title appear more often in Internet searches and thus find interested readers. This is especially important to niche publications like this, so please do write a review, no matter how brief. Thank you!

Visit our website *www.nslavinski.com* to find interesting and informative blog posts, links, and resources. That's also where you can contact us or sign up to receive updates on new content and releases. Our travel blog is at *www.namaniatsea.org*.

**Also by Nadine Slavinski**:

- *Lesson Plans Ahoy! Hands-on Learning for Sailing Children and Home-Schooling Sailors*

- *Cruising the Caribbean with Kids: Fun, Facts, and Educational Activities*

- *Lesson Plans To Go: Hands-on Learning for Active and Home-Schooling Families*

**Coming soon by Nadine Slavinski**: watch for Nadine's sea adventure novels, *The Silver Spider* and *Rum for Neptune*.